Managing Development and Application of Digital Technologies

T0181058

Eva-Maria Kern
Heinz-Gerd Hegering
Bernd Brügge
(Editors)

Managing Development and Application of Digital Technologies

Research Insights in the Munich Center
for Digital Technology & Management (CDTM)

With 91 Figures

 Springer

Dr. mont. Dr.-Ing. habil. Eva-Maria Kern
TU Hamburg Harburg
Institut für Logistik
und Unternehmensführung
Schwarzenbergstraße 95
21073 Hamburg
e.kern@tu-harburg.de

Professor Dr. Heinz-Gerd Hegering
Leibniz-Rechenzentrum/Institut für Informatik
der LMU
Boltzmannstraße 1
85748 Garching b. München
hegering@lrz.de

Professor Bernd Brügge, Ph.D.
Technische Universität München
Institut für Informatik/I1
Lehrstuhl für angewandte
Softwaretechnik
Boltzmannstraße 3
85748 Garching b. München
bruegge@in.tum.de

Cataloging-in-Publication Data

ISBN 978-3-642-07055-6   e-ISBN 978-3-540-34129-1

This work is subject to copyright. All rights are reserved, whether the whole or part of the material is concerned, specifically the rights of translation, reprinting, reuse of illustrations, recitation, broadcasting, reproduction on microfilm or in any other way, and storage in data banks. Duplication of this publication or parts thereof is permitted only under the provisions of the German Copyright Law of September 9, 1965, in its current version, and permission for use must always be obtained from Springer-Verlag. Violations are liable for prosecution under the German Copyright Law.

Springer is a part of Springer Science+Business Media

springeronline.com

© Springer Berlin · Heidelberg 2010
Printed in Germany

The use of general descriptive names, registered names, trademarks, etc. in this publication does not imply, even in the absence of a specific statement, that such names are exempt from the relevant protective laws and regulations and therefore free for general use.

Hardcover-Design: Design & Production, Heidelberg

Foreword

This collection of research contributions documents the scope of topics investigated by researchers at and connected to the *Center for Digital Technology and Management* (CDTM) in Munich. It shows the effective collaboration between various scientific disciplines and, in turn, demonstrates the potential of interdisciplinary work in a field that is of utmost importance for the socio-economic future all over the globe.

Digital technology determines today's world and will be one of the key technologies of the future. Non-stop technological change demands constant innovation at tremendous speed. While information technology offers great opportunities, it poses quite a few challenges to managers. The ability to integrate business and technology decisions will become a crucial core competence.

Consequently our vision was to create CDTM as an innovative cross-disciplinary institution qualifying promising students for their further managerial career in nowadays business environment. It offers an experience that opens new ideas, new views, new opportunities by combining the abilities of business administration, computer science and electrical engineering students.

CDTM, an interdisciplinary establishment of education and research, was founded in 1998 as a joint venture between the Technische Universität München and the Ludwig-Maximilians-Universität München. Building on the specific strengths of both universities, the CDTM provides highly qualified and ambitious students with an excellent honour's academic education in the field of Technology Management. Since 2004 it is part of the newly founded Bavarian Elite Study Program (see www.cdtm.de).

As a research institution it focuses on topics around the development and application of digital technologies, closely cooperating with industry partners within the TIME sector (Telecommunication, Information Technology, Media, and Entertainment).

Even eight years after its foundation the CDTM is unique in the German academic scene. The ongoing interest of the industry and the students are indicators of its promising strategic positioning and its enduring success.

We wish the CDTM, its staff, students, its graduates, and its partners a bright future in the fascinating field of digital technology and management!

We thank all the authors for their valuable contributions, and in particular Dr. Eva-Maria Kern who with great enthusiasm managed to make this book become a reality.

Manfred Broy   Jörg Eberspächer   Arnold Picot

Founding Professors of CDTM

Munich, March 2006

Preface

Digital Technology plays an important role in today's world. Successful technology development, introduction and management are not only a question of technical issues. Due to their complexity a close cooperation between various scientific disciplines is required to discuss meaningful aspects, arising consequences, chances and risks from manifold points of view as a base for the development of adequate solutions.

The *aim of this anthology* is to highlight a selection of current research topics in the field of digital technology and management, which are investigated in the scientific environment of the *Center for Digital Technology and Management*.

The book is structured in six chapters in which the following topics are discussed:

- *Digital Technology and Management*: This chapter deals with the design of the innovation process. One paper describes a systematic approach for an efficient and user oriented development process. Two contributions deal with the problem how to integrate customers successfully in the innovation process by using a specific toolkit or as active participants in user communities. Another paper describes an approach of preparing IT students for their future job by engaging them in a distributed software engineering course.

- *Digital Rights Management (DRM)*: Intellectual property right is a research issue closely connected to innovation processes and their results. One paper describes the effects of DRM on software innovation in Open Source and proprietary software development processes. Additionally, an architecture for a DRM framework based on OpenTC is introduced.

- *IT Service Management (ITSM)*: Providers of connectivity and value-added services in the IT domain must adopt a service-oriented view of their operations to improve their customer relationships. IT Service Management has become an important part of this strategy. The contributions in this chapter explain the technical components for implementing ITSM and describe two approaches to realize intra- and cross organizational ITSM.

- *Future Communication Networks*: The rapidly evolving network technologies play a key role in information management. Beside technological characteristics cost aspects become more and more relevant. Key trends of future communication networks are described and an approach to cost-efficient core networks is introduced.

- *Mobile Services*: Many applications used by end consumers are based on mobile services. Therefore users need to be integrated in the innovation process. The contributions in this chapter describe a toolkit architecture for involving users in service creation and an approach for using their knowledge in the development of mobile games. Another paper describes the use of ontologies in virtual organizations and distributed teams.

- *Location Based and Ubiquitous Services*: A recent focus in the domain of digital services is on the development of context sensitive and ubiquitous services. This chapter provides a critical discussion of the business potentials of RFID (Radio Frequency Identification Devices), introduces a novel approach to ubiquitous location-based service architectures and describes a test case for context-sensitive service provision.

We hope that our book illustrates the variety of aspects, which have to be considered in the development and application of digital technologies - and therefore the strong need for interdisciplinary research in this scientific domain. We also hope that the articles demonstrate the interdisciplinarity of CDTM and its contribution to research in the field of digital technology management. We cordially thank all the authors for their articles. We would also like to express our thanks to Barbara Karg and Barbara Feß from Springer Verlag who supported us in the final phase to make this book a reality.

Eva-Maria Kern   Heinz-Gerd Hegering   Bernd Brügge

Editors

Munich, March 2006

Table of Contents

I Digital Technology and Management

1. Digital Technology and Management

Innovation in Engineering Software Intensive Systems

Manfred Broy

1 Introduction

In many technical products, software plays a dominant role today. In cars, for instance, this applies even to the extreme. Today software in cars is a dominant factor for the car industry, bringing various problems but being nevertheless decisive for innovation and competition.

Software construction develops continually into a key technology of the 21st century for engineering complex technical systems. More and more critical infrastructures are crucially depending on the reliable functioning of software. Today the reliability of software is often insufficient. Nevertheless, software intensive systems in avionics show impressive reliability. However, this is only achieved by high efforts and costs according to careful quality assurance and system redundancy aiming at error tolerance.

Over the past years, we have witnessed a slow but steady decrease in the gap between the theoretical and practical sides of the software engineering community. We are confident that this trend will continue and will accelerate improvements in the state of software engineering practice and theory.

The continued doubling of computing speed and memory capacity every 18 months according to Moore's law and the improvement in the capacity of communication links implies that the only constancy for large distributed systems, technology, tactics and doctrine may well be the idea that change is always inevitable. The dynamic aspect of systems is not supported by current practice and is seldom emphasized in current research. Software evolution research is extremely important for achieving modifiable and dependable systems in the future. Improved methods for reengineering are also needed to bring legacy systems to the condition where they can benefit from improvements in software evolution technology.

Thirty years ago, when the term software engineering was coined, there was lack of theoretical foundation for many practical concepts in computing. That is no longer true. A solid body of foundational work is available now that addresses many challenging issues related to software and computing, including:

- Specification and modelling techniques for requirements,
- specification and modelling techniques for systems and data,
- models and logical calculi for concurrent, distributed, and real time systems,
- logical concepts related to interactive systems, and
- formal models of programming language semantics with a variety of inference systems as well as
- formal models for implementation infrastructure in terms of hardware.

The challenge is to put these results to work, to develop theories that better support engineering needs, and to improve practice. This will require cooperation and a concerted effort from both theoreticians and practitioners. We will need advances in education and improvements in theoretical approaches to meet the increasing demand of practical engineering for computer software. To be attractive to practitioners, formal methods, mathematical foundations and automated engineering tools need to provide return on investment. These approaches must be cost effective to successfully compete with other development methods, and the benefits they provide in terms of software quality must have sufficient economic value to justify investment in them.

These goals require some uncomfortable changes in the research community. Mathematical elegance is not enough for the success of an engineering theory: applicability, tractability, and ease of understanding are often more important in practice than logical completeness or conceptual elegance of the principles that guarantee the soundness of the methods. We must carefully separate the application of mathematics to demonstrate the soundness of a formal software model or to construct automated tools for engineers from the formal models that will be used "by engineers as design representations".

Foundations of software engineering cannot be studied in isolation without precise knowledge of the current state of the art and feedback from practice if we are to have practical impact. The different aspects of technical, educational, and management issues are so closely intertwined in software engineering practice that it is risky and ineffective to study and develop them in isolation if practical applicability is a prominent goal. This puts interdisciplinary requirements on researchers and lends importance to interactions between experts from different specialties.

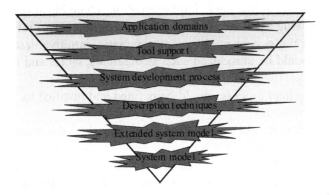

Fig. 1. The stack in software engineering

Software development capabilities lag far behind society's demands for better, cheaper, more reliable software. Since the gap is so large, and even widening, it is unlikely that "business as usual" will be able to meet this need. Engineering automation based on sound and scientific methods appears to be our best chance to close the gap.

Software engineering being originally very much restricted to the idea of programming develops more and more into a universal discipline of systems engineering.

2 The Structure of Software Engineering

As shown in Fig. 1 software engineering techniques need a variety of ingredients including:

- Foundations formed by a universal mathematical system model that defines what a system essentially is, as well as basic its notions such as component, interface, composition, decomposition, architecture, ways to represent systems by mathematical models leading to a theory of the system model.
- The system model should offer and support essential system views:
  - Data model,
  - state and state transition model,
  - interface (users' view),
  - distribution and structure (architecture),
  - process and interaction.
- The system model has to be extended to domain specific issues such as real time, mobility, exception handling etc.
- Based on the system model methodological foundations such as stepwise property refinement, implementation, changing levels of abstractions showing essential properties such as modularity of refinement.
- Based on the system model more pragmatic, intuitive description techniques should be introduced such as diagrams, tables and tuned formalisms.
- A development process should be defined and justified by the theory of the system model.
- Tool support should be provided and justified by the theory of the system model.
- For individual application areas the system model should be extended to more sophisticated aspects such as performance, quality of service, real time etc.

This way a rich software engineering technology is created always justified on scientific grounds where at the same time it has to be validated by practical experiments and experience. Only by gathering experimental and heuristic data we are able to understand the benefits and drawbacks of the individual methods.

In the remainder of the paper we mainly concentrate on issues of software technology and do not treat issues of practical experiments, experience, or management.

3 Hot Spots in Software Technique

Studying large software projects we easily recognize always the same critical points:

- Requirements
- Architecture
- Management of change
- Quality and reliability

A systematic model-based development process effectively supports all these issues.

4 Modeling in Software Engineering

In a systematic development of distributed interactive software systems we work with a basic system model and description techniques providing specific views and abstractions of systems such as their data, interfaces, distribution, process, interaction, and state transitions. Each of these views is helpful and has its place in the systems development process. The development of systems concentrates on working out these views that lead step by step to an implementation. For large systems, the development is carried through several levels of abstraction. Clearly, working with different system views and abstractions supports the entire spectrum between top-down and bottom-up approaches to system development; this is necessary for scalable and realistic development processes. The system model we work with allows us to relate all the artifacts we produce during systematic development.

Whatever conceptual system model we use in software development we need a mathematical system model as a basis for justifying the methods and design patterns we rely on. Just as the physicist relies on a thorough mathematical foundation to describe, quantify, and understand phenomena of the complex "real world", the software engineer must be able to found modeling and design decisions made for complex software systems on a solid basis – instead of on quicksand.

5 The Strive for Quality

Software development always means creating a formal model – be it at the level of code and machines or at a very abstract logical level. It is a commonplace by now that apart from very specific small projects modeling at the code level does not suffice.

Software is complex, error prone, and costly. Quality management (QM) is one of the three key issues in the magic triangle of cost, quality, and time. Quality is never an unconditional value. Achieving a high level of quality for software systems we have to solve two major problems:

- *Quality requirements engineering* (QRE): Specification of quality aspects and attributes of a software product.
- *Quality assurance* (QA): Guarantee of specified quality aspects and attributes by the development process.

Higher quality is never for free! Every decision of the inclusion of quality requirements may increase the costs and is to be justified in the application scenario. Issues of QRE can be put into the following categories:

- Functional requirements (behavioral requirements): Properties of software related to its behavior, its offered services, and its performance.
- Product requirements: Properties of software related to its representation and documentation as well as the way of its realization and distribution.
- Process requirements: Properties of the software development process.

Making requirements precise always leads into a modeling task. If we cannot quantify, model, specify, give test cases, and verify a requirement, then it is dubious whether it is of any value or relevance.

6 Real Life Software Quality

Although it is not a secret that many commercial software projects and products suffer from poor quality it cannot be overstressed how far away most real life and even large-scale software projects are from implementing acceptable quality standards.

While some spectacular software bugs, like the overflow that caused the ARIANE 5 rocket failure, became widely visible and lead to an increased awareness for specific techniques in certain situations (e.g. rigorous testing of critical systems and advanced verification techniques) the bulk of commercial software still seems to be built with little quality considerations in mind. We draw this conclusion from our own personal experiences as well as statistical material.

6.1 Functionality and Correctness

The Standish Group reports on software project cancellations, and cost overruns in 80% of the cases are well known. According to these empirical studies, more than 30% of the projects investigated produced software that provided at most 50% of the originally specified functionality. In addition to this, one can expect that many of the 80% cancelled and late projects had severe quality deficits, too.

The issue of functionality and correctness is of course crucial. But what does complete functionality and correctness mean precisely? One could argue that all of the stated requirements (and no others) had to be implemented the way they were specified. This road leads to the techniques that our colleagues in formal methods develop; i.e. develop a precise formal specification and then do a formal, or even automated verification of the implementation against the specification. Though this sounds promising, it underestimates the most important issue: getting the right requirements and getting them right. Only after the functional requirements are appropriate and formalized verification becomes an issue. But since we do not really know how to judge whether we got "the right requirements" and due to the inherent troubles to confirm the validity of a requirements specification against the actual desires of users providing correct functionality remains a challenge.

6.2 Maintainability

Even in the rare cases that a software project could be considered successful according to these criteria, that is complete functionality in time and budget, the quality of the outcome deserves a second, separate look.

The bulk of the costs for a software system – 80% – does not go into initial development but into maintenance. Because of this, the maintainability of a software system is of paramount importance to many organizations whose processes depend on software. Despite of this fact, our survey on software maintenance practices in 2003 revealed that 70% of the participating software organizations did not regard the maintainability of the software they produce at all.

To us, it is still a mystery how large companies deliberately mobilise capital over and over again to replace old "legacy" systems with new ones. As a matter of fact, some of the new systems expose many of the undesirable properties of a typical "legacy" system, just after being released.

6.3 Efficiency and Performance

Efficiency is another example for frequent shortcomings though processing speed and memory consumption are rather intuitively comprehensible. At least three large scale commercial projects are known to the authors where the performance of the software is unacceptable for delivery. In all of these three cases, it is tried to solve this problem by switching to more powerful hardware; hence, without tackling the root of the actual quality shortcoming.

Again, the reason for this is a lack of understanding what software quality is, what the criteria are and how it can be influenced.

6.4 Possible Explanations

Why is it that the need for quality is widely known and accepted but quality seems to be missing in practice?

First of all, quality costs. Higher efficiency and increased security may easily multiply development costs. At the same time our software engineering discipline is still unable to answer basic economic questions such as "how much more costs 10% increased processing speed?" or "how many more bugs will be detected before shipping if we increase our testing efforts by 20%". Other industries are able to precisely explain the increased price and its corresponding benefit. For example, a 3 litre car may cost 3.000$ more than its 2 litre counterpart. You therefore receive a 20% improvement in acceleration and a 30mph increased top speed.

Since we are unable to reason about the costs and benefits of software quality in a similarly precise way it is not surprising that the average software customers is usually unwilling to accept explicit charges for quality issues. As a consequence, quality requirements remain often unspecified though the target quality profile depends on the individual needs of the users of the software system and the specification of the quality requirements was obviously part of a proper requirements engineering process.

Another major source for quality shortcomings is the simple fact that we still do not know what the right criteria for high quality software are. For example, it is accepted that GOTO is harmful. But, does a comprehensive documentation really increase program comprehension? Does UML modelling contribute to better architectures? We argue that most of the rules commonly used during quality management have not been derived from a quality goal but selected for one of the following two reasons: 1) seen elsewhere ... so it cannot be wrong or 2) easy to check. Consequently, many of the common rules hardly match the actual quality needs. Since most software developers are aware of the little impact of these rules, they simply ignore them.

In fact, many software organizations frankly admit that the primary purpose of their quality management efforts is to get an ISO 9000, CMM, or some other certificate that can be used as a selling point. The actual improvement of the quality of their products plays a secondary role. Though this attitude tastes bitter it is indeed comprehensible considering the debatable impact of the existing quality guidelines.

It should not be left unmentioned that there are of course many other reasons for the lack of quality in software products, such as weak qualification of development personnel, which we do not elaborate in greater detail, here.

7 The Situation in Practice

In practice, many methods for modeling and specification have been suggested (SA, SADT, SSADM, SDL, OMT, UML, ROOM, ...). Of course the design of universal modeling languages is a great idea. A closer look shows, however, how ad hoc most of these "methods" are. At best, they reflect deep engineering insights in engineering particular applications. But never have they been justified on the basis of a comprehensive mathematical foundation. Thus we run into endless discussions what an obscure graphical or textual phrase could "really" mean. As a result, tool support is shallow, development steps are ad hoc and descriptions are ambiguous. A bad example is UML with its statecharts dialect with its endless discussions about its semantics. We claim that identifying and exploiting methodical potential present in modeling gain lots of benefits; this requires a look beyond the individual syntax and isolated semantics of a given notation. A solid mathematical basis is a significant aid in discovering such potential, and in justifying the value of corresponding methodological suggestions.

Moreover, often the suggested methods are too weak and offer only little help. A striking example is the situation of modeling and specifying interfaces of classes and components in object oriented modeling techniques in the presence of call backs – where "specifying" means not only to list all methods and attributes, but a precise description of their functioning. None of proposed so-called practical methods around gives convincing answers to that question.

A third example is concurrency and cooperation. Most of practical methods especially in object orientation seem to live in the good old days of sequential programming and do not properly address the needs of highly distributed, mobile, asynchronously cooperating software systems.

What is needed beyond innovative engineering methods is a systematic collection of heuristic data to learn from these about their efficiency and effectiveness. Only this way we achieve controlled learning curves.

8 Reducing Complexity

One of the biggest problems in software industry today is the overwhelming complexity of the systems they face today. How can we reduce complexity?

Of course, we can use classical techniques from software engineering, which is structuring, separation of concerns, and abstraction. Structure is what we have achieved if we get an appropriate architectural view with the levels as described above. Abstraction is what we gain if we use models. Model orientation remains one of the big hopes for the software industry to improve its situation.

A key issue is process orientation and software development processes. So far the processes in the software industry are not adapted to the needs of software intensive systems and software engineering. Process orientation will introduce a much higher awareness for processes.
A good example is the introduction of Spice and CMMI techniques into the software industry, which already has helped a lot to improve the competencies there.

Actually, a deep process orientation on the long run would need a well-understood handling of the product models. The product data of course need a comprehensive coherent and seamless model chain.

9 Academic Contribution

In academic research we find a concentration on formal methods. There we find logic based system models and verification techniques. Much concentrates on logical theories for system and program modeling including a particular notation ("syntax"), rules for manipulating it ("deduction rules") and a notion of model ("model theory"). This has often been criticized as purely theoretical and not practically applicable work. This criticism is valid as far as proponents of formal methods have claimed that their logical theories can be applied immediately as engineering methods. This is a claim that is nearly always unjustified.

However, seeing adequate logical and mathematical theories as the scientific basis of engineering methods including specification and modeling techniques, methods, design patterns, process models, and support tools makes them a key contribution to software development as an engineering discipline. For that, we have of course to find out the most appropriate theories, as well as where and how they apply.

Good examples for those achievements are models of time. While not being available 20 years ago we have now a rich body of time models at hand and also logical methods for their usage in specification.

10 The Research Challenges

Much has been achieved in researching logical and mathematical models of programs, software, and systems. Much of it is fractional and incomplete. Here are three major challenges for researchers:

- Enlarging the models to fields not properly covered yet like performance, security, resource requirements etc.
- Evaluating and comparing existing logical methods to identify which are most appropriate for what.
- Combining existing approaches into comprehensive foundations as a basis for engineering approaches.

In fact, we can achieve a lot more along these lines.

11 The Practical Challenges

The practical challenges are obvious: design practical modeling and specification methods on the basis of a well-worked out theory, implement tools with deep and comprehensive support.

Only if we do that and gain practical experience with the application of such methods we can go to the necessary trial and error loops. This way we get the needed feedback from practice to guide and inspire the academic research.

We can and should dream of much more powerful tools, precise and nevertheless readable specifications and a flexible toolbox of models, notations, and methods based on well-understood theories.

12 Conclusion

Software intensive systems need a much more systematic development approach based on well-worked out, well-chosen scientific foundations and validated engineering principles. Model oriented approaches contribute here.

The conclusion is straightforward: we need a much deeper and more intensive interaction between researchers in the foundations, the designers of practical engineering methods and tools, and the programmers and engineers in charge of the practical solutions.

Acknowledgements

It is a pleasure to acknowledge helpful remarks by members in our group, in particular Ingolf Krüger and Bernhard Schätz.

References

Brodie ML, Michael Stonebraker (1995) Migrating Legacy Systems: Gateways, Interfaces & the Incremental Approach. Morgan Kaufmann, March 1995

Broy M (1991) Towards a formal foundation of the specification and description language SDL. Formal Aspects of Computing 3, 1991, 21-57

Broy M (1997) Refinement of Time. In: Bertran M, Rus Th (eds.): Transformation-Based Reactive System Development. ARTS'97, Mallorca 1997. Lecture Notes in Computer Science 1231, 1997, 44-63

Broy M, Stølen K (2001) Specification and Development of Interactive Systems: Focus on Streams, Interfaces, and Refinement. Springer 2001

Herzberg D, Broy M (2003) Modeling layered distributed communication systems. Applicable Formal Methods. Springer Verlag, Volume 17, Number 1, May 2005

Broy M, Deißenböck F, Pizka M (2005) A Holistic Approach to Software Quality at Work. 3rd World Congress for Software Quality (3WCSQ), 2005

Dijkstra EW (1968) Go To statement considered harmful. Communications of the ACM, 11(3), 1968.

Fenton N (1994) Software measurement: A necessary scientific basis. IEEE Trans. Softw. Eng., 20(3):199–206, 1994.

IEEE (1998) Standard for a software quality metrics methodology. IEEE 1061, 1998

Jones C (2000) Software Assessments, Benchmarks, and Best Practices. Addison Wesley, 2000.

Katheder K (2003) A Survey on Software Maintenance Practices, Technische Universität München, November 2003

Lions JL (1996) ARIANE 5 – Flight 501 Failure. European Space Agency (ESA), July, 1996.

Paulk MC, Weber CV, Curtis B, Chrissis MB (1995) The capability maturity model, guidelines for improving the software process.Addison-Wesley 1995.

Parnas D (1972) On the criteria to be used to decompose systems into modules. Comm. ACM 15, 1972, 1053-1058

Pigoski TM (1996) Practical Software Maintenance. Wiley Computer Publishing, 1996

Selic B, Gullekson G, Ward PT (1994) Real-time Object-oriented Modeling. Wiley, New York 1994

SEI (2004) Software Engineering Institute, Carnegie Mellon University. Maintainability Index Technique for Measuring Program Maintainability. January 2004, (http://www.sei.cmu.edu/str/descriptions/mitmpm.html)

SEQ (2001) Software engineering – Product quality – Part 1: Quality Model. ISO/IEC 9126-1, June 2001.

SEQ (2003) Software engineering – Product quality – Part 3: Internal metrics. ISO/IEC 9126-3, July 2003.

Standish (1995) Standish Group International, Inc. CHAOS. 1995

Standish (1999) Standish Group International, Inc. CHAOS: A Recipe for Success. 1999

Zave P, Jackson M (1997) Four dark corners of requirements engineering. ACM Transactions on Software Engineering and Methodology, January 1997

Zuse H (1996) A Framework of Software Measurement. Walter de Gruyter, 1998

Outsourcing Innovation in Digital Service Creation: What Software Engineering Can Learn from Modern Product Development

Bernhard Kirchmair

1 Introduction

The considerably fast-paced diffusion of information technology throughout the last decade has had not only a huge impact on how companies optimize their businesses by leveraging the potential IT offers, but also had vast implications on the types of product and service concepts created and offered to market actors (Grover et al. 1994, 1998; Weill and Broadbent 1998; Powell and Dent-Micallef 1999). The diffusion of products that rely on software rather than on material components has gained significant momentum (Fichmann 2000; Naher et al. 2002). In fact, a whole new class of products has evolved which can be referred to as digital services. A digital service includes characteristics of both, immaterial services and material products. Although a digital service is based on software and, thus, constitutes a product with respect to design and development activities, it also shows inherent characteristics of a service when it comes to its commercialization and consumption.[1]

It has been recognized by academics and practitioners alike that the path to the development of successful need-oriented products and services includes an involvement of customers in the development process (e.g. Sioukas 1995; Neale and Corkindale 1998; Campbell and Cooper 1999; Brockhoff 2003; Callahan and Lasry 2004).

However, collecting customer needs can be very costly and time-consuming as these needs are often subtle, complex, and not stable (Thomke and von Hippel 2002). Traditional approaches for involving customers in software development mainly focus on collecting customer needs efficiently by various means during requirement analysis, but suffer from various shortcomings when required to trigger true innovation as they put customers into a rather passive, creativity-hindering role.

Recently, research in the field of innovation theory suggested that customers themselves might be a unique and fruitful source of innovative ideas. Instead of generating ideas for innovative products in-house and assigning an evaluator role to customers, companies may want to enable them to design, create, and adapt their own products according to their very needs. This approach has become known as user innovation (von Hippel 1998).

This article elaborates on the background of user innovation and suggests its application to the development of immaterial software, particularly digital services. Digital services created according to the proposed approach can be expected to fulfil customer requirements more accurately,

---

[1] A comparison of general differences between products and services can be found e.g. in (Storey and Easingwood 1998) or (Venkatraman and Dholakia 1997).

to be more innovative, and to follow a cheaper and faster development process than possible with traditional software engineering methods. Above all, their development is less risky.

2 Digital Services and Innovation

In this article, a digital service is defined as an abstract concept that is realized by a software entity. This entity is the specific piece of software that implements a digital service. A digital service itself can be considered as a resource characterized by the abstract set of functionality that is provided to the service consumers. Software constituting the technical basis of such a digital service consists of a set of communication interfaces, application logic, and metadata. To illustrate this distinction between a service's abstract functionality and its realization, one may consider a digital service as being implemented by a certain software entity one day (e.g. written in a specific programming language), and a different software entity (e.g. written in a different programming language) realizing the same functionality the other day. Digital services are consistently realized by electronic means: No human interaction is necessary on the service provider's side to facilitate any provision or consumption process. Services are provided and consumed exclusively electronically. No media or individual discontinuity appears.

With the vast diffusion of information technology, digital services are rather ubiquitous nowadays. This evolution goes along with the transformation from an economy focused on the production of material goods to an information- and service-oriented economy (Houghton and Sheehan 2000). A prototypical example for the latter is the mobile telecommunication industry where service providers offer intangible mobile digital services to their customers. Whereas this industry has experienced strong growth during the last couple of years, a recent slowdown mainly caused by market saturation has put industry into a state of tough competition (Beaubrun and Pierre 2001; Doganoglu and Grzybowksi 2005). A business strategy for companies acting in such highly competitive market environments and aiming at achieving sustainable economic success is to innovate constantly (Downes 2002). Product innovation implies differentiation which may lead to sustainable competitive advantage (Porter 1998). Innovation can be considered as the power of the engine of the economic value chain. New and innovative products, however, have to meet actual customer needs in order to be really successful. Hence, it is particularly important for companies providing digital services and facing cut-throat competition to find ways to quickly and efficiently develop services that are both truly innovative and highly customer need-driven.

Innovation can be defined as any idea, practice, or object that is perceived as new by an individual or other unit of adoption within the relevant environment (Biemans 1992; Rogers 2003). The original concept of innovation, as introduced by Schumpeter, designates innovation as the activity of developing an already invented element into a commercially useful element that is accepted in a social system, for instance, a company or a society (Schumpeter 1939). Innovation implies a change in the economic environment, or a change in the behavior of consumers. The distinction between invention and innovation is important to note. Whereas invention denotes the creation of an idea of how to do or to make something, innovation refers to the act of making this idea real and putting it into practice (Ruttan 1959). Correspondingly, the result of innovation is a new product, service, or process - or a qualitative change in an existing product, service, or process which constitutes a substantial difference as compared to the previous state.

The question now is how true innovation could be achieved in the development of digital services. In today's innovation literature the school of thought that regards customers as the primary source for true innovation has gain momentum (von Hippel 2005). If one accepts the corresponding premise that the most innovative ideas originate from customers, it seems reasonable to assign customers an active role in the innovation process. However, even though the involvement of customers in the development of material products has been explored extensively in literature, the integration of customers in the development of intangible digital services is an almost unexplored field (Magnusson et al. 2003).

3 Modern Product Development

In the following, it is examined, firstly, how customer-oriented development of innovative products is conducted in the field of material products and, secondly, which problems occur and how these problems can be solved. This discussion will serve as the rational basis for investigating the application of respective methods to trigger innovation in the development of intangible software-based digital services.

3.1 Traditional Approaches of Customer Involvement

It is crucial for companies to learn about user needs first in order to be able to develop adequate products. A company may want to find out as much as possible about these needs when aiming at bringing a successful product to the market. Various methods can be used by companies to collect need information from users. The selection of a specific method depends on the type of product to be developed. Generally two forms of customer involvement can be distinguished: a company may simply want to listen to customers, for instance by conducting interviews, or it may want to establish a closer connection to its customers by directly interacting with them (Jeppesen 2002).

Listening to customers limits their role to being simple information providers. A passive role is assigned to them. Examples are interviews, qualitative surveys, quantitative surveys (Woodruff and Gardial 1996) or focus groups (Krueger 1994). Besides surveys, interviews and focus groups, a number of other methods of listening to customers to stimulate innovation can be exercised in the course of product development. For instance, the collection of consumer complaints can serve as an indicator for product flaws and may give impulses to add innovative features.

The direct interaction with customers involves mostly advanced users. Those are users who recognize benefits, shortcomings, and problems with a product or a technology faster and more accurately than mainstream customers. The approach of interacting with advanced users is similar to the listening to customer approach, but differs in the fact that it lets users generate innovative ideas rather than letting in-house product developers do it (Jeppesen 2002). A well known method involving advanced users is the lead user method (von Hippel 1986; Herstatt and von Hippel 1992). Lead users are advanced users who face needs that will become general in a market, but face them months or years before other market actors encounter them. Since lead users are familiar with conditions that lie in the future for most others, they can serve as a need-forecasting resource during product development. Moreover, lead users often attempt to fill the need they experience and, thus, might provide innovative product concepts as well.

3.2 Problems with Traditional Approaches of Customer Involvement

Whereas traditional approaches employed in the process of innovative product development proved to be valuable and sufficient in the past, with respect to today's market characteristics they are often not. Since many markets today are characterized by heterogeneous user needs and, thus, heterogeneous user demand, companies are increasingly moving towards serving markets of one instead of serving mass markets. Consequently, companies adapt their production processes in order to produce customer-unique products rather than standardized mass products. Traditional methods of understanding and responding to customer needs, however, were effectively designed for homogeneous markets (Franke and Schreier 2002). Studies have shown that ideas and products created by utilizing traditional methods are rarely breakthroughs (Eliashberg et al. 1997). The respective results may be too ambiguous or overly simplistic (Jeppesen 2002). In general, traditional market techniques often fail, since they do not stimulate and foster a user's creativity which, as described above, may be an excellent source for innovative ideas.

The most severe problem for the development of innovative products though, remains to find out how future customer needs for innovative technical products can be identified with this technological environment constantly changing (von Hippel 1988). Changing technological conditions cause user needs to change as well. This complicates the integration and realization of an innovative product in case the specific realization process takes a long time to be accomplished (Reichart 2002).

Another fundamental problem of innovative product development is related to the users' experiences with currently available products. Users selected to provide input data to market analyses in the product development context have an important limitation: Their insights into new product or service needs and potential solutions are constrained by their own real-world experience (Hondrich and Vollmer 1983). Their personal context is considered as a very limited frame of reference which hinders them from generating highly innovative ideas (Ulwick 2002). This phenomenon is often referred to as *functional fixedness*, a term coined by Adamson (Adamson 1952). His empirical studies have demonstrated that once a certain object or process is familiar to a user, this experience will limit his capability to think of new, innovative ways to handle the object or process. Hence, users steeped in the present are unlikely to generate novel product concepts which differ from actual solutions (von Hippel 1988). Moreover, it often is questionable whether customers know exactly what they are looking for. In fact, customers may not be aware of their own needs; or customers may not fully understand their needs until they try out prototypes to explore exactly what does, and does not work for them (Thomke and von Hippel 2002). But even if customers do know what they need, they may not be able to describe or encode their needs precisely enough for the manufacturer to produce the respective product (von Hippel 1998). They rather have problems giving the manufacturer a clear and complete

picture of what they want. Particularly in high-technology markets, customers may often not have enough knowledge and experience to define a
product specification that corresponds exactly to their needs (Huffman
1998). Generally, it seems to be very difficult to translate need-related information into solution related information, such as a product development
specification (Urban and Hauser 1993).

3.3 The Information Problem of Modern Product Development and its Solution

Frequently, customer needs fall into the class of *sticky information*, which
is defined as information that is costly to transfer, to acquire, and to use at
a new location (von Hippel 1994). The degree of information stickiness
corresponds to the incremental expenditure required to transfer it to a
specified locus in a form that is usable by a given information seeker. Information stickiness is low, when this cost is low. Accordingly it is high,
when this cost is high. As particularly information used in problem solving
activities is highly sticky (von Hippel 1998), the need information called
upon by product developers can only be transferred at high costs. In the
worst case, the need-information is so sticky, that "unsticking" the information, i.e. reducing the stickiness of this information, and transferring it
to another locus is hardly possible at all. This may be particularly the case,
when users are not even aware about their own needs at all as mentioned in
the last section. Besides the fact that the process of transferring, i.e. collecting, user needs is costly, it may also be imprecise and error-prone when
dealing with very sticky information: User needs may be misinterpreted by
the manufacturer leading to products which, as a consequence thereof, will
fail in satisfying these needs. Research has shown that particularly information used in technical problem solving, i.e. problem solving occurring
during the innovation of technical products, is often sticky (Pavitt 1987;
Nelson 1990).

The solution to this problem is to simply shift the locus of problem solving activity, or at least some part of it, to the locus of the sticky information (von Hippel 1998). The overall product development task could be
partitioned into subtasks, whereas each subtask is either assigned to user or
manufacturer-based problem solvers. Subtasks requiring local sticky
manufacturer information (as how to actually produce a product) are assigned to the manufacturer. Subtasks requiring local sticky user information (as what are the user's needs and wishes) are assigned to the user.
Hence, the costly transfer of the respective sticky information can be bypassed giving rise to cheaper and faster product development resulting in

products or services which truly satisfy the users' needs and which even have the potential to be really innovative.

This promising idea of repartitioning product development tasks is the grounding reasoning behind a product development strategy actively employed by an increasing number of companies: letting user innovate.

3.4 The Concept of User Innovation and Toolkits

User innovation is about managing the development process of innovative products in a flexible way by assigning innovation related design tasks to the user. The concept's goal is to provide customers with enough creative freedom to design custom products that, first, truly satisfy their needs and, second, are potentially innovative. In contrast to established mass customization systems (Piller 2001), users are not restricted to a couple of alternatives to choose from, rather they are equipped with such powerful design tools that true innovation becomes possible - ideally without overstraining them with the tools' potential complexity (Maes 1994). Such tools allow users to convert their ideas into products which then are producible by the manufacturer. According to the thoughts outlined above, manufacturers of a particular type of product are the locus of expertise with respect to problems common to many designs. Users, however, possess the deepest understanding of a particular application. Therefore, it is reasonable to outsource innovation-related tasks of the product development process directly to users.

A proper tool for user innovation would shield users from technical details of the production process, but would provide functionality to allow them to drive innovation. Von Hippel and Katz (2002) concretize this notion by introducing the toolkits for user innovation approach.

Generally, toolkits for user innovation are coordinated sets of user-friendly design tools that enable users to develop new product innovations by themselves (von Hippel and Katz 2002). Accordingly, those toolkits support the repartition of innovation-related problem solving tasks and provide users with corresponding co-design means. Within their fields of use they give users real design freedom which may result in new innovative solutions. A toolkit for user innovation should encompass five important elements as identified by von Hippel in several exploratory studies (von Hippel 1999):

- First, a toolkit should allow customers to run complete cycles of trial-and-error learning. A user designs a first solution which is then built (or simulated by software). The user may find flaws of his newly designed product by using it (or using the simulation thereof). Then a properly designed toolkit would enable the user to refine his design, which is then instantly built and can be tested and evaluated again. These cycles can be repeated until the user is satisfied with the new product. Hence, the entire iterative design process including testing, evaluation, and the incorporation of any necessary improvements can be carried out by the user himself. No sticky need information has to be costly transferred between the manufacturer and the user at all. The information remains solely at the user locus.

- Second, the resulting custom user design shall be producible by the manufacturer without requiring revisions by manufacturer-based engineers. This implies that the language of such a toolkit must be translatable automatically and error-free into the language of the intended production system at the conclusion of the user's design work (von Hippel and Katz 2002). This aspect is essential as otherwise the manufacturer had to manually imitate the user's design by using the language of the respective production system. This process would be error-prone and could even result in a loss of user-defined requirements for the product.

- Third, a toolkit should provide libraries of commonly used design elements to make the initial design work easier and to prevent users from having to start from scratch with each new design or refinement thereof. Thus, users do not have to do everything on their own wasting time and resources, but rather are able to focus their creative work on those aspects of a product or service that are really novel. One may even think of providing users with standard design templates as a starting point for further design work.

- Fourth, it should offer users a concrete delimited solution space that encompasses the designs they want to create. With respect to production process constraints, economic production of custom products is only achievable when a custom design falls within the pre-existing capabilities and degrees of configuration freedom built into a given manufacturer's production system (von Hippel and Katz 2002). This is termed the solution space offered by that system. Hence, a toolkit has to constrain the users' design freedom to ensure resulting designs are indeed producible.

- Fifth, a toolkit should be intuitively usable by users. Users should be able to express their needs in a highly intuitive manner. This can be achieved by allowing users to work with an easy to understand design language – or even their own design language.

Empirical studies on successful real world projects indicate that this approach can indeed be very efficient in triggering innovation in modern product development. To better understand how toolkits for user innovation work and how they benefit the development of innovative products, the Nestle USA Food Services Division's ingredients toolkit for custom food design shall be introduced.

One of Nestle's businesses includes the production of custom food, e.g. custom sauces, for restaurant and food chains. If a customer is in need of a new sauce differing from existing sauces say in flavor, color, or consistency, the proceeding to create this new sauce is usually as follows: the chain's executive chefs compose the new sauce by using common food ingredients available to individual customers and restaurants and restaurant-style cooking equipment. Afterwards they hand this sauce over to Nestle Food Services and ask them to produce the sauce they have designed. However, this proceeding gives rise to several problems encumbering the seamlessly integration between innovation and production processes: Being an industrial food producer, Nestle can only use ingredients that are obtainable in quantity at a consistent quality. These ingredients may possibly not taste the same as those used by the executive chefs to mix their sauce. With industrial ingredients differing in taste and plenty of other attributes from the restaurant ingredients, the resulting sauce may most probably differ from the chefs' creation as well. Therefore, Nestle cannot simply reproduce the chefs' recipe as-is under factory conditions. Instead, the production chefs carefully analyze the customer's sauce and then try to make something which approximates the taste and texture of the original sauce by using their factory ingredients and methods. However, the problem persists: the chain's chefs are seldom satisfied with the initial version of the factory sauce. Longsome and costly iterations of this production-and-evaluation process are necessary. The design of truly innovative sauces is hindered. This is where the toolkit approach came into play. Nestle simply assembled a set of standard industrial food ingredients as each of them being the factory version of an ingredient traditionally used by chefs during recipe development. Of course these factory ingredients differ slightly from the fresh ingredients, but these differences are discovered immediately via learning by doing. So the chefs can adapt the sauce to their taste and particularly can be sure that the final result, the sauce Nestle produced according to their recipe, will taste exactly the same as their sauce prototype. In sum, the application of the toolkit approach to the domain of custom food resulted in more satisfied customers, shortened the time of custom food development from an average of 26 weeks to three weeks, and gave rise to innovative sauces (von Hippel and Katz 2002).

4 Modern Software Development

Starting from the raised question of how true innovation could be achieved in the development of intangible software-based digital services, it was shown in the previous section how innovation is fostered in the development of material products. The user innovation approach was introduced as a very promising strategy for triggering innovation in the context of material products.

However, as explored in more detail in this chapter, the development of innovative software as an intangible product suffers from similar problems as the development of material products does in respect of innovation matters. Interestingly, just as traditional product development methods have certain shortcomings in stimulating true innovation, software development methods commonly used today have so as well. Why this is the case, why those methods may not be able to cope with the stressed necessity of triggering true innovation and, consequently, why the need for a new alternative, or complementary, approach is given, shall be outlined in the following.

4.1 Traditional Approaches of Customer Involvement

As much as the development of material products relies heavily on considering customer needs and wishes, the development of successful software as an intangible product does so as well. Hence, it is reasonable to involve customers at a very early stage in the software development process for the purpose of minimizing risk and reducing costs. The earlier in the development process a software system is changed, the easier and cheaper these changes can be realized: The complexity and, thus, the costs of incorporating changes into a software system increases exponentially with the system's development progress. The earlier customers get involved, the lower the probability that significant changes are necessary later on and the lower the risk that their expectations and requirements are not met in the end.

However, as it is the case with material product development, involving customers solely during the first stages of a development project leaves several issues unaddressed. First, customer requirements for a software system often change or evolve during the course of a system's development, which makes them a moving target difficult to capture and to track. This is especially true for long lasting development projects due to a system's complexity and size or due to a changing technological environment. Second, customers might not have a clear understanding of their own needs and, hence, of the requirements for a specific software. The problem of sticky information is also highly relevant in this context. Another problem relates to the fact that customer requirements have to be captured in an unique and precise manner in order to prevent misunderstandings between customers and developers.

For those reasons, the elicitation of customer requirements solely in the initial phase of a development process, as suggested by software development process models[2] such as the basic *waterfall model* (Royce 1970), is not recommended. The basic waterfall model is a structured, strictly sequential, and non-iterative model that breaks the development process down into several phases as shown in Fig. 1. Only when one phase is completed, the next one can begin. Any analysis of customer requirements is conducted solely within the first phase. After the completion of that phase, no changes to the identified set of requirements are allowed.

Modern software development process models already take problems outlined above into account and allow for customer integration at several points during the development process. *Boehm's spiral model* (Boehm 1988) or the *Rational Unified Process* (Kruchten 1999) in conjunction with *rapid prototyping* (Thomke 1998) are popular examples for such models.

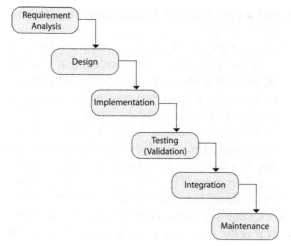

Fig. 1: The waterfall model

---

[2] The main function of a software development process model is to establish the phases in which major tasks are performed within a software development project, and to establish the transition criteria for proceeding from one task or phase to the next (Pawlowski 2001).

Latter, rapid prototyping is a widespread approach to rapidly generate prototypes[3] of a system that then can be tested and validated against the specifics of an use environment in an iterative process. This iterative process constitutes one form of experimentation and can be regarded as a four step iterative learning cycle as visualized in Fig. 2.

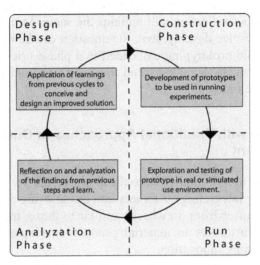

Fig. 2: The four step learning cycle

In the design phase, requirements are identified. In the construction phase, these requirements are incorporated into a physical or virtual prototype. In a third step, the run phase, the prototype is evaluated in a real or simulated use environment. Finally, in the analysis phase, the evaluation results are analyzed to determine whether additional modification and, thus, additional iterations are necessary. By conducting such experiments, information is collected about both the requirements for new functionality and the adequacy of possible designs. Furthermore, an iterative verification of whether the software meets the customer's expectations is conducted.

By considering this information throughout the remainder of the development process, uncertainties and, hence, risk can be minimized, the overall project costs reduced, and the development time shortened (Thomke and Bell 2001). It is recognized that rapid prototyping often is more benefiting than other techniques of other phase-oriented software development process models. Customer needs can be met more accurately and even the

---

[3] A prototype is an experimental design or implementation of a system that incorporates those very aspects of the system that shall be evaluated by a target audience.

problem of sticky information can be solved to a certain degree by increasing the number of prototyping iterations.

However, a problem that still remains unaddressed is the precise and formal capturing of user requirements. By increasing the number of iterations, the problem of bad defined requirements is not really solved. Even though requirements are approximated through iterations, the fundamental problem of bad specification still remains the same. Moreover, in the context of digital service development, the question can be raised whether the approach of rapid prototyping embedded in a phase-oriented development process does provide developers and users with enough freedom to actually achieve true innovation.

4.2 Problems with Traditional Approaches of Customer Involvement

In general, the newer models introduced above are recognized as being well suitable for integrating customers into the software development process. Still they suffer from drawbacks similar to those, traditional methods for involving customers in material product development face when it comes to promoting innovation.

True innovation requires the support for trial-and-error cycles (Baron 1988; Tyre 1995) to allow for learning by doing (Rosenberg 1982). In the course of traditional rapid prototyping techniques, a prototype is generated by developers, which is presented to and evaluated by customers who may then suggest improvements leading to a new prototype generation cycle. This proceeding involves an ongoing interaction between software developers and customers and implies shifting problem solving back and forth between these two instances during each trial-and-error cycle. As it is the case in material product development, this shifting is costly and inefficient. Customers have to articulate their requests for changes explicitly and in a manner developers are able to understand. Generally, this implies that it is not easily possible for a user to experiment with different variants of a software's functionality in an ad-hoc manner. Rather, a prototype has to get modified and rebuilt by software developers every single time the customer wants to try out something new, even if it is only a minor or temporary change to the software. Hence, the flow of consecutive learning by doing is broken and innovation is slowed down in the best case, or even made impossible in the worst case – but constrained in any case as, in fact, it is exactly this process of easily conducted instant and continuing modification and verification of new functionality that fosters innovation.

Another problem affects the selection of user groups for evaluating a prototype. The environments in which digital services are provided may be characterized by heterogeneous and constantly changing user needs. This gives rise to the question of how to select a proper user group efficiently when there is a diverse mass of users with slightly different needs. Selecting a too narrow or too broad group may hinder innovation as well.

By considering these problems with involving customers in the software development process when aiming at innovation, it gets obvious that a new approach is needed.

4.3 Solving the Problem of Innovation Inefficiencies in Digital Service Creation

In chapter 3.4, the toolkit for user innovation approach as recently employed to leverage the potential of user innovation in the development of material products was introduced. So far, this approach has mainly been applied to the development of material goods and products like industrial food, embedded chips or kite-surfing, even though there is a huge potential in utilizing this approach for the development of innovative intangible products such as software, and particularly digital services. Subsequently, it is shown how this approach can solve the problem of innovation inefficiencies in the development of digital services.

Even though it seems to be a long way from innovative food design in the custom food industry to a solution for the problem of innovation inefficiencies in the software industry, the application of the toolkit approach to the development of innovative digital services is well reasoned.

Intuitively, one can consider a complex service as consisting of several less complex services which are composed in some way. Provided that each of these single services as well as their composition is executable, a user might get easily enabled to compose a service on his own by giving him access to proper tools. One of the current paradigms in software engineering states that the reuse of certain pieces of software is desirable. Re-use across software systems is possible whenever redundancy of particular aspects is inherent to these systems. Services, when broken down to single functional units, are often characterized by redundancy. For instance, mobile services involving positioning and tracking of user locations make use of certain positioning functionality which is essentially the same in all services. Hence, it suggests itself to operationalize this redundancy in the development of digital services by making these redundant functionalities available as toolkit module libraries. If then a method for describing such compositions of functionalities is utilized that is so fundamental that it is suitable to capture any service in many service domains, the respective toolkit would be highly generic and applicable to many different instances of digital services.

Besides fostering innovation, a toolkit can also serve as an excellent means to ship around the problem of collecting user requirements and capturing them explicitly in an unique and formal manner: By utilizing the toolkit approach, software developers may acquire a user's need information and requirements for a service implicitly without forcing him to specify his needs explicitly in a formal way. This is because all user requirements are already contained in the user's service design that he creates. Thus, this service design can be expected to fulfil his very needs quite accurately. From a service design a detailed and formal requirement specification can then be derived. This specification could be modified by in-house software developers to whatever extent required. For instance, there might be certain refinements necessary such as incorporating security or safety features. In case a user creates an obviously new and innovative service whose high potential for market success is recognized by the provider, this service might serve as a basis for continuing product development efforts resulting in a final service which then can be offered to a major market.

Another advantage of the proposed approach relates to the risk of failure and associated costs in the development of software. Those are barriers for innovation. It may simply not be affordable for a company to generate an arbitrary number of "hit or miss" development projects in the hope that there will be an innovative output sometime. Rather, usually new development projects are preceded by a phase of precise planning and risk assessments. A toolkit, on the other hand, once implemented, enables users to try out new ideas and create new services on a large scale with virtually no consequential costs for the toolkit provider. The risk of failure in the development of a new digital service is, in fact, shifted to customers who use the toolkit and invest their own time and resources. A comparison between a traditional prototype-based development approach and the toolkit for user innovation approach for digital service creation is illustrated in Fig. 3.

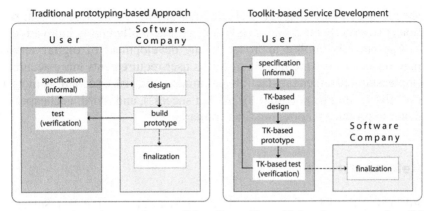

Fig. 3: Digital service creation: traditionally and by utilizing the suggested toolkit for user innovation approach

5 Summary

This article sought to answer the question of how true innovation could be achieved in the development of intangible software-based digital services. And, consequently, what software engineering can learn from modern product development. For this purpose, it was examined how customer-oriented development of innovative products is done in the field of material products. Traditional approaches of customer involvement in development and innovation processes in the context of material products suffer from various shortcomings when it comes to fostering true innovation. Related problems include the problem of functional fixedness and the information problem of modern product development. The concept of user innovation was introduced as a means to tackle those problems. User innovation refers to innovations developed by consumers and end users, rather than manufacturers.

It was shown that modern software development models suffer from similar shortcomings as the development of material products does when it comes to innovation matters. True innovation is often hindered due to costly and error-prone communication and information transfer processes between customers who articulate requirements and software engineers who implement corresponding functionality in prototypes.

As a solution to the identified problems and challenges, an adoption of the toolkit for user innovation approach for the development of digital services was suggested. Toolkits for user innovation are integrated sets of design, prototyping, and testing tools intended for use by end users. Nonspecialist users are enabled to create high-quality, producible custom solutions that exactly meet their needs and are potentially highly innovative.

Applying the toolkit approach to the development of digital services may result in software that, first, fulfils user requirements more accurately (increasing customer satisfaction and minimizing risk), second, is more innovative (rising its potential for market success), and, third, is cheaper and faster to produce (shortening time-to-market).

References

Adamons RE (1952) Functional Fixedness as Related to Problem Solving: A Repetition of Three Experiments. In: Journal of Experimental Psychology 44(4):288-291

Baron J (1988) Thinking and Deciding. Cambridge University Press, New York

Beaubrun R, Pierre S (2001) Technological Developments and Socio-Economic Issues of Wireless Mobile Communications. In: Telematics and Informatics 18:143-158

Biemans WG (1992) Managing Innovation with Networks. Routledge, New York

Boehm BW (1988) A Spiral Model of Software Development and Enhancement. In: IEEE Computer 21(5):61-72

Brockhoff K (2003): Customers' Perspectives of Involvement in New Product Development. In: International Journal of Technology Management 26(5):464-481

Campbell AJ, Cooper RG (1999) Do Customer Partnerships Improve New Product Success Rates? In: Industrial Marketing Management 28:507-519

Callahan J, Lasry E (2004) The Importance of Customer Input in the Development of Very New Products. In: R&D Management 34(2):107-120

Doganoglu T, Grzybowksi L (2005) Estimating Network Effects in Mobile Telephony in Germany. Working Paper. University of Munich

Downes L (2002) The Strategy Machine: Building Your Business One Idea at a Time. HarperBusiness, New York

Eliashberg J, Lilien GL, Rao V (1997) Minimizing Technological Oversights: A Marketing Research Perspective. In: Garud R, Nayyar PR, Zur S (eds) Technological Innovation: Oversights and Foresights. Cambridge University Press, New York, pp 214-230

Fichman RG (2000) The Diffusion and Assimilation of Information Technology Innovations. In:Framing the Domains of IT Management Research: Glimpsing the Future through the Past, Zmud R (ed), Pinnaflex Educational Resources

Franke N, Schreier M (2002) Entrepreneurial Opportunities with Toolkits for User Innovation and Design. In: The International Journal of Media Management 4(4):225-235

Grover V, Fiedler KD, Teng JTC (1994) Exploring the Success of Information Technology Enabled Business Process Reengineering. In: IEEE Transactions on Engineering Management 40(3):276-284

Grover V, Teng JTC, Segars A, Fiedler KD (1998)The Influence of Information Technology Diffusion and Business Process change on Perceived Productivity: The IS executive's Perspective. In: Information & Management 34:141-159

Herstatt C, von Hippel E (1992) From Experience: Developing New Product Concepts via the Lead User Method: A Case Study in a "Low Tech Field". In: Journal of Product Innovation Management 9:213-221

von Hippel E (1986) Lead Users: A Source of Novel Product Concepts. In: Management Science 32(7):791-805

von Hippel E (1988) The Sources of Innovation. Oxford University Press, Oxford

von Hippel E (1994) Sticky Information and the Locus of Problem Solving: Implications for Innovation. In: Management Science 40(4):429-439

von Hippel E (1998) Economics of Product Development by Users: The Impact of Sticky Local Information. In: Management Science 44(5):629-644

von Hippel E (1999) Toolkits for User Innovation. Working Paper No. 4058. MIT Sloan School of Management, Boston

von Hippel E, Katz R (2002) Shifting Innovation to Users Via Toolkits. In: Management Science 48(7):821-833

von Hippel (2005) Democratizing Innovation. The MIT Press, Boston

Huffman C, Kahn B (1998) Variety for Sale: Mass Customization or Mass Confusion. In: Journal of Retailing 74:491-513

Hondrich KO, Vollmer R (1983) Bedürfnisse - Stabilität und Wandel. Westdeutscher Verlag, Opladen

Houghton J, Sheehan P (2000) A Primer on the Knowledge Economy. Report. Centre for Strategic Economic Studies, Victoria University

Jeppesen LB (2002) The Implications of User Toolkits for Innovation. Working Paper No. 2002-09 (in IVS/CBS Working Papers Series). Department of Industrial Economics & Strategy, Copenhagen Business School

Kruchten P (1999) The Rational Unified Process: An Introduction. Addison-Wesley, Upper Saddle River

Krueger RA (1994) Focus Groups: A Practical Guide for Applied Research. Sage Publications, Thousand Oaks

Maes P (1994) Agents that Reduce Work and Information Overload. In: Communications of the ACM 37(7):31-40

Magnusson P, Matthing J, Kristensson P (2003) Managing User Involvement in Service innovation - Experiments with Innovating End Users. In: Journal of Service Research 6(2):114-124

Naher N, Kakola T, Huda N (2002) Diffusion of Software Technology Innovation in the Global Context. In: Proceedings of 35th Annual Hawaii International Conference on System Sciences (HICSS'02) 7:178-187

Neale MR, Corkindale DR (1998) Co-developing Products: Involving Customers Earlier And More Deeply. In: Long Range Planning 31:418-425

Nelson R (1990) What is Public and What is Private About Technology? Consortium on Competitiveness and Cooperation Working Paper No. 90-9. Center for Research in Management, University of California at Berkeley

Pawlowski J (2001) The Essen Learning Model. Dissertation. Fakultät für Wirtschaftswissenschaften, Universität Essen

Pavitt K (1987) The Objectives of Technology Policy. In: Science and Public Policy 14(4): 182-88

Piller FT (2001) Mass Customization. Gabler, Wiesbaden

Porter ME (1998) On Competition. Harvard Business School Press, Cambridge

Powell TC, Dent-Micallef A (1999) Information Technology as Competitive Advantage: The Role of Human, Business, and Technology Resources. In: Strategic Management Journal 18(5):375-405

Reichart SV (2002) Kundenorientierung im Innovationsprozess: Die erfolgreiche Integration von Kunden in den frühen Phasen der Produktentwicklung, Deutscher Universitäts-Verlag, Wiesbaden

Rogers ME (2003) Diffusion of Innovations. The Free Press, New York

Rosenberg N (1982) Inside the Black Box: Technology and Economics. Cambridge University Press, New York

Royce W (1970) Managing Development of Large Scale Software Systems. In: Proceedingsof IEEE WESCON

Ruttan VW (1959) Usher and Schumpeter on Invention, Innovation, and Technological Change. In: Quarterly Journal of Economics 73(4):596-606

Schumpeter J (1939) Business Cycles. McGraw-Hill, New York

Sioukas AV (1995) User Involvement For Effective Customization: An Empirical Study on Voice Networks. In: IEEE Transactions on Engineering Management 42:39-49

Storey C, Easingwood CJ (1998) The Augmented Service Offering: A Conceptualization and Study of its Impact on New Service Success – A Means-End Model and Synthesis of Evidence. In: The Journal of Product Innovation Management 15(4):335-351

Thomke SH, Bell DE (2001) Sequential Testing in Product Development. In: Management Science 47(2):308-323

Thomke S, von Hippel E (2002) Customers as Innovators: A New Way to Create Value. In: Harvard Business Review 80(4)

Thomke SH (1998) Managing Experimentation in the Design of New Products. In: Management Science 44(6):734-762

Tyre M (1995) How "Learning by Doing" is done: Problem Identification. In: Novel Process Equipment, Research Policy 24(1):1-12

Urban GL, Hauser JR (1993) Design and Marketing of New Products. Prentice-Hall, New Jersey

Ulwick AW (2002) Turn Customer Input into Innovation. In: Harvard Business Review 80(1):91-97

Venkatraman M, Dholakia RR (1997) Searching for Information in Marketspace: Does the Form – Product or Service – Matter? In: Journal of Services Marketing 11(5):303-316

Weill P, Broadbent M (1998) Leveraging the New Infrastructure: How Market Leaders Capitalize on Information Technology. Harvard Business School Press, Boston

Woodruff RB, Gardial SF (1996) Know Your Customer: New Approaches to Understanding Value and Satisfaction. Blackwell Publishers, Cambridge

Motives and Perception of Fairness in Commercial User Communities

Philip Mayrhofer

1 Introduction

Rather recently, the widely discussed example of software development in open source projects has intensified research in the economic field of public goods. Lerner and Tirole (2002, p.198) bring forward a puzzle that an increasing body of literature aims to understand and explain: "Why should top-notch programmers contribute freely to the provision of a public good?". Scholars argue theoretically[1] and provide empirical evidence[2] that innovators derive various and additional benefits from their innovative activity than the primarily monetary ones postulated in traditional economic theory. Indeed, studies, also covering other industries than software, find that user communities emerge, which exhibit a mix of benefits such as reputation effects and reciprocity among contributing users. In the context of this article, user communities are understood to be innovation communities, meaning "nodes consisting of individuals or firms interconnected by information transfer links which may involve face-to-face, electronic, or other communication" (von Hippel 2005, p.96).[3] The benefits inherent in such communities are generally argued to provide the answer to the economic puzzle stated.

A current phenomenon in practice has found considerably less attention in literature so far but might upset the incentive system found to work for innovative communities. Commercial firms increasingly develop business models in order to capitalize systematically on innovative activity of user communities. In early 2005, for example, the technology firm Sun Mircosystems Inc. released the source code of its commercial operating system Solaris to the programming community (Shankland 2005a). By doing so, the firm attempts to tap on an enormous development pool that user communities provide and aims at substituting internal development effort. Similar business models exist and become especially interesting if they change the notion of open access to property that prevails in open source communities (Weber 2004). If firms take openly accessible innovations from a user community and put them in their private domain, it may disrupt the community's stable incentive system. Specifically, if benefits of

---

[1] See for example Johnson (2001), Harhoff et al. (2003), Mustonen (2003) and von Hippel and von Krogh (2003).

[2] See for example Hars and Ou (2001), Ghosh et al. (2002), Franke and von Hippel (2003), Hertel et al. (2003), and Lakhani and Wolf (2003).

[3] Those communities often exhibit qualities of communities of a more traditional definition, i.e. understanding networks as "networks of interpersonal ties that provide sociability, support, information, a sense of belonging, and social identity" (Wellman et al. 2002, p.4).

the innovative activity in the community are perceived to be distributed unfairly between the contributors and the commercial firm, users may turn away. Fairness in this context is defined in reference to economics literature which considers "fair" agents to be averse against cooperation settings with inequitable benefit distribution (Fehr and Schmidt 1999).

The survey described in this article aims at contributing to a first understanding of both aspects brought forward in this introduction. Both the motives and the perception of fairness of contributors to a user community with an adjunct commercial firm shall be studied. It shall be examined to what extent members of this community are similarly motivated as contributors to open source projects and whether they find benefits to be distributed fairly.

The article proceeds as follows. In a first step, a literature review summarizes findings of empirical studies on open source communities. It follows a section with a case study of StataCorp, the vendor of a statistical software package, and its user community. The section also contains an explanation of the method used to examine the user community in more detail as well as descriptive results and discussion of the participants' motives and perception of fairness. The article ends with a conclusion and outlook for further research areas.

2 Motives to Contribute in Open Source Communities

Theoretical papers and empirical studies of open source projects show that determinants of motivation can be both extrinsic and intrinsic.[4] This section provides a short overview of both forms of motives in open source communities.[5]

Generally, the primary example of extrinsic motivation is *monetary compensation*. In fact, Lakhani and Wolf (2003) find in a study of 684 open source developers that approximately 40% of the contributors receive some form of monetary compensation for their work on open source projects. This confirms a previous study by Hars and Ou (2001) with similar

---

[4] A common categorization of motivational determinants is to distinguish between extrinsic and intrinsic motivation (Osterloh and Frey 2000). Agents are extrinsically motivated, if the activity allows for indirect compensation (primarily through monetary rewards). If an agent acts due to his immediate need satisfaction and the activity is valued for its own sake, one speaks of intrinsic motivation (Lakhani and Wolf 2003).

[5] See Brügge et al. (2004) for a detailed overview of empirical studies on the determinants of motivation of contributors to open source projects.

findings and results reported by Hertel et al. (2003) on contributors to the Linux kernel. However, the three reported studies do not find that monetary rewards directly motivate developers to contribute. Determinants of monetary compensation also rank last in a study by Henkel and Thies (2003). A second extrinsic determinant of motivation is *personal use* of the contribution. As Raymond (1999, p.32) states: "Every good work of software starts by scratching a developer's personal itch." Empirical evidence for this statement is brought forward by Lakhani and Wolf (2003) who report that 58% of their study's respondents regard "user need" as the most important reason for contributing to open source projects. *Career advancement* is a third determinant argued to be important for contributors (Lerner and Tirole 2002). However, Henkel (2003) concludes after reviewing several empirical studies that Lerner and Tirole's (2002) emphasis on this aspect might be too strong.[6] A final extrinsic determinant stems from *skill improvement* through active peer-review. Contributions to open source projects are typically subject to intense peer review both before and after a submission. For example, Ghosh et al. (2002) find in their study of 2784 developers that the most important reason (78.9% of respondents) is to learn and develop new skills. 33.7% of the contributors report that the reason for joining was to improve products of other developers. An earlier study by Hars and Ou (2001) confirms these findings.

There also exist various studies that examine contributors' intrinsic determinants of motivation. Intrinsic motivation can be distinguished in enjoyment and obligation based motivation (Lindenberg 2001). The former is in detail studied by Lakhani and Wolf (2003). First, the authors find that *creativity* is the single most important reason why programmers contribute to open source projects.[7] Second, *fun* appears to be particularly important for contributors who program to improve their skills and for intellectual stimulation (Lakhani and Wolf 2003).

If individuals act on the basis of principle or are socialized to act according to a group norm, one speaks of obligation or community based intrinsic motivation (Lindenberg 2001). In this category, *reciprocity* has been proposed to play an important role (Kollock 1999). In their study on contributors to the Apache Usenet, Lakhani and von Hippel (2000) find that reciprocity is the most important reason for users to provide answers.

---

[6] Empirical studies have found determinants such as "professional status" (Lakhani and Wolf 2003) and "improve my job opportunities" (Ghosh et al. 2002) to rank quite low among other determinants.

[7] In the same study as cited above, 44.9% of the respondents regard the following reason to be important: "Project code is intellectually stimulating to write" (Lakhani and Wolf 2003).

Contributors either have been helped in the past or expect others to help them in turn in the future. An unconditional determinant of motivation, *altruism*, is empirically examined by Hars and Ou (2001). However, this determinant ranks in the lower third of alternatives provided in the questionnaire. On a related note, *community identification* is of relatively low importance to contributors in the same study (Hars and Ou 2001). Lakhani and Wolf (2003) provide differing results. In their study, 83% of the respondents agree with the statement that the hacker community is a primary source of their identity (Lakhani and Wolf 2003). Community related motives rank in the mid-field in the study by Ghosh et al. (2002). Finally, *reputation within the community* is investigated in various studies. Raymond (1999) observes that contributors have a strong strive for "ego satisfaction". Hars and Ou (2001) find empirical evidence for this claim. In their study, "peer recognition" ranks third among eight reasons to contribute to open source projects (Hars and Ou 2001). Absolutely contrary to this finding is the result reported by Ghosh et al. (2002). The authors find that reputation is of low importance to contributors. Only 9.1% of the respondents see reputation in the community as one of their four most important reasons why they joined an open source project (Ghosh et al. 2002). Reputation effects in the community also rank low in the study by Lakhani and Wolf (2003) and Henkel and Thies (2003). Table 1 again lists the determinants described above. It was shown that career advancement, monetary compensation and altruism are not major determinants of motivation in open source projects. Strong influence, however, was observed for personal use, skill improvement through active peer-review, fun, creativity and reciprocity. Other determinants, such as community identification and reputation, seem to matter in some studies whereas they do not in others.[8]

Table 1. Determinants of motivation in open source projects[9]

extrinsic motivation	**intrinsic motivation**	
active peer-review	*enjoyment-based*	fun / flow
career advancement		creativity
monetary compensation	*obligation-based*	altruism
personal use		community identification
skill improvement		reciprocity
		reputation

[8] Note that studies of motives of open source contributors exhibit an inherent subjectivity of the respondents' assessments, self-serving biases and low response rates (Lerner and Tirole 2004). As a consequence, it is no surprise that self-reported motivations vary considerably across studies.

[9] The categorization of this section and of Table 1 is based on Lakhani and Wolf (2003).

3 Survey on StataCorp's User Community

3.1 Motivation and Object of Study

This survey of StataCorp's user community aims at contributing to the understanding of user communities which exhibit a strong and vivid interaction with a commercial firm. There are two sets of questions which shall be explored specifically. First, the motives of Stata contributors are examined analogously to studies of open source communities. Are contributors similarly motivated in both settings? For successful communities, this is expected to be true. And, furthermore, do signaling effects within the community or in relation to the firm hosting the community play an important role? Second, the concept of fairness in the sense of inequity aversion shall be tested exploratively in this setting. Do contributors indeed perceive benefits to be distributed fairly and, thus, contribute freely?

The Stata user community was chosen and is an appropriate object to study in the context of this article because the vibrant community interacts closely with the commercial vendor of the statistical software, StataCorp. The case study of the following section will show the modular concept of the software. Whereas the majority of add-on modules are simply shared in a user-maintained online-repository, StataCorp selects particularly successful modules and integrates them in subsequent versions of the software. Thus, it is a good example of the integration of innovations from an open to a proprietary innovation system. Though limited to a single case and to solely contributing users, the following case and explorative empirical study provide first insights in the incentive structure of users as well as their perception of fairness.

3.2 StataCorp and Its User Community

StataCorp, based at College Station (Texas/USA) and located near the Texas A&M campus, has been a leader in developing statistics, graphics, and data-management solutions for over 20 years. Since 1984, the company produces and distributes the statistical software package Stata. Originally designed by William Gould as a DOS program, Stata is now available for a variety of operating systems and marketed to a diverse set of customers. It caters primarily academics and researchers in health sciences, social sciences and econometrics (Baum 2002). Version 8.1 added a completely new graphics subsystem with powerful control over publication-quality graphs as well as enhanced "menu-and-icon" functionality. This extends the former command-line mode of operation and places Stata on an "interesting middle ground" (Baum 2002, p.3) between predominantly "menu-and-icon"-based and "command-line"-based systems.[10]

A highly frequented medium of the Stata community is the mailing list called Statalist, which was initiated in 1994 and currently has over 1,500 subscribers.[11] The mailing list is hosted at the Harvard School of Public Health and used to ask for and provide help on general statistics or Stata specific questions. Contributions are very frequent and it is not uncommon that help-seekers receive extensive answers (often with exemplary code) within hours. Statalist is also used to announce and distribute user-written modules to the statistics package, so-called ado-files.

Since 1997, ado-files distributed via Statalist are collected and supplied for download by another user initiative. The so called "Boston Archive" is stored on RePEc (Research Papers in Economics) servers and can be accessed via two web-based services (IDEAS and EconPapers). In addition, the browser functionality of Stata allows users to directly search and install ado-files within Stata.[12] As of end of 2003, the Boston archive consists of 836 packages of ado-files contributed by 131 Stata users.[13]

The process of publishing ado-files on Boston Archive is as follows. Stata contributors send their written ado-file to the maintainer of the archive who uploads it to the RePEc repository. The program must be documented with appropriate help files and may be accompanied by additional files such as a sample dataset. There is no review of the file's functionality and the material in the archive is warranted by their authors who are urged

---

[10] Former are represented amongst others by Stata's broadly based competitors SAS and SPSS and latter by extensible matrix languages like MATLAB and GAUSS. See Renfro (2003b) for a detailed categorization of statistical packages. A short historical overview and review of Stata's capabilities is provided by Renfro (2004a).

[11] See StataCorp web page: http://www.stata.com/statalist/; last accessed: 2006/03/13.

[12] This procedure is encouraged by both prominent Stata users and StataCorp since it automatically places the ado-file in the correct directory and consequently prevents mistakes in the installation process of downloaded add-ons.

[13] The data was retrieved from Boston Archive via the IDEAS web interface. The archive provides information on the date of contribution, the contributor's name, e-mail-address and institution. Ado-files added between 1997/02/06 and 2003/12/31 were considered. Files stored in the archive but not in ado-file format were excluded.

to correct appearing deficiencies. Once it is uploaded to the archive, the ado-file's availability is announced via Statalist.[14]

Apart from Boston Archive, there exist two more ways to grant other users access to personally developed programs. First, users may provide their ado-files on personal web pages. Some selected of these private repositories are linked to on StataCorp's web page. Analogously to the procedure described above for Boston Archive files, any directory with public access rights can be accessed within Stata, which eases the integration of these personal repositories for other users. It has to be noted, that in many cases, the most sophisticated ado-files published via personal web pages are also contributed to Statalist and are consequently stored on Boston Archive. Second, ado-files are distributed via StataCorp's journal publications. The Stata Technical Bulletin (STB) served as a means of distributing new commands via diskettes between 1991 and 2001. In the last years of its publication, however, the distribution of ado-files was mainly performed via the web and as a result, the editors, predominantly Stata users who are also prominent contributors to Statalist, decided to reorganize the publication. Stata Journal (SJ), which is also published by StataCorp and edited by Stata users, succeeded STB and is now a quarterly publication with focus on more substantial articles on statistics rather than small programs.[15]

3.3 Survey Method and Response Rate

The choice of survey method fell on an Internet-based questionnaire because it is argued that virtually all Stata users have access to the Internet and possess an e-mail-account. The questionnaire was online from November 1st, 2004 until December 31st, 2004. The majority of the closed questions cover the respondents' motives as well as their perception of StataCorp. Those questions are presented in five-point rating-scales. Furthermore, within the questionnaire, respondents are given the option to provide their name as used on Boston Archive. The name is used to match data of the archive with the one collected via the Internet-survey. Finally, no rewards or gifts besides a synthesis of the study's results were offered.

---

[14] See the web page "Submitting and retrieving materials from the SSC Archive" for further details: http://www.repec.org/bocode/s/sscsubmit.html (last accessed: 2006/03/13).

[15] See StataCorp web page: http://www.stata-journal.com/editors.html for a list of the editors (last accessed: 2006/03/13); http://www.stata-journal.com/sjfaq.html #stb for FAQs concerning Stata Journal and Stata Technical Bulletin (last accessed: 2006/03/13).

The final mailing-list consisted of 120 entries and the questionnaire produced 53 responses. With 110 invitations delivered successfully, the response rate is at 48.18%. A more detailed examination of the responses
shows that only eight Stata users did not provide their name for a matching
of the survey's results with data from Boston Archive.

3.4 Survey Results and Discussion

3.4.1 Stata Contributors and Their Use of the Community

This section provides an overview of the contributors to Stata community
as well as their use of the community's ado-files and services.

Survey respondents are on average 41 years old and predominantly live
in the developed Western world (52% of respondents from North America
(US and Canada) and 44% from Europe). The majority of respondents
work in academic institutions (62% of respondents). The second and third
most frequently named employers are the government (15%) and independent research organizations (10%). Their field of research or work is
primarily in social science (46%) and health science (35%). Another 4% of
respondents are engaged in natural sciences and 15% in other fields.

Furthermore, respondents are using Stata since eight years and on average 13 hours per week. They perform the considerably more challenging
task of writing ado-files on average since six years and about four hours a
week. The vast majority finds Stata easy to use (96% of respondents) and
Stata commands easy to learn (94%). 51% of the respondents agree to the
statement that "standard commands and ado-file programming are too limited" for some applications. Hence, 53% of the respondents have in the
past used other programming languages for tackling problems not easily
solved in Stata language. This suggests that Stata contributors exhibit a
high level of skill. When asked to report on their level of skill, 43% of the
respondents consequently claim to be advanced in both using Stata and
programming ado-files. This is further underlined by 34% who are advanced in using Stata and intermediate in programming ado-files.

There are various channels which Stata contributors use to access Stata
related information. 77% are subscribed to Stata's mailing list and 38%
read Stata News. StataCorp's publication, Stata Journal, is read by 66% of
the respondents. Finally, a quite high 34% of respondents have attended
Stata user meetings which are held in North America and many countries
in Europe since 1997. This shows that Stata contributors are interested in
keeping up-to-date in recent developments regarding Stata.

In a last step of this overview, the Stata contributors' use of Boston Archive as a repository for ado-files as well as their perception of the quality of ado-files shall be examined. Stata contributors have downloaded about 18 (s.d.: 29.44; median: 10) ado-files in a 90-day period prior to the survey.[16] The answers range from one to as many as 150 ado-files. 38% of the respondents have downloaded their last ado-file in the week prior to the survey and 9% even on the same day. This suggests a high usage of the archive's resources.

3.4.2 Determinants of Motivation

The questionnaire provided the participants of the survey with two lists of statements referring to their motivation to write and publish ado-files.[17] Stata contributors were asked to refer their answers to the last incident they wrote and published an ado-file. This avoids undesirable "average perceptions" that may blur the results. Table 2 summarizes the results which are described in the following.

Motives to write ado-files
It becomes apparent that personal need is the strongest motive to write an ado-file. Statements A1 ("functionality not available in Stata") and A2 ("specific problem") rank highest with means of 4.81 and 4.77 respectively. Fun ranks third (A3) with a mean of 4.31. 50% of respondents chose "agree strongly" when answering to this statement. Furthermore, the motive of skill improvement (A4) exhibits a solid agreement with a mean of 4.02. Statement A5, which relates to current career effects, ranks last with a mean of 2.21.

---

[16] s.d. abbreviates standard deviation.

[17] The participants were asked to indicate to what extent they agree or disagree with the statements. They were provided with a five-point rating scale ranging from 1 ("disagree strongly") to 5 ("agree strongly"). A sixth option for "Don't know" was provided but excluded when computing the statistics of Table 2).

Table 2. Determinants of motivation to (A) write and (B) publish the ado-file last contributed to the community

	n	mean	s.d.	strong agreement
(A) I wrote this particular ado-file because ...				
... Stata didn't offer the functionality. (A1)	53	4.81	0.44	83.02%
... I had a specific problem. (A2)	53	4.77	0.51	81.13%
... it is fun for me to program ado-files. (A3)	52	4.31	0.88	50.00%
... by doing so, I improve my Stata knowledge. (A4)	53	4.02	0.84	26.42%
... by doing so, I can show my employer that I am productive. (A5)	53	2.21	1.28	5.66%
(B) I published this particular ado-file because ...				
... I want to do something for the community per se; no reward needed. (B1)	52	4	0.86	28.85%
... I like to be an active member of the Stata community. (B2)	51	3.84	1.01	31.37%
... I hope somebody else will contribute too. (B3)	52	3.75	0.97	19.23%
...others then have the opportunity to improve it or report bugs. (B4)	52	3.73	0.97	21.15%
... I want to communicate with like-minded people. (B5)	52	3.67	0.98	21.15%
... you only get something when you give something yourself. (B6)	51	3.51	1.08	13.73%
... I hope that my developments are integrated in future releases. (B7)	52	3.4	1.07	15.38%
... I want to appear as a good member of the community. (B8)	52	3.21	1.14	7.69%
... gaining prestige within the community is important to me. (B9)	52	3.21	1.26	13.46%
... it is beneficial for my professional status. (B10)	50	2.74	1.32	8.00%
... it increases my attractiveness for future employers. (B11)	51	2.49	1.36	7.84%
... publishing modules makes me known at StataCorp. (B12)	51	2.47	1.21	1.96%

notes: - five-point rating scale: 1 strongly disagree; 5 strongly agree
          - variation in n due to missing answers in some items.

Motives to publish ado-files

Surprisingly, altruism is the highest ranking motive for publishing the last ado-file (statement B1; mean: 4). This is startling when considering other studies of open source projects in which altruism seems to be of lower importance. Clear indication is also brought forward for the feeling of belonging to a community, which ranks high among the statements provided. Stata contributors like to be active members of the community (statement B2; mean: 3.84) and to communicate with like-minded people (statement B5; mean: 3.67). As expected, reciprocity (statements B3 and B6) is important for Stata contributors. However, it also becomes apparent that agreement to these motives is less strong than to the ones pointed out above. Even though reciprocity ranks third and sixth among twelve motives, agreement to the statements is only moderate (compare means of 3.75 and 3.51 respectively). Furthermore, reputation in the community plays a minor role (statements B8 and B9; mean: 3.21 (both)). Finally, motives regarding potential signals sent to current and future employers rank last. Current career effects, represented by statement B10 ("beneficial for professional status"; mean: 2.74), is of equally low importance as future career effects (B11; "increased attractiveness for future employers"; mean: 2.49) and recognition from the commercial entity (B12; "makes me known at StataCorp"; mean: 2.47).

Discussion

The above presented results show that solving a personal need and altruism[18] are the most important determinants of motivation to contribute to Stata's user community. The high importance of these two determinants is somewhat startling in the light of past empirical studies on open source software. However, considering the characteristics of Stata contributors and their differences to purely open source projects, these results are sensible. Stata contributors predominantly use Stata in order to solve statistical problems in their respective field of science or work. Stata is the means to an end. If a Stata user encounters a problem, which cannot be solved with Stata's standard functionality, he develops a solution in form of an ado-file. Publishing the ado-file on Boston Archive incurs low costs of effort and competitive disadvantage. Consequently, the "costs of altruism" are quite low. The results concerning the other determinants studied are conform with surveys examining motivation in open source communities. Thus, these findings confirm the expectation that the incentive system of a user community remains predominantly unaltered in its most important determinants.

---

[18] Note that altruism is a determinant that may be particularly affected by biases known as "self presentation" and "social desirability" (Bortz and Döring 2002). Respondents are inclined to give answers that make themselves look "good" or which they believe to be the most accepted ones.

Another important finding of this section is the low importance of signaling for future career effects in the Stata community. This is contrary to an intuitive expectation as well as findings of Jeppesen and Frederiksen (2004) who provide empirical evidence that contributors in firm-established user communities do care about recognition from the firm. This expectation turns out to be not the case among respondents answering to the questionnaire. A reason for the low importance of signaling can be seen in the specific characteristics of the community. Stata community is primarily frequented by users in need for sophisticated statistical methods. However, the users in the community are not primarily statisticians interested in the method itself. Rather, they are experts who use statistics to produce results in a variety of unrelated fields. Thus, writing ado-files as a signal for their primary field of work is not likely. One exception, however, remains: academics may signal their ability on the academic labor market. Stata users from one university may recognize the strong statistical competencies of a colleague in a related field. An analysis of the variable "attractiveness for future employers", in fact, provides evidence for this proposition. Academics see this motive to be more important (mean: 2.77; s.d.: 1.41; median: 3) than non-academics (mean: 2.05; s.d.: 1.19; median: 2). The difference is statistically significant at the ten per cent level. However, it has to be noted that a mean of 2.77 expresses a weak disagreement with the statement regarding the motive to increase one's "attractiveness for future employers".

3.4.3 Description and Discussion of Perception of Fairness

In this section, it shall be examined whether Stata contributors in fact view the benefits to be distributed fairly between StataCorp and the community. Both data from closed and open questions is utilized. In the questionnaire, participants of the survey were asked to indicate to what extent they agree or disagree with the statements listed in Table 3. The statements aim at measuring the perception of StataCorp's commercial interest in user written ado-files. Apparently, the respondents welcome StataCorp's approach. 57% strongly agree with the statement that this strategy helps to improve the product (mean: 4.49; s.d.; 0.67; median: 5). Furthermore, almost equally strong agreement is indicated for the statement that it is a fair deal because both parties benefit from it (mean: 4.27; s.d.: 0.7).

Finally, reversely formulated respondents exhibit disagreement with the statement that they are annoyed by StataCorp's strategy (mean: 1.89; s.d.: 1.9; median: 1).

Table 3. Perception of StataCorp's Commercial Interest in User Contributions

	obs.	mean	s.d.	median	strong agreement
I am glad because it helps to improve the product.	53	4.49	0.67	5	56.60%
It is a fair deal with them – both the users and StataCorp gain from incorporating ado-files in new versions.	51	4.27	0.7	4	41.18%
I am annoyed because they take user contributions and make money with it.	53	1.89	1.9	1	0.00%

The relatively high standard deviation suggests, however, that there are larger differences in this response than in the ones before. And indeed, six respondents (11.32%) report that they somewhat agree to being annoyed because StataCorp makes money with user contributions. Disagreement to the other two statements is practically non-existent.

These quantitative results are supported by additional remarks which respondents stated when asked for their opinion on StataCorp benefiting from the community's work. For example, one respondent simply states: "It is a brilliant design. Neither SAS nor SPSS easily allow people to contribute to their packages". Another respondent has a similar attitude by referring to the fair licensing policy offered by StataCorp as opposed to SAS and SPSS. He believes that StataCorp cares very personally about their product and, thus, he is happy to contribute code. "In short, everybody wins" finds another respondent and notes that StataCorp benefits from the users' free labor which allows the company to grow more quickly. This, he believes, in turn benefits the community. Finally, one respondent points out that StataCorp can incorporate ado-files as long as the price of the package remains unaffected by user written add-ons.

The results presented in this section indeed provide evidence for the proposition that contributors in successful communities find benefits to be equally distributed between the community and the firm. This is a promising finding for companies pursuing business models which rely on the development effort of an external community. It suggests that, if done correctly and with appropriate measures of compensation, user communities are manageable.

However, there is one evident and important caveat to this study. By including only users who have contributed in the past, one can not know whether there are users who decided not to contribute due to their perception of fairness. Consequently, this study needs to be extended to non-contributing users in order to get a comprehensive understanding. In addition, problems of self-reporting biases do also apply here.

4 Conclusion and Outlook

Motives of Stata users to contribute to the community were shown to be similar to the ones found in studies of open source projects. The determinants personal use and altruism were identified to be most important. However, the empirical results do not provide evidence for the proposition that signaling effects to future employers and the firm hosting the community are more pronounced in a firm-user community setting. The empirical study furthermore showed that the vast majority of Stata contributors feel treated fairly by StataCorp.

These findings have implications for firms in product industries that exhibit a high degree of modularization of the product as well as clearly defined interfaces and standards between core products and additional modules. It appears that, if done correctly, an open innovation and proprietary model may coexist and a user community may be managed by a firm. If this was found true in a variety of settings, firms could begin to explore new arrangements of value creation and develop business models relying on the external development efforts of an adjunct user community. In any business model, management will certainly have to consider a fair distribution of the benefits. This implies understanding the needs and expectations of the firm's users as well as internal processes that succeed in economically fulfilling these expectations.

Whereas the findings of this paper provide first insights, there are various further aspects to investigate. An extension of this particular study, i.e. including Stata users who have not contributed in the past, appears to be rewarding and is currently pursued. Additional empirical studies of cases similar to Stata's community are important in order to validate the findings of this article and to examine its potential of generalization. The concept of fairness, as exploratively introduced in this article, is in need of further theoretical development. Finally, an aspect, which was only considered to a minor degree in this article, concerns the commercial entity in such a user community. In order to allow a user community to innovate, the firm has to provide an interface. However, this implies a higher degree of openness of the firm's closed and proprietary innovation process. The firm's organizational setup and the impact of differing intellectual property regimes pose manifold research questions for further investigation as well as managerial challenges in this respect.

References

Baum CF (2002) Facilitating applied economic research with Stata. Working Paper 2002/01, Boston College

Bortz J, Döring N (2002) Forschungsmethoden und Evaluation: für Human- und Sozialwissenschaftler. 3rd edition, Springer, Berlin

Brügge B, Harhoff D, Picot A, Creighton O, Fiedler M, Henkel J (2004) Open-Source-Software-Eine ökonomische und technische Analyse. Springer, Berlin

Fehr E, Schmidt K (1999) A Theory of Fairness, Competition, and Cooperation. Quarterly Journal of Economics 114, 3: 817-868

Franke N, von Hippel E (2003) Satisfying heterogeneous user needs via innovation toolkits: the case of Apache security software. Research Policy 32: 1199-1215

Ghosh RA, Glott R, Krieger B, Robles G (2002) Free/Libre and Open Source Software: Survey and Study. In: Part 4: Survey of Developers, http://www.infonomics.nl/FLOSS/report/, International Institute of Infonomics, University of Maastricht

Harhoff D, Henkel J, von Hippel E (2003) Profiting from voluntary information spillovers: how users benefit by freely revealing their innovations. Research Policy 32:1753–1769

Hars A, Ou S (2001) Working for Free? Motivations for Participating in Open-Source Projects. International Journal of Electronic Commerce 6, 3: 25–39

Henkel J (2003) Open-Source-Aktivitäten von Unternehmen – Innovation in kollektiven Prozessen. unpublished Habilationsschrift, Munich School of Management, Ludwig-Maximilians-University, Munich

Henkel J, Thies S (2003) Customization and Innovation – User Innovation Toolkits for Simulator Software. Working Paper, 2003/03, University of Munich

Hertel G, Niedner S, Herrmann S (2002) Motivation of Software Developers in Open Source Projects: An Internet-Based Survey of Contributors to the Linux Kernel. Research Policy 32: 1159–1177

Jeppesen LB, Frederiksen L (2004) Why firm-established user communities work for innovation: The personal attributes of innovative users in the case of computer-controlled music instruments. Working Paper, 2004/06, Copenhagen Business School

Johnson JP (2001) Economics of open source software. Working Paper 2001/05, MIT Sloan School of Management

Jokisch M (2002) Open Source Software-Entwicklung-Eine Analyse des Geschaeftsmodells der STATA Corp. unpublished master thesis, Munich School of Management, Ludwig-Maximilians-University Munich

Kollock P (1999) The Economies of Online Cooperation: Gifts and Public Goods in Cyberspace. In: Smith MA. / Kollock P (eds.) Communities in Cyberspace, chapter 7, London, Routledge

Lakhani KR, von Hippel E (2000) How Open Source software works: "Free" user-to-user assistance. Working Paper 4117, MIT Sloan School of Management

Lakhani KR, Wolf RG (2003) Why Hackers Do What They Do: Understanding Motivation Effort in Free/Open Source Software Projects. Working Paper 4425-03, MIT Sloan School of Management

Lerner J, Tirole J (2002) Some Simple Economics of Open Source. The Journal of Industrial Economics L, 2: 197-234

Lerner J, Tirole J (2004) The Economics of Technology Sharing: Open Source and Beyond. Working Paper 10956, NBER

Lindenberg S (2001) Intrinsic motivation in a new light. Kyklos 54, 2-3: 317-342

Mustonen M (2003) Copyleft - the economics of Linux and other open source software. Information Economics and Policy 15: 99–121

Osterloh M, Frey BS. (2000) Motivation, knowledge transfer, and organizational firms. Organization Science 11, 5: 538-550

Raymond ES (1999) The Cathedral & the Bazaar: Musings on Linux and Open Source by an Accidental Revolutionary. O'Reilly, Cambridge

Renfro CG (2004a) A Compendium of Existing Econometric Software Packages. Journal of Economics and Social Measurement 29, 1-3: 459-509

Renfro CG (2004b) Econometric software: The first fifty years in perspective. Journal of Economic and Social Measurement 29, 1-3: 9-107

Shankland S (2005a) Sun to release first OpenSolaris tidbit Tuesday. ZDNet News, 2005/01/24, http://news.zdnet.com/2100-9593_22-5548394.html, last accessed: 2005/02/19

Von Hippel E (2005) Democratizing Innovation. MIT Press, Cambridge, M.A.

Von Hippel E, von Krogh G (2003) Open Source Software and the "Private-Collective" Innovation Model: Issues for Organization Science. Organization Science 14, 2: 209–223

Weber S (2004) The Success of Open Source. Harvard University Press, Cambridge, M.A.

Wellman B, Boase J, Chen W (2002) The Networked Nature of Community On and Off the Internet. Working paper, Centre for Urban and Community Studies, University of Toronto

Engaging Students in Distributed Software Engineering Courses

Christoph Angerer, Michael Nagel,
Bernd Brügge, Thomas Gross

1 Introduction

Nowadays, academic education is not only expected to teach abstract scientific working methods. In fact, it is desired that students become prepared for working in real companies, on real projects. For this reason, pedagogy has developed various problem-oriented and situation-oriented approaches to teach students the necessary problem solving and group interaction skills.

Constructivist paradigms, for example, aim at teaching such problem solving skills by embedding the whole educational process into real-life situations and problems, thus dissolving the common distinction between the lecture and the corresponding exercises.

One particularly successful concept for teaching based on authentic activities and natural social interaction is *cognitive apprenticeship*. Cognitive apprenticeship requires a close master-novice relationship between the teacher and the students. However, such a structure is costly in terms of time and personal care. We investigate how to apply this method to teaching software engineering in the university environment, where a teacher typically faces several dozens, if not hundreds, of students.

We start with the assumption that cognitive apprenticeship is applicable even in large academic courses if we enable communication between course participants. To realize communication between all participants, we envision a computer aided learning environment that encourages students to dynamically form groups during the lecture on a demand basis. In these groups the instructor, a teaching assistant, or even a fellow student may play the role of the expert ("master") for a certain period of time. Due to its focus on practical issues, software engineering has a great demand for distinct problem solving skills – not only because programming computers is a structured process in itself, but also because building large and complex systems requires an engineering approach as well.

The skills that are considered relevant depend on the concrete goals of the individual course. However, the ability to analyze and design complex systems by collaborating with other members in distributed teams is clearly an important skill for computer scientists. As cross-cultural and inter-regional teams become common practice in the design of software systems, we want to provide the students with an opportunity to gain experience with this style of work while still enrolled in the university. Given the importance (and difficulty) of sharing design ideas, we emphasize the sharing of high-level views in the context of a distributed class: In the course on "Design Patterns for Mobile and Distributed Applications", organized by ETH Zürich and the Center for Digital Technology & Management

(CDTM) we try to test the ideas of cognitive apprenticeship in an academic course, including remote student collaboration in a distributed setting. Such a course requires specialized tool support for realizing such scenarios and our goal is to leverage the start-up investment in tools into an improved teaching scenario in the future.

2 Pedagogical Background and Related Work

As a pedagogic methodology, the psychologists Collins, Brown, and Newman coined the term "cognitive apprenticeship" (Collins et al. 1989). The original objective was to teach problem-solving skills by assigning exercises based on real-live problems to the students. As such, cognitive apprenticeship lives in the tradition of constructivist approaches and situated learning and is one of the major responses to the problems of traditional frontal lectures (Krapp and Weidemann 2001, pp 603–646).

The educational principles of cognitive apprenticeship can be traced back to a centuries-old Japanese educational tradition that roots in such diverse pursuits as martial arts, flower arranging, and puppetry: The educational three-staged *shu-ha-ri* process (Cockburn 2002, p 17). Shu-ha-ri literally means 'embracing the form', 'diverging from the form', and 'discarding the form', where the term *form* (Japanese: *kata*) denotes a single exercise and the "most visible representation of a school's knowledge packaged into one seemingly simple set of movements or concepts" (Takamura 1986).

The pervasiveness of shu-ha-ri in Japanese culture can be seen in many plots of martial arts movies: An initially clumsy student is forced by his (rarely her) master to train (apparently useless) exercises (shu), such as coloring fences, carrying stones, or polishing an automobile (of course to the advantage of the master who desires a clean home or car). After an initial crisis the student begins to understand and starts to use the experience actively, even trying out some variations: The student makes progress because the ha-level has been entered. In the end, the student succeeds over the master and becomes a master on his own – ready to accomplish the task he failed to do in the very beginning and which initially made him to call on his master. Only after undergoing the complete process the student is capable to teach these ideas to other students; he then becomes a teacher – a *sensei*, or "one who has gone through before."

Traditional methods to teach handcrafts are based on the same principle. The master (expert) builds up an educational relationship with an *apprentice* (novice) who has to pass three stages: the cognitive stage, the associative stage, and the autonomous stage (shu, ha, and ri). In traditional hand-crafting, the master-apprentice relationship was usually one-to-one or at most one-to-few due to the intensive and time-consuming care the master must give to the novices.

Modern pedagogy takes up the very same fundamentals of shu-ha-ri and teaching handcrafting. The cognitive apprenticeship approach was formu-lated with the initial goal to improve the teaching quality of reading, writ-ing, and mathematics in public schools. Like education in traditional hand-crafting, this approach is deeply rooted in an intense teacher-student relationship; however, class size now becomes a big problem: To monitor and coach students and their cognitive processes, courses should be smaller than they often are. To overcome this drawback, some pedagogues have proposed using technology to replace the teacher's role or to aid the teacher in creating simulated and authentic examples (Cleary and Schank 1995).

Our work is based on the assumption that constructivist approaches – especially cognitive apprenticeship – and cooperative learning are benefi-cial to the purpose of academic education. A meta-analysis of 43 studies verified the positive effects of problem-oriented teaching claimed in con-structivist theories (Dochy et al. 2003). Cooperative learning techniques were also subject to various studies that demonstrated that intensified and active communication between peer students leads to so-called co-cooperation processes that activate learning processes (Fischer 2001).

In the context of e-learning numerous applications have been developed to increase the involvement of students in lectures. For example, the *ETH Lecture Communicator* allows instructors to conduct instant in-class sur-veys where students can fill out online questionnaires with their wireless notebooks or PDAs and see the result of the survey in real-time on the presentation screen (Gross et al. 2003). Since its first release in 2003, the ETH Lecture Communicator has been successfully used in several courses at ETH.

Another application that aims at facilitating more efficient and more stimulating modes of learning is *Lifenotes* (Kam et al. 2005). Lifenotes en-ables students to interact with each other by taking lecture notes coopera-tively. Lifenotes also augments student note-taking by providing instructor slides in the background to annotate. However, Lifenotes allows only free-form annotations on presentation slides.

The Tablet PC-based *Classroom Presenter* combines the survey ap-proach of the ETH Lecture Communicator with the possibility to annotate presentation slides in Lifenotes (Anderson et al. 2006). In this setup, both the instructor and the students use Tablet PCs to write questions that are sent to all students. They then can send back their handwritten (or drawn) solutions. The instructor can view all responses, select one or more, display them to the class, and annotate them with ink as they are being displayed.

The *Ubiquitous Presenter* enhances Classroom Presenter by common web technologies to support non-Tablet PC users and to improve student control (Wilkerson 2005). Students using the Ubiquitous Presenter can participate by using a standard web browser; furthermore, an archiving capability allows the instructor to publish the annotated slides on a portal page after the lecture took place.

GroupUML aims to enable distributed collaborative UML modeling (Boulila et al. 2004). A user interface similar to CASE tools allows software engineers or students in different locations to model UML class diagrams collaboratively on a shared space. The shared model can be annotated by pen, but the application doesn't support shape recognition or other advanced pen-tailored input modes. GroupUML is designed for SMART-Board input devices, but may also be used with Tablet PCs.

3 Design on a Napkin: When Software Engineers Learn

The Institute of Electrical and Electronics Engineers (IEEE) defines software engineering as the "application of a systematic, disciplined, quantifiable approach to the development, operation, and maintenance of software" (IEEE 1990). At first, it seems that such a "purely" technical discipline has not much in common with a social science like pedagogy; but at a closer look, both disciplines, pedagogy and software engineering, can complement each other quite well in the field of education:

- Pedagogy developed sophisticated process models of how students learn, and it provides concrete means for designing courses to teach them;
- Software engineering provided broad experience with different process models for software development; it researched their effects on staying in time and budget while meeting project objectives; furthermore, software engineering can provide software support for implementing education processes.

However, the commonalities between students learning subject matter and developers programming software are much deeper than the above list may indicate. The computer scientist Peter Naur described the mental processes of a software developer during designing and coding a program as a process of building up a personal theory of the problem and its solution (Naur

1992). Problems arise when no appropriate theories exist: Programmers can hardly communicate about the same issues and ambiguities occur easily.

In this sense, one crucial task in software development is to build up theories about the application and solution domain, i.e., to learn, the software engineers must construct knowledge. The resulting system then reflects the knowledge of the programmers regarding the application domain; for this reason, software has also been called *executable knowledge* (Armour 2003).

It is this fundamental relation between learning and software engineering that motivates us to explore the pedagogic paradigms and to develop educational software tools that can be used in software development projects. Often, software development is described as a highly formalized process incorporating well-defined phases and carefully designed and documented work products. In contrast Al-Rawas and Easterbrook show in a field study that communication often happens informally and therefore remains undocumented (Al-Rawas and Easterbrook 1996). Informal knowledge that is transferred in coffee breaks or drawn on a napkin usually does not find its way into any knowledge management system.

The desire for formalized processes led to a vast variety of both process definitions, such as the Unified Process, and specified notations for work products, such as the Unified Modeling Language (UML). These ideas also influenced today's curricula in software engineering: Most curricula aim at teaching students skills for creating specifications and mechanical drawings. But there is also a pressing need for software *architects* who can actually analyze requirements, design software, and manage progress – all highly creative tasks.

4 A Plan for Action

In software engineering, where problem solving skills are especially important, a situated learning environment is beneficial for both students and instructors: The students do not only receive factual knowledge but are required to use it for solving practical tasks; the instructor on the other hand must carefully prepare the topic and provide a clear outline to the students – a chance to externalize and stabilize expert knowledge.

The learning experience can be further intensified by alternating the assignments of the instructor role and by supporting direct collaboration between the students; students then not only learn from the instructor, but also from each other. In turn, the teaching activity directly leads to the creation and improvement of practical experiences for the instructor (Krapp and Weidemann 2001, p 385).

We are offering such a distributed education scenario in a joint course "Design Patterns for Mobile and Distributed Applications", organized co-operatively by ETH Zürich and CDTM. Students from different disciplines, as well as from different countries, will collaborate locally *and* remotely to learn about the design of mobile applications. By realizing this joint course we intend to verify the following four hypotheses:

1. Students benefit from being actively involved in the teaching process. Skilled students can discuss advanced topics with each other and help less experienced students with basic problems. In addition, carefully mixed groups support the exchange of lecture-relevant information between all participants. We expect that this will improve their problem solving skills.

2. Flexible mentoring settings, where not only the teacher can teach a student but also students can help each other, facilitate the direct exchange of knowledge between students. This exchange is expected to have a positive learning effect and may reduce the instructor's workload.

3. The offer of cutting-edge technology in students' education raises their motivation, especially in engineering disciplines and adds factual knowledge that they can apply directly.

4. The experience we will gain during the development of the course infrastructure and the evaluation of the results will help to pave the way for other teachers to start similar classes; and it will help with packaging a software toolkit that supports preparing and conducting such future courses.

Through this course we intend to develop, apply, and evaluate techniques that support cooperative learning in different mentoring settings. By mentoring setting we mean the expert-novice relationship between the instructor and the student (or groups of students) that exists for a certain period of time with the purpose of transferring a defined set of skills and knowledge. The instructor is believed to have a deeper knowledge of the particular subject matter that has to be transferred to the students. This knowledge stems either from prior experience or is gained as a result of preparing the topic. By mentoring, the instructor teaches the student this knowledge and trains them to apply it in different scenarios. The mentoring relationship is dynamic; it can change depending on time or subject. Imagine, for example, a seminar-style course, where each student must research a certain topic and present the results to the others. In this case, all students play the role of the expert during one lecture when they present their topic.

5 Software for Education: Supportive Technology

The realization of a distributed course as the one described above requires the employment of specialized software tools: Tools that help with managing all the distributed resources like students, student groups, and learning material, as well as tools that enable students to communicate and collaborate efficiently, be it locally or remotely. The toolkit contains existing off-the-shelf software, such as content management solutions, standard video conferencing software, and the ETH Lecture Communicator, as well as custom software for specific collaboration purposes where no standard solution is yet available. Defining the requirements and specifications for this software toolkit is an important aspect of this distributed course.

In a university environment one can distinguish two types of collaboration between the lecturer and the students: Synchronous (real-time) collaboration during live events such as lectures, exercises, or office hours; and asynchronous collaboration in between the live events. In practice, of course, hybrid forms such as asynchronous communication in a lecture exist as well. Synchronous as well as asynchronous collaboration has been researched for decades: In the field of computer supported collaborative work (CSCW), numerous *text-* and *form-based* interfaces have been proposed, implemented, and tested (Krapp and Weidemann 2001, p 639).

Real-time collaboration in graphical ("diagram-based") environments for computer-mediated learning, however, is still not well explored. One reason is that it makes high demands on compute times and usability. Controlling the application must integrate seamlessly into the collaborative workflow even when multiple persons concurrently draw on the same document. For this, human-machine interfaces must be both intuitively understandable and intuitively usable.

Tablet PCs and pen-based user interaction can provide such an interface: The users draw with real pens on the screen that acts as virtual paper. Drawing with a pen is a well-known metaphor. Advanced Tablet PC applications provide means for handling strokes as graphical input, recognizing strokes as geometric objects such as rectangles or connections between objects, and recognizing special pen-gestures to trigger the most important editor or application specific actions and provide fast access to workflow control and collaboration features.

While intuitive user interfaces are *necessary* for real-time collaboration, they are not *sufficient* for a successful employment of such technology in a real course. An important question that also must be resolved is what type of communication protocols can effectively been used between the instructor and the students during a lecture. Imagine, for example, a frontal lecture attended by more than thousand students. Should the protocol be based on a public electronic whiteboard that everybody is allowed to use at any time? Or should the protocol be based on a forum with moderator that grants exclusive access to the forum? Furthermore, should the protocol make it possible for the students to dynamically form small working groups for discussing the – ongoing – lecture? How could this be accomplished without disturbing the others or keeping the noise level low?

Fig. 1 shows the pen-based application *Brainchild*[1] (currently under development). In Brainchild, the presenter (the instructor, a teaching assistant, or a student) selects one slide at a time to be shared with the audience. All participants then can edit (i.e., draw on) the slide jointly with their pen-based application. Changes on the slides are traced for each participant, that is, students and instructor can simultaneously enter their remarks onto the slide during the discussion. Because the pen position of each participant is displayed as a small pen icon on all screens, everyone is kept in sync about what the others are doing; so even vague references like "that box over there" are clarified.

Brainchild allows the formation of a peer-to-peer network: Students can organize themselves without a central authority involved. This approach also works in ad-hoc networks – networks that rely only on the end-user devices instead of a given infrastructure such as base stations or routers. As a result, off-campus scenarios become realistic: Students can participate in the lecture regardless of their current location.

The application is intended to support different diagram styles, suited for different purposes. For example, in a project course a mind-mapping editor can be used collaboratively to generate ideas in the early stages of the project. More specialized diagram editors, such as for UML class diagrams, then supplement the mind maps for discussing more detailed issues later in the project.

In a distributed lecture the students can form and break up learning groups dynamically, even when there is no public network infrastructure available.

---

[1] visit http://wwwbruegge.in.tum.de/static/projects/brainchild for details

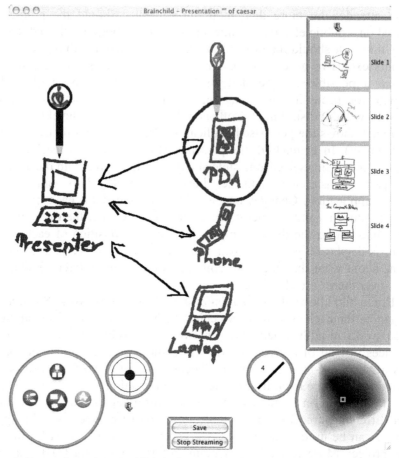

Fig. 1. Screenshot of Brainchild during an ongoing discussion showing the main controls: The pens denoting the current mouse positions of the collaborating participants (in the drawing); the slides list containing the prepared presentation (on the right); and controls for selecting the diagram style and scrolling (bottom left), saving and streaming the application (bottom center) and choosing line thickness and color (bottom right)

6 Concluding Remarks

Constructivist theories, with cognitive apprenticeship as one prominent example, are pedagogic responses to problems arising from pure frontal lecturing. In these theories, situated learning environments are set up for teaching problem solving skills by requiring students to work on realistic problems. As a technical discipline, software engineering requires structured approaches to problem solving and therefore students need to train these particular skills. The distributed course "Design Patterns for Mobile and Distributed Applications", organized jointly by ETH Zürich and CDTM, requires students from different disciplines to form local and remote teams to cooperatively solve practical problems. The students are supported by software tools that allow in-class communication, remote and local collaboration, recording of design ideas, and management of course resources. The experience we gain by conducting and evaluating this course will help us in improving subsequent courses, may animate other teachers to start similar – distributed – classes in the longer run, and will provide students with a unique learning experience before starting their professional careers.

References

Al-Rawas A, Easterbrook S (1996) Communication problems in requirements engineering: A field study. In: Proceedings of the first Westminster Conference on Professional Awareness in Software engineering, pp 47–60

Anderson R, Anderson RE, Chung O, Davis KM, Davis P, Prince C, Razmov V, Simon B (2006) Classroom Presenter – A Classroom Interaction System for Active and Collaborative Learning, In: Proc. of WIPTE 2006

Armour PG (2003) The Laws of Software Process: A New Model for the Production and Management of Software. Auerbach Publications, Boston

Boulila N, Dutoit A, Bruegge B (2004) Towards a Unified Object-Oriented CSCW-Framework for Supporting Distributed Group Modeling of Software. In: Proc. of International Conference on Applied Computing, pp. 613-621

Brügge B, Dutoit AH (2003) Object-Oriented Software Engineering: Using UML, Patterns and Java. edn 2, Prentice Hall, New Jersey

Cleary C, Schank RC (1995) Engines for Education. Hillsdale, NJ: Lawrence Erlbaum Associates, Inc.

Cockburn A (2002) Agile Software Development. In: Cockburn A, Highsmith J (eds), Agile Software Development Series. Addison-Wesley

Cohen EG (1994) Restructuring the classroom: Conditions for productive small groups. J Review of Educational Research 64: 1–15

Collins A, Brown JS, Newman SE (1989) Cognitive apprenticeship: Teaching the crafts of reading, writing and mathematics. J Knowing, learning and instruction. Essays in the honor of Robert Glaser: 453–494

Dochy F, Segers M, van den Bossche P, Gijbels D (2003) Effects of problembased learning: A meta-analysis. J Learning and Instruction 13: 533–568

Fischer F (2001) Gemeinsame Wissenskonstruktion – Analyse und Förderung in computerunterstützten Kooperationsszenarien. Unveröffentlichte Habilitationsschrift, Ludwig-Maximilians-Universität München

Gross T, Szekrenyes L, Tuduce C (2003) Increasing Student Participation in a Networked Classroom. In: Proc. of Frontiers of Education

IEEE (1990) Standard Glossary of Software Engineering Terminology. IEEE Standard 610.12–1990. New York

Kam M, Wang J, Iles A, Tse E, Chiu J (2005) Lifenotes: A System for Cooperative and Augmented Note-Taking in Lectures. In: Proc. of the SIGCHI conference on human factors in computing systems, pp 531–540

Krapp A, Weidemann B (2001) Paedagogische Psychologie. edn 4, Beltz Psychologie Verlags Union, Weinheim

Naur P (1992), Programming as Theory Building. In: Computing: A Human Activity. ACM Press, pp 37–48

Takamura Y (1986) Teaching and Shu-Ha-Ri. J Aikido Journal, published online, http://www.aikidojournal.com/article.php?articleID=222

Wilkerson M, Griswold W, Simon B (2005) Ubiquitous Presenter: Increasing Student Access and Control in a Digital Lecturing Environment. In: Proc. of ACM SIGCSE 2005

II   Digital Rights Management

Digital Rights Management and Software Innovation

Arnold Picot, Marina Fiedler

1 Introduction

In order to avoid an undersupply of immaterial goods (e.g. content or software) and to reach a balance between the creator's interest (control of property rights) and the interest of the public (access to an immaterial product as a public good), the government has various possibilities to foster innovation. Governmental action can supply the public good through a governmental agency; it can induce production of the public good by paying the inventor ex ante; it can reward the inventor ex post for providing the public good; it can create and enforce institutions in order to protect the inventor against imitation or undue competition; or it can assist the inventor in designing devices that increase the excludability of the immaterial good (e.g. Fisher 2004).

Following the latter two paths, governments have installed the institutions of copyright and patent right. As a result, the creator is granted the exclusive right to benefit from the fruits of his or her invention for a certain period of time, whereas the public profits by obtaining access to the intellectual good. This "natural" property right of one's own ideas goes back to the Venetian Statute of 1474 when the first patent rights were granted (http://en.wikipedia.org/wiki/Patent).

This article focuses on digital rights management and its impact on innovation and competition in the software sector. Due to the variety of potential innovators in this area, such as proprietary software firms, open source software firms, complementary asset owners and even code developing software users, one can assume that software innovation is not only triggered by commercial motivations, such as the prospect of monetary and material benefits from innovation, but also by access to, and experimenting with information and its application, as well as non-commercial motivations such as the pleasure of having created and implemented something new and useful (Brügge et al. 2004; Picot and Fiedler 2006).

Digital Rights Management (DRM) prohibits all production or distribution of circumvention devices intended to bypass copy protection of computer programs (Picot and Fiedler 2004a). It consists of the definition and enforcement of property rights (e.g. copy right and contract law) by means of mandatory technology routines on the one hand and of enforcing law (such as the Digital Millennium Copyright Act (DMCA) and the EU Directive 2001/29 EG) on the other. Thus, DRM helps, at comparatively low costs, to define and enforce rights on digital goods according to the rightholders preferences. Hence, according to economic theory, DRM should foster innovation in the area of software due to more complete definition and enforcement of rights and, thus, increased commercial motivation (Coase 1960).

On the other hand, contrary to traditional copyright and patent law, the combination of DRM technologies and legal norms like the Digital Millennium Copyright Act does not grant first sale, fair use and first sale rights to the public (Picot and Fiedler 2003). DRM systems enable right holders to protect their material in a way that has never been possible with copyright law alone (e.g. Chicola et al. 1998; Lessing 2001; Bechtold 2002). Therefore, the combination of DRM technology and law can effectively stop public access to useful information. This concern is even added to when we take into consideration the fact that software has inherent positive network externalities that tend to lead towards the creation of natural monopolies (see e.g. Microsoft products such as Windows, Excel and Powerpoint). Once a product or system sets a de-facto standard, Digital Rights Management enhances this effect by making it even more difficult for new firms to attack. As monopolists do not have to defend themselves against competitors, the incentive for investment in research and development seems in turn very low (e.g. Shavell and v. Ypersele 2001). Thus, Digital Rights Management threatens to lock out other potential innovators in the IT sector, such as small proprietary software firms, open source software firms, developing software users and complementary asset owners, thereby reducing competition for monopolists and leading to even less innovation in the software area. (Lessig 2001; Picot and Fiedler 2004b; Samuelson and Scotchmer 2001).

Thus, DRM seems contradictory: it appears to provide an incentive for the development of software and, at the same time, to hinder access from competitors as well as non-commercially oriented innovators, thereby potentially reducing innovation. To resolve this conflict, there is a very vivid debate among the different stakeholders regarding the potential pros and cons of Digital Rights Management regarding software innovation as well as the optimal legal design of DRM.

Therefore, we would like to analyze the effects of Digital Rights Management on software innovation in more detail.

The remainder of this paper is organized as follows: Section two gives basic information on Open Source Software (OSS) and DRM. Section three analyzes the effects of Digital Rights Management on Open Source and proprietary software developers and section four concludes this article.

2 Open Source Licensing and Digital Rights Management

2.1 Open Source Software Licensing and Innovation

Open Source software (OSS) is a fascinating phenomenon in many respects (Lakhani and Hippel v. 2000; Kuan 2000; Lerner and Tirole 2002; Krogh 2003; Brügge et al. 2004). It allows the merging of competition and collective ownership, the integration of the consumer into the generating process of the product, the participation of individual programmers as well as of large corporations, the simultaneous pursue of competition and cooperation, the pooling of altruistic preferences with calculated economic benefits. Lakhani et al. (2002) found out that approximately 50% of all OSS code stems from profit oriented firms, while another 50% comes from non-commercial developers such as students, system administrators and IT Managers who work on the development of Open Source software in their spare time.

While the roots of Open Source software lead back to the 1960s, the concept itself officially exists only since 1998, when the Open Source Initiative (OSI) was founded. According to the OSI, software can only be designated as Open Source software if it is protected by a license that is acknowledged by the OSI.

Regarding the importance of the Open Source licenses, Bruce Perens (1999) states the following:

„The volunteers who made products like Linux possible are only there, and the companies are only able to cooperate, because of the rights that come with Open Source. The average computer programmer would feel stupid if he put lots of work into a program, only to have the owner of the program sell his improvement without giving anything back. Those same programmers feel comfortable contributing to Open Source because they are assured of these rights: The right to make copies of the program, and distribute those copies; the right to have access to the software's source code, a necessary preliminary before you can change it; the right to make improvements to the program."

Similarly Bob Young (1999) from Red Hat points out:

"If Red Hat builds an innovation that our competitors are able to use, the least we can demand is that the innovations our competitors build are available to our engineering teams as well."

In order to become acknowledged by the Open Source Initiative as an Open Source software license, a license must fulfil ten requirements (see www.opensource.org for an overview of the criteria). [1]

58 licenses have been certified by OSI until September 2005. Among the most popular OSS-licenses are GNU General Public License (GPL), GNU Lesser/Library General Public License (LGPL), Berkeley Software Distribution (BSD) and Artistic License. Fig. 1, which is based on the information of the largest Open Source Portal "SourceForge.net"[2] shows that the frequency of adoption of the various types of OSS-Licenses varies remarkably.

One explanation of the frequency of use of the various license models is the pattern of rights that are granted with a specific model.

All the licenses have in common that they entitle the right holder or the user of the software respectively to read, use, change and distribute the source code of the software without any restriction. Among others, this implies that every programmer processing an OSS can make the software available for distribution. Furthermore, this concept involves that other software connected with OSS programs without being an integral part of the OSS program may remain proprietary.

However, Open Source software licenses differ with respect to regulations on whether they can be integrated with proprietary software, whether modifications must be revealed in case of distribution and whether they grant certain rights to the original developer.

As Fig. 1 shows, with a usage rate of 69%, the GNU GPL is by far the most frequently used license. In 1989 Richard Stallman created the GPL in order to protect software that had been created within his GNU-Project from commercial "hijacking" (http://www.gnu.org/press/2001-05-04-GPL.html). The key idea of GPL is to prevent an open software code from being made proprietary. If a GPL protected software is integrated in a non-GPL-protected software, the entire new software package must be fully handled under GPL-conditions. This characteristic is often referred to as "viral".

---

[1] These criteria are: free redistribution of the software, access to the source code, the possibility to modify the source code, integrity of the author's source code, no discrimination against persons or groups as well as fields of endeavour, distribution of license, the license must not be specific to a product or restrict other software and the license must be technology-neutral.

[2] SourceForge.net contained on September, 20 2005, 67.580 OSI-approved-Projects. Please note that this information on frequency does not involve any weight regarding the economic or technical relevance of the projects. Projects like Linux and Apache have their own websites and are not included in SourceForge.net.

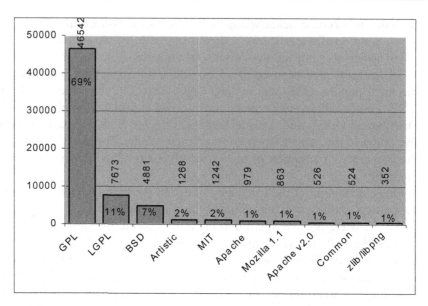

Fig. 1. Frequency of adoption of 10 most popular OSS-Licenses according to
SourceForge.net (n=67.580 projects)

The second most popular license, the Lesser/Library General Public License (LGPL), was originally developed in order to grant libraries involved in the GNU-project a less rigorous protection when using proprietary programs in connection with GNU programs. Thus, software that is licensed under the LGPL may be connected with proprietary software and distributed without an OSI license.

While GPL and LGPL prohibit the integration (after a possible modification) in proprietary software and further distribution of the new software package as a proprietary good, the third group of OSI licenses, the so called BSD type-licenses and the Artistic license allow a strong degree of property rights appropriation.

A fourth group of OSI approved licenses reserve particular rights to the original right holder. Examples for this group are the MPL (Mozilla Public License) and SPL (Sun Public License). The following table depicts the main differences between the most often applied OSS-licenses (Fig. 2).

All things considered, the license that allows for the least personal appropriation of property rights and the highest amount of external effects is the GNU GPL while the license that allows for the most personal appropriation of property rights and only small external effects is the BSD-type license. Given the fact that the one in wider usage is the more open GPL, one can assume that innovating and creative actors are not solely motivated by commercial preferences, but also by other motives.

	Unlimited reading, use, modification and distribution of source code	Possibility of integration with other proprietary software and redistribution without OSS-License	Modifications of OSS-Source Code may remain proprietary in case of redistribution	Special privileges for the copyright holder regarding modifications of other contributors
GPL	X			
LGPL	X	X		
BSD-Type (x11, apache, w3c ...)	X	X	X	
MPL	X	X		X

Fig. 2. Characteristics of OSS-Licenses (following Perens 1999)

Several studies reveal that people developing Open Source software have commercial as well as non-commercial motivations (e.g. Fiedler 2004; Brügge et al. 2004 for a summary on the motivations of Open Source software developers).

Non-commercially oriented actors develop Open Source software mainly for the benefit of improved software functionality, the wish for learning and development, peer recognition as well as altruistic preferences like being a "good citizen" in the OSS community.

Profit oriented actors participate in the development of Open Source software because they wish to set a standard, reduce maintenance cost, increase sales of complements, increase pricing pressure on competitors, and also learn, develop and a acquire a higher reputation in the OSS community (Henkel 2004).

Since the GPL does not allow for personal appropriation, it has a greater appeal to developers with non-commercial preferences, whereas BSD type licenses appeal more to profit-oriented actors. This is exemplified by the change from the GPL to the more proprietary oriented LGPL in January 2002 in the context of the project "Mono", which led to an investment of source code from Hewlett Packard as well as Intel (see Pal and Madanmohan 2002 ; Lerner and Tirole 2002).

Lerner and Tirole (2005) found out by analysing 40.000 OSS projects, that Open Source projects oriented towards non-commercial end-users tend to have more open licenses like the GPL, while projects oriented towards developers and designed to run on commercial operating systems are more likely to have BSD type licenses.

Thus, depending on the preferences of the innovator, licenses like the GPL that do not allow for personal property rights, can have positive or negative consequences on the degree of innovation. Developers with non-commercial preferences are motivated to innovate by the GPL, whereas actors with commercial preferences have a reduced incentive for innovation by such a restrictive license and prefer the BSD.

2.2 Digital Rights Management

Digital Rights Management aims at increased security and correctness for holders and users of digital goods' property rights, by employing technical components enforced by legal measures, like copyright and patent law, with the objective to help reduce external effects.

Technical Digital Rights Management systems fulfil the following three tasks: 1) encryption and decryption, 2) authenticity and 3) the definition and enforcement of rights. DRM technology can consist of a pure software solution, as well as of a combination of software and hardware approaches. A lot of competing technological DRM solutions exist, ranging from pure software on an OSS-basis, to a hardware-based industry solution where every authentication costs money. So far, no standard application has emerged.

Theoretically, any technology managing to accomplish the above stated tasks can be considered a Digital Rights Management technology. However, DRM technology is understood in business practice as a technology based on mandatory software and hardware routines, which allow the lawful owners to define and enforce rights associated with a good on a mandatory basis.

Examples for this are SIMlocks, which prevent customers from switching mobile carriers, and "software use controls", which let the company decide what software is allowed to run on the customers hardware device, and are used in cell phones or game consoles (see Lessig 2001; https://www.trustedcomputinggroup.org for further examples).

DRM technologies are protected by accompanying legal measures such as the Digital Millennium Copyright Act (DMCA) and the EU Directive 2001/29 EG, which had to be transformed in national law by all EU states and led to § 95a UrhG (German Copyright Law) in Germany. §95a section 1 prohibits factual circumvention of DRM-components and section 3 prohibits the production and distribution of devices for a circumvention of these components (Bechtold 2002, 2003). These provisions refer to classical protected good like text, music and films. With regard to software, German copyright law prohibits circumvention of protection measures in

§69a-g and §87a-e UrhG (Copyright Law). These regulations prohibit all production or distribution of circumvention devices intended to bypass copy protection of computer programs.

Violation of the mentioned provisions in German copyright law can lead to administrative or criminal penalties depending on the specific facts of the case and the importance of the violation (see § 108b and §111a UrhG).

This brief sketch of DRM technology and enforcing legal measures indicates that DRM helps to define and enforce rights of digital goods according to the right-holders preferences with comparatively low costs. Thus, the emergence of positive externalities can be avoided efficiently and, according to theory, innovation in the area of digital assets should be fostered.

On the other hand, contrary to traditional copyright and patent law, the combination of DRM technologies and legal norms like the Digital Millennium Copyright Act do not grant first sale, fair use and first sale rights to the public[3]. DRM systems enable right holders to protect their material in a way that has never been possible with copyright law alone (e.g. Chicola et al. 1998; Lessig 2001; Bechtold 2002). Other than copyright or patent laws, which, together with the above stated norms, enable the access of the public to copyrighted works, the combination of DRM technology and law can effectively stop public access to useful information. Many authors state their concern that this could lead to a gradual concentration around certain trusted DRM-platforms which couldn't be bypassed because of mandatory routines under the sole control of the original rights holder (e.g. Chicola et al. 1998; Gillmor 2002).

In the following, we want to take a brief look at potential effects of DRM on innovation in the software area, specifically Open Source soft-

---

[3] See Committee on Intellectual Property Rights and the Emerging Information Infrastructure (2000) and Picot; Fiedler (2003) for a more detailed explanation. "Fair use" refers to the right to reproduce at least some limited portion of a copy-righted work for legitimate purposes, including critical commentary, scientific study, or even parody or satire. In other words, fair use enables an agent to quote from previous works in order to comment or report news about them. The "first sale" rule is a limitation on the right of rights holders to control copies of their works that have been distributed to the public. This rule stipulates that the first sale of a writer's copy to a member of the public "exhausts" the rights holder's ability to control further distribution of that copy. Thus, a library is free to lend or even rent or sell its copies of books to its members. Bookstores, art galleries, and auction houses also depend on it, as does the practice of sharing copies of books or magazines with friends or of giving purchased books to friends.

ware developers and firms whose business model is mainly based on proprietary software.

3 Digital Rights Management and Software Innovation

3.1 Impacts of Digital Rights Management on Open Source Software Developers

As stated before, Open Source software developers consist of a variety of agents such as students, IT and system administrators, software users and profit oriented soft- and hardware firms.

Since developers with non-commercially oriented preferences explicitly value the openness of Open Source software, one can assume that DRM technology that helps to enforce property rights doesn't appeal to these kinds of Open Source developers and, thus, will not enhance innovation coming from them.

However, in the case of commercially oriented OSS developers such as Hewlett Packard, IBM, Novell/SuSe, Red Hat and Sun, consequences for the degree of innovation are less obvious. Theoretically, DRM has the potential to lead to increased security for the OSS developer through better transparency regarding the developers involved; contributions of these developers and congruence with provisions of software licenses can be better ensured; thus, DRM could be beneficial for software development even in OSS-environments. Bruce Perens (Perens 1999), founder of GNU/Linux-distribution Debian and a leading promoter of Open Source software, once acknowledged certain advantages of rights management technologies:

"Having good identification of the people who submit software and modifications is our best defence, as it allows us to use criminal law against the perpetrators of Trojan horses. While I was manager of the Debian GNU/Linux distribution, we instituted a system for all of our software maintainers to be reliably identified, and for them to participate in a public-key cryptography network that would allow us to verify whom our software came from. This sort of system has to be expanded to include all Open Source developers."

Linus Torvalds (Torvalds 2003), founder of the Linux kernel, once stated similarly:

"In short, it's perfectly ok to sign a kernel image – I do it myself indirectly every day through the kernel.org, as kernel.org will sign the tar-balls I upload to make sure people can at least verify that they came that way. Doing the same thing on the binary is no different: signing a binary is a perfectly fine way to show the world that you're the one behind it, and that you trust it. And since I can imagine signing binaries myself, I don't feel that I can disallow anybody else doing so."

However, critics state that the granted monopoly rights from patent and copyright laws, in combination with DRM systems, only raise entry barriers for innovators without adding value for society (e.g. Kitch 1986; Lessig 1999, 2001). DRM increases transaction costs for Open Source software developers through (frequent) costs of authentication for Open Source-engineering-activities.

One can assume that, if the developer abandons the use of Digital Rights Management authentication, the capability of participation in software development, interoperability, cloning and reverse engineering is restricted (e.g. Gilmore and John 2001; Samuelson and Scotchmer 2001). Thus, Digital Rights Management bears the potential to lock out competition and can result in a smaller amount of innovation in the software area.

In addition, commercial Open Source developers mostly benefit from selling complementary assets and services or setting a standard, in short from constantly adding to already developed software. This reflects the incremental nature of the lion's share of software development. The role of DRM, on the contrary, is to protect the status quo, thus making it difficult to continue developing existing software. It is therefore highly questionable whether Open Source software developers have an increased motivation for software development due to improved rights management possibilities offered by DRM. On the contrary, Digital Rights Management seems to conflict with the aims of OSS developers and thus not to be beneficial for the motivation to invent software.

3.2 Impacts of Digital Rights Management on Proprietary Software Companies

At first glance, since protecting digital content in the Internet is becoming increasingly difficult, DRM, by helping with the protection of digital goods, seems to heighten the probability of an invention's commercial exploitation leading to a higher motivation for invention. Also, as innovations involve a high degree of uncertainty regarding the estimation of costs incurred and of future demand as basis for cash flows (Landes and Posner 1989), there is apparently a higher potential in large companies to convert ideas into products, since those companies have the means to fund research. At the same time, it is necessary to remember that software development is, in truth, relatively low in capital needs and therefore has relatively low entry barriers. Therefore, the probability to realize an idea in the field of software development does not necessarily increase with the volume of funds available.

Nevertheless, considering the commercial motivation for invention, DRM seems to lead to a higher level of innovative activity by commercial software firms, which is especially important for costly innovations.

However, immaterial resources like software have inherent positive network externalities that tend to lead towards the creation of natural monopolies (see e.g. Microsoft products such as Windows, Excel and Powerpoint)[4]. Once a product or system sets a de-facto standard, Digital Rights Management enhances this effect by making it even more difficult for new firms to attack. As monopolists appear not to have to defend themselves against competitors, the incentive for investment in research and development seems in turn very low (e.g. Shavell and Ypersele 2001).

Therefore, DRM seems to be Janus-faced: it provides an incentive for the development of software and it leads to a stand still once a company has acquired a certain position.

Now, some may argue that without DRM, new innovators can enter the market, but without protection of their goods they are not motivated to do so. Even though this cannot be excluded from the outset, there are results which refute that argument. For instance, Cohen and Levinthal show that companies invest in research and development even if they know that imitators will also benefit from their invention. They explain this with the interest of the firm to enhance its absorptive capacity (Cohen and Levinthal 1990). Bloom and Griffiths report that higher education accounts for about one fifth of all R&D done (Bloom and Griffith 2001). This sort of invention is motivated by a love of knowledge, by satisfaction gained from puzzle-solving and most of all by the desire to establish priority and status (Dixon and Greenhalgh 2002).

The innovation effect of mandatory Digital Rights Management on proprietary software companies is conflicting. On one hand it could be expected that a lower imitation potential can lead to increased motivation for proprietary software companies. On the other hand one can assume that DRM has a considerable lock out potential for competitors and thus that software protected by efficient DRM could lead to less innovation by proprietary software companies and by independent software developers as well.

---

[4] see Zerdick et al. 2000, pp. 107f. for the Laws of Sarnoff and Metcalfe

4 Conclusion

Innovation is crucially connected to the advantage an innovator expects from the creation. However, the expected gain differs depending on the innovator's preferences. Non-commercially oriented software developers or scientific researchers expect an increase in reputation and attention for their works. Commercial companies on the other hand expect profitgenerating opportunities, but not necessarily only from the software itself but also from complementary assets. Therefore, systems enforcing personal property rights are beneficial for inventors wanting an exclusive rights position. At the same time such systems often raise entry barriers for innovators with non-commercial interests and are, thus, obstructive to inventors interested in wide and fast distribution of their ideas.

However, governmental intervention with intellectual property law does not reflect this open preference structure of innovators, but is still designed in a way that only accounts for the interest of commercially oriented actors. In areas such as software development, where little financial resources are needed, and knowledge is more important for the development of something new, this could be more inhibiting than stimulating for socially beneficial innovation and diffusion of knowledge. To foster innovation of digital assets in the areas of business information and technology open interfaces, open standards and minimal costs for licensing seem a necessary and important ingredient to allow a socially beneficial degree of innovation. This is especially true in the field of cross sectional software and file formats like operating systems and office applications. Therefore, in those areas, governments should not exclusively protect the inventor against competition and assist him in deploying devices that increase excludability, but also provide sufficient and reliable room for free exchange of ideas among those who prefer this kind of innovative collaboration. Whether and under what circumstances the invention should be supplied by governmental bodies, whether the government should pay the inventor ex ante to produce an innovation or reward the inventor ex post for the provision is a question that cannot be answered in the context of this contribution. The work of Open Source software developers does not only contribute to innovation in the Open Source area but also to innovation of proprietary software firms via an increased competition and learning potential. Overall, to spur innovation, intellectual property law must allow for the participation of various agents, not only commercially oriented ones. This seems especially important in areas where not traditional financial resources, but intellectual capital and individual motivation are key for innovation.

References

Barlow J (1994) The Economy of Ideas. WIRED, March/1994, URL: http://www.
wired.com/wired/archive/2.03/economy.ideas.html

Bechtold S (2002) Vom Urherber- zum Informationsrecht - Implikationen des Digital Rights Management. Beck, München

Bechtold S (2003) The Present and Future of Digital Rights Management - Musings on Emerging Legal Problems. In: Becker, Buhse, Günnewig & Rump (eds) Digital Rights Management – Technological, Economic, Legal and Political Aspects. Lecture Notes in Computer Science 2770. Springer, Berlin pp 597-654

Bessen J, Hunt R (2003) An empirical look at software patents. URL: http://www.
idei.asso.fr/Commun/Conferences/Internet/Janvier2003/Papiers/Besssen.pdf

Bloom N, Griffith R (2001) The Internationalisation of UK R&D. Fiscal Studies 22: 337-355

Brügge B, Harhoff D, Picot A, Creighton O, Fiedler M, Henkel J (2004) Open Source Software - eine ökonomische und technische Analy-se. Springer, Berlin

Buhse W (2004) Wettbewerbsstrategien im Umfeld von Darknet und Digital Rights Management. DUV Gabler, Wiesbaden

Chicola J, Farber D, Karatsu M, Liu J, Richter K, Tilly J (1998) Digital Rights Architectures for Intellectual Property Protection - Le-gal/Technical Architectures of Cyberspace. URL: http://www.swiss.ai.mit.edu/6805/student-papers/fall98-papers/trusted-systems/trustsys.html

Coase R (1937) The Nature of the Firm. Economica 4: 386-405

Coase R (1960) The problem of social cost. Journal of law and economics 3: 1-44

Cohen W, Levinthal D (1990) Absorptive capacity: a new perspective on learning and innovation. Administrative Science Quaterly 1/35s: 128-153

Committee on Intellectual Property Rights and the Emerging Information Infrastructure (2000) The digital dilemma: intellectual property in the information age. Washington D.C. URL: http://www.nap.edu/html/digital_dilemma/

David P (2000) A tragedy of the public knowledge "commons"? All Souls College, Oxford & Stanford University

Dixon P, Greenhalgh C (2002) The economics of intellectual property: a review to identify themes for future research.
URL: http://www.oiprc.ox.ac.uk/EJWP0502.html, EJWP

Fiedler M (2004) Expertise und Offenheit. Mohr Siebeck, Tübingen

Fisher W III (2004) Promises to Keep. Technology, Law, and the Future of Entertainment. Stanford University Press URL: http://www.tfisher.org/PTK.htm

Furubotn EG, Richter R (1991) The new institutional economics: An assessment. In: Furubotn EG, Richter R (eds) The new institutional economics. Mohr Siebeck, Tübingen, pp 1-32

Furubotn EG, Richter R (1994) The New Institutional Economics: Bounded Rationality and the Analysis of State and Societs. Journal of Institutional and Theoretical Economics 150: 11-17

Gilmore J (2001) What's Wrong With Copy Protection. URL: http://www. toad.com/ gnu/ whatswrong.html

Hardin R (1982) Collective action. Baltimore, MD

Henkel J (2004) Open source software from commercial firms – tools, complements, and collective invention. Zeitschrift für Betrieb-swirtschaft (ZfB)

Hippel E (1987) Cooperation between rivals: Informal know-how trading. Research Policy 16: 291-302

Hippel E (1988) The sources of innovation. New York, NY

Hippel E (2005) Democratizing Innovation. MIT Press, Cambridge, MAS

Kitch E (1986) Patents: monopolies or property rights?. Research in Law and Economics 8: 31-49

Krogh G v (2003) Open source software development. MIT Sloan Management Review 44: 14-19

Kuan J (2000) Open Source Software As Consumer Integration into Production. URL: http://opensource.mit.edu/online_papers.php

Lakhani K, Hippel Ev (2000) How Open Source software works: "Free" user-to-user assistance. URL: http://opensource.mit.edu/papers/lakhanivonhippeluser-support.pdf

Lakhani K, Wolf B, Bates J (2002) The Boston Consulting Group Hacker Survey. URL:http://www.osdn.com/bcg/BCGHACKERSURVEY.pdf, Version 0.3

Landes W, Posner R (1989) An Economic Analysis of Copyright Law. URL: http://cyber.law.harvard.edu/ipcoop/89land1.html

Lerner J, Tirole J (2002) Some simple economics of open source. Journal of Industrial Economics 2/50: 197- 235

Lerner J, Tirole J (2005) The scope of Open Source Licensing. Journal of Law, Economics, & Organization 1/21: 20-56

Lessig L (1999) Code and other laws from cyberspace. Basic Books, New York, NY

Lessig L (2001) The future of ideas: the fate of the commons in a connected world. Random House, New York, NY

Machlup F, Penrose E (1950) The patent controversy in the nineteenth century. The Journal of Economic History 1/10: 1-29

Olson M (1985) Die Logik des kollektiven Handelns - Kollektivgüter und die Theorie der Gruppen. Mohr Siebeck, Tübingen

Ostrom E (1990) Governing the commons: the evolution of institutions for collective action. New York, NY

Pal N, Madanmohan TR (2002) Competing on Open Source: Strategies and Practise. URL: http://opensource.mit.edu/online_papers.php

Perens B (1999) The open source definition. Opensources: Voices from the open source revolution. In: DiBona C, Ockman S und Stone M, Sebastopol (eds) O´Reilly, pp 171-188

Picot A, Fiedler M (2003) Impacts of DRM on Internet based Innovation. In: Becker, Buhse, Günnewig & Rump (eds) Digital Rights Management – Technological, Economic, Legal and Political Aspects. Springer, Berlin, pp 288-300

Picot A, Fiedler M (2004) Digital Rights Management. Medienwirtschaft 3: 125-129

Picot A, Ripperger T, Wolff B (1996) The Fading Boundaries of the Firm: The Role of Information and Communication Technology. Journal of Institutional and Theoretical Economics 1/152: 65-79

Plant A (1934) The economic theory concerning patents for inventions. Economica 1: 30-51

Richter R (1994) Institutionen ökonomisch analysiert. Mohr Siebeck, Tübingen

Richter R (1998) Views and Comments on the New Institutionalism in Sociology, Political Science, and Anthropology. Journal of Institutional and Theoretical Economics 154: 694-789

Samuelson P, Scotchmer S (2001) The law and economics of reverse engineering. URL: http://ist-socrates.berkeley.edu/~scotch/re.pdf

Savage D (1995) Protecting intellectual property - A warning to the soft-ware industry about patents. URL: http://www.redherring.com/mag/issue19/property.html

Shavell S, Ypersele T (2001) Rewards versus intellectual property rights. The Journal of Law and Economics 2/XLIV: 527-543

Tirole J (1999) Incomplete contracts: Where do we stand. Econometrica 4/67: 741-781

Torvalds L (2003) Flame Linus to a crisp. URL: http://groups.google.de/groups

Young R (1999) Given it away: How Red Hat software stumbled across a new economic model and helped improve an industry. In: DiBona C, Ockman S, Stone M (eds) Opensources: Voices from the open source revolution. Sebastopol pp 113-125

Zerdick A, Picot A, Schrape K, Artopé A, Goldhammer K, Lange U T, Vierkant E, López-Escobar E, Silverstone R (2000) E-conomics: strategies for the digital marketplace. Springer, Berlin

Open Standards – a Cure for Digital Rights Management?

Michael Pramateftakis, Klaus Diepold

1 Introduction

Digital Rights Management (DRM) systems govern the use of content by describing per-user rights in machine-readable licenses and enforcing them by using cryptographic methods. The public's conception of the term "DRM" today does not extend beyond a copy-protection system of the content industry. DRM systems are seen as means to just restrict copying and sharing of multimedia content and are thus viewed negatively. Much of the negative impression comes from the fact that current systems offer very little transparency and convenience to the user. One way leading into the future for DRM could be to foster standardization for DRM and the introduction of trusted computing. Along those lines we propose an approach for DRM towards the introduction of a standardized license-processing core that is open to the public and common to a variety of DRM-related applications. We hope that the trusted environment, in which the DRM core and applications are executed, together with the open architecture, will help to introduce clarity and convenience in the DRM process and thus give a positive spin to the topic.

2 Digital Rights Management

Since the advent of digital media formats users have enjoyed the possibility to make lossless copies of their media data such as music, images, video and the like. Also, Audio CDs don't wear out by playing them, which is a big change compared to the user experience with vinyl records. The distribution of digital content has also significantly changed the landscape of the content industry since going digital has become the motto of the day, mainly because the digital technology allows to decouple the distribution technology from the service offered. Telephone networks are not limited to offer analog voice services, but can also distribute any type of digital content including music and video. If producing seamlessly identical copies of content is combined with the distributing the corresponding bits over widely available data networks we arrive at situation of uncontrolled private sharing of digital media which causes dramatic financial losses to content owners and distributors. Media houses publish and disseminate reports and spread-sheet calculations that are meant to prove that the ongoing violation of copy-rights as committed by millions of users attached to the Internet is going to kill their business and, which is much worse, the business of all content creators, artists, composers etc.. The International Federation of the Phonographic Industry (IFPI) issued a Commercial Piracy Report 2005 where one can read quite dramatic statements such as "One in 3 discs sold worldwide is a pirate copy." or "Illegal music traffic in 2004 is worth US $4.6 billion." or "In 31 countries, fake recordings outsell the legitimate alter-native." The creators of content deserve a fair remuneration of their work and that is what media companies and their organizations are determined to fight for.

One means of accomplishing their mission is to apply various forms of copy-protection mechanisms to audio CDs, DVDs, such that making copies of CDs is not feasible any-more. Digital Rights Management (DRM) is a more general concept, which allows for rights holders to the content to control the use of digital content throughout its entire lifecycle, a concept that goes far beyond a bland copy protection mechanism. In other words, DRM represents a technology that ensures that digital content is consumed by the end user only in accordance with copyright laws and with the consent from the holder of the rights to the content. The content owner can issue a license that is associated with the content, and which describes how the user may consume the intellectual property of the content owner. In return, DRM is advertised to represent an approach that allows for the development of entirely new business models and remuneration mechanisms for a variety of uses of digital media and for trading digital goods in general. The content owner can issue a license that restricts the rights of a user. Restricting the rights to access to digital media is not necessarily a bad thing, if the associated price is reduced accordingly. However, DRM is suffering from a number of problems. Consumers do not embrace the idea of DRM, which causes problems of acceptance. The same applies to the open source community, who dismiss and combat the entire idea of DRM as an attack to free speech and democracy, inhibiting innovation and the spread of culture and new ideas. Practically deployed DRM systems demonstrate a number of conceptual shortcomings and technical defects, which further fuel the criticism of the technology. On the other side, the content industry is determined to build up DRM empires to protect their markets and business models. The jurisdiction is contemplating on how to adopt copyright laws to successfully cope with the challenges posed by digital technology. New players enter the markets who start to position themselves in the scene claiming a share of the business, notably the companies developing and deploying DRM systems.

Will DRM eventually solve the problems associated with the trade of digital media and digital goods? As it turns out, the DRM topic comes in the shape of a three legged stool, the legs being labelled business, law and technology as depicted in Fig. 1.

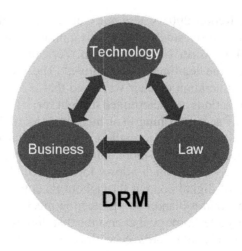

Fig. 1. The three legged stool of DRM

Any workable solution to DRM needs to balance those three domains, arriving at a solution that all stake holders involved can easily agree to. After all, DRM is not a concept for law enforcement but a means to do business between stake holders. If the power between content owners and consumers is out of balance no sustainable market will evolve.

In this article we try to discuss a few of the issues around DRM and we try to present an idea and a concept that we hope can contribute to a more amenable solution for DRM systems.

3 Digital Rights Management Technology

There are already a number of DRM systems in the market such as Windows Media DRM, Apple iTunes and Real Network's Helix DNA DRM. Besides those proprietary systems there exist standardization efforts to produce DRM standards such as the system specified by the Open Mobile Alliance (OMA DRM), the standardised components from MPEG-21 and proposals made by the Digital Media Project (DMP), to name a few. DRM promises to offer more control and more flexibility over the trade with digital goods for the rights holders. Take as an example the Windows Media DRM system. The WM-DRM home page solicits its solution with statements such as *"WM-DRM enables **content service providers** to **offer new business models**... ",* or *"**Content providers** can remain confident that their digital media files will **stay protected**, no matter how widely they are distributed. "* There are also promises being made that claim that DRM provides benefits to consumers such as expressed again by Windows Media DRM: *"WM-DRM ensures that **consumers** will be able to **enjoy** even **greater flexibility and choice** by allowing them to acquire and/or transfer their subscription content to the **devices of their choosing**."*

3.1 Principle of DRM Systems

The technical details of proprietary DRM systems are not published. However, all DRM systems are working according to the same basic principle that is depicted in Fig. 2. A content creator issues a piece of content, e.g., a piece of music, and sends the file in an unprotected media format to the Packager ①. The Packager takes the unprotected media data and produces an encrypted media ② data along with a corresponding key ③. The encrypted media data is forwarded to the Distributor while the key is forwarded to the License Issuer. The Distributor offers the encrypted content via a mechanisms of content distribution to the Consumer, who can, e.g. download the encrypted content from a server ④. The License Issuer takes the encryption key necessary to decrypt the protected content and wraps it into a license. The license contains a description of the rights that the content owner wants to be granted to the consumer if he buys the license. If the Consumer wants to have access to the encrypted music, she needs to pay the License Issuer ⑤ in order to receive a license ⑥, which contains the key for decryption.

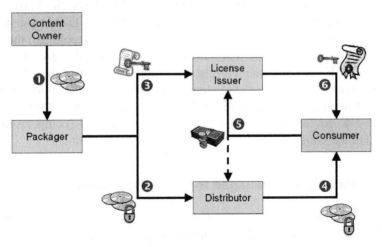

Fig. 2. Principle operations of a DRM system

After this process has been completed, the Consumer can decrypt and enjoy the digital content. In Fig.3 Apple iTunes is shown as an example for an existing DRM system.

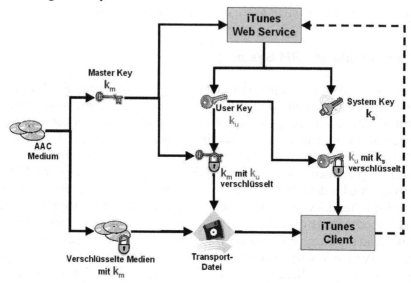

Fig. 3. Example for an existing DRM System - Apple Fairplay (iTunes)

It becomes apparent that this DRM system mainly acts as a key management system, using a hierarchy of three encryption keys, the Master Key, the System Key and the User Key. In Fig. 3, Apple's DRM system used for the iTunes/iPod System is schematically depicted. Apple call the DRM system "Fairplay", a name that indicates the fair terms that are supposedly supported. Looking at the Fairplay it becomes apparent that this DRM mainly consists of a key management system. The encryption uses the symmetric encryption standard AES with a key length of 128 bits. The example also reveals that iTunes delivers the music files (compressed with AAC) to the consumer along with the keys for decryption.

3.2 Describing the Managed Rights – the License

The rights that a content owner is willing to grant to a consumer are described in a license that the consumer needs to accept and conform to in order to consume digital goods. A license is issued for each consumer individually and is therefore a personalized contract between the content owner and the consumer. For the user to accept the license terms it needs to be presented in human readable form. For the use in a DRM sys-tem the license needs to be processable by a machine and therefore a machine readable language is used to represent the license. There are several Rights Expression Languages in existence the Open Mobile Alliance has picked up ODRL as a starting point for standardization to create the OMA REL specification. MPEG has chosen Content-Guard's XrML language as the basis to specify MPEG-21 REL. Both languages are expressive in the sense that they are able to express a wide range of rights and conditions in order to facilitate current and future business model in need of a Rights Expression Language. Typical examples for rights which can be associated with digital content in a meaningful way are Modify, Enlarge/Reduce, Move, Adapt, Embed/Extract, PlayPrint, Execute, Install/Uninstall, Delete.

4 Problems with DRM

If illegal copying of media data is the problem, is DRM the answer? To a large extend the necessary technology is readily available and this should pave the way for the deployment of DRM. However, there seem to be a few problems with DRM that are widely discussed. Those problems can be divided into two main categories – problems with the acceptance of DRM by consumers and technical problems. In this section we will discuss a few of those problems.

4.1 Acceptance Problems

Over the years, consumers got used to deal with media and digital media in particular. Many of those uses go along with a common understanding of what it means to "buy media". It causes problems with the acceptance of DRM if those traditional uses of media shall not be permissible anymore. Any DRM solution that does no longer support common uses with media will have acceptance problems. Examples for traditional uses of digital media are: second hand trading with CDs, shifting digital media on port-able devices or other devices within a household, sharing content with friends and family or making a private copy etc. Today, most existing DRM systems collide with those traditional forms of usage which creates a certain uneasiness within consumers.

One way to improve this situation out could be if under the regime of DRM new business models are offered that appear attractive to consumers. For example, consumers might be accepting a restriction of the permissible rights if the price for the content is adjusted accordingly. No one has made a profit by setting a price that is higher than people are willing to pay, and price ultimately depends on competition. If it comes to trading digital media there are three dimensions of competition: competition in content, competition in set of rights offered to user, competition in convenience of access.

Typical rights a consumer acquires in terms of a license from a download music store are to playback a certain piece of music a certain number of times (mostly unlimited playback on a computer), or that the consumer can burn a song onto a CD a certain number of times (3-10). It often is also allowed to transfer songs onto a portable player. However, the number of portable players may be limited and the players must be compatible with the format offered by the music store. Those rights cover the needs of typical user. She can listen to the music on her computer, in her car or while jogging. But it may turn out that other uses of media are suppressed, such as borrowing content to a friend, resell content, re-use the music while creating e.g. one's own slide show, creating your own party remix etc. This is perceived as a lack of comfort. Circumvention of those restriction expressed in the license is problematic from a legal perspective.

Another source of acceptance problems are the licensing terms. Take as a prominent example the following excerpt from Apple's iTunes license (paragraph 13b): „*Removal of Apple Content or Other Materials.... Apple and its licensors reserve the right to* **change, suspend, remove, or disable access to any products, content, or other materials** *comprising a part of the Service* **at any time without notice. In no event will Apple be liable for** *the removal of or disabling of access to any such Products, content or materials under this Agreement. Apple may also impose limits on the use of or access to certain features or portions of the Service,* **in any case and without notice or liability.** "

This means that whatever I have bought at some point of time, I may not own anymore in the future. Nobody will inform me if there occurs a change in the license and the company will not be liable. That's certainly different from what a common person associates with the term "buying". It is also in strong contrast to the advertisement statement on iTunes' Web site, which states: "*.. now features music videos and TV shows to buy and own forever.* "

Another perceptual weakness of DRM is that every paying customer is per default considered a potential criminal and thief and that all in all it is the honest consumer who runs in problems with the DRM system, who experiences the mentioned limitations. Customers of the "illegal alternative" via peer-to-peer networks don't suffer from those weaknesses. In summary, one cannot but agree that the negative connotation with DRM is justified if seen from a consumer perspective.

4.2 Technical Problems

Besides the acceptance problems there are also technical problems that need to be overcome before DRM can widely succeed. Those technical problems are on a conceptual level and not simple implementation issues that will go away as the products out there will be updated. For once, there is the need that any device must be trusted, that is, a trusted player must not be able to create an unprotected copy of the protected content. There must be mechanisms to assert the trust in a device. For this purpose a public key infrastructure is not in place, and even if it were, then it would be to expensive to be operated and additional problems will be incurred. The solution taken on today is the concept of "security by obscurity". For example, the specification of Windows Media DRM is not published. As another example, consider the Apple iTunes/iPod system, which is a closed system, that does not allow other manufacturers or content owners to freely use this platform. Another conceptual challenge is that the key for decrypting the protected content needs be delivered to the consumer somehow. The key needs to be protected e.g. with another encryption mechanism such that the user can't have control over the content. But the key for the second line of defence also needs to be delivered somehow. In the end the ultimate key for decryption needs to be sitting somewhere on the users machine; it is only hidden somewhere on the machine. Therefore, there will be always individuals who will successfully spot the key and hack the system. Therefore, a hacked system needs to be updated in order to neutralize such attacks – this again leads to further issues concerning longtime compatibility and durability.

One of the candidate remedies for this set of conceptual technical problems is trusted computing. However, trusted computing is currently also suffering from bad press and has an acceptance problem. Even if trusted computing may provide solutions to some of the more urgent computer security problems (viruses, Trojan horses, worms, spam, etc.) for and also for DRM there exists substantial distrust that it may be abused to a level where users loose control over their own computer system. Another consequence is that in the context of trusted computing the Open Source Community is widely excluded, or rather excludes itself by rejecting any notion of DRM. This deplorable effect may inhibit innovation.

4.3 Legal Issues with DRM Systems

Besides the problems mentioned before there are also legal issues associated with the DRM topic. There are more legal issues that we can cover in the article and the authors are certainly not sophisticated in legal matters. The examples brought up in this section mainly serve to demonstrate that there are numerous legal issues that go along with DRM.

4.3.1 General Public License Version 3

The General Public License (GPL) is the license under which most Open Source Software is released including e.g. Linux. Parts of the Open Source Community wholeheartedly reject DRM and call it the "Digital Restriction System". Recently, a Version 3 of GPL has been proposed, which is now under debate. This new proposal makes it practically impossible to release DRM software as Open Source Software under GPL v3. This is only possible if the user herself is allowed to modify the source code of any DRM component. But such a modified DRM software basically means that there is no functional DRM at all. This is no artefact, but again reflects the tough-minded opinion of the Open Source Community about DRM.

4.3.2 SONY Root Kit

Sony BMG has recently gained some dubious fame by introducing to the music CD market a more than questionable approach to DRM in the form of a Root Kit. When running a CD on a computer a piece of software is installed on the consumers machine, even if he denies to accept the license terms. This software is typically invisible to the user, it cannot be uninstalled and it can communicate to a central server of Sony if connected to the net. This way it creates a major security vulnerability for the user's machine, since hackers have started to exploit this vulnerability for installing malicious software. From a legal point of view this is a case of computer sabotage, such that several users have filed a lawsuits against. For this case there exists now a settlement agreement, but Sony has made a number of startling statements in this context ("Consumers don't know what a Root Kit is. So why should they care about it ?"), which again do not help DRM to find more acceptance among consumers.

4.3.3 Real Networks vs. Apple – the Harmony System

Real Network's own DRM system labeled Helix tried to offer interoperability with the existing major DRM systems. Real licensed Microsoft's Windows Media DRM and integrated it successfully. Apple did not agree to license their Fairplay system. As a response, Real circumvented the Fairplay system such that Helix could also utilize Apple's iPod platform. Real also threatened to license their Helix technology to other companies.

Apple responded by changing the firmware of the iPod to close their DRM system. It took a while but Real succeeded again to by-pass those changes. The case between Real Networks and Apple is an interesting case, since this represents an approach of one company (Real Networks) seeking to achieve interoperability with another companies' systems with a dubious outcome.

5 Basic Features of a Fair DRM System

After we discussed a long list of negative aspects and problems of DRM the question is if there is a future for DRM. DRM works to defend the interests of content owners, who have full control of licensing terms and who dictate the conditions for the trade. So far the interests of consumers have not been taken into account to a satisfactory level. In order to gain acceptance DRM systems need of support fairness in the sense that the consumers aspects need to be respected to a higher degree. We believe that there is a chance for DRM to take off if the future solutions incorporate features that support such a kind of fairness. What are the basic fairness features future DRM system should support? The restrictions imposed by the license should not be visible for the standard consumer. The consumer should be free to choose the content and the playback devices independent of each other. The business models offered to consumers should be transparent and provide a clear value proposition, the price for digital content should be commensurate with the rights granted in the licensing terms.

After all we should keep in mind that digital media like music or movies are mainly entertainment material and that DRM is not supposed to enforce copyright legislation for altruistic reasons. Also, the value of digital media differs to a large degree depending on the content. It doesn't seem to be reasonable to dedicate a heavy duty protection system for a piece of music or a movie that only a few people are interested in. Finally, it needs to be acknowledged that there will never be a 100% secure solution for DRM. As stated earlier, finding balanced and workable solutions for DRM is not a merely technical issue.

6 Standardisation – a Road to Fair DRM Systems?

It is interesting to analyse to what extend the struggle between proprietary DRM systems interferes with the competition in the market place. In the long run it may turn out to be politically much more important to ensure competition than securing rights.

From this point of view competition may be ensured by standardising the DRM, which will eliminate competition in the provision of the DRM system. But what is the alternative? A proprietary system would privilege those who control it, which will inhibit competition. If there is an open and non-proprietary standard for DRM this will facilitate competition. Consider MPEG, TCP/IP or GSM as representatives of such open standards, which definitely have created markets full of competition. But watch out – open standards need work and a lot of balance checking.

The benefits of standardisation are rather obvious. All content-producers and device manufacturers are producing for one standard. This helps to reduce cost for development and to reduce the risk of making wrong decision for any particular technology. Consider the situation as it was prevailing for media streaming, where most web sites need to offer their video clips in three different streaming formats (Real, Windows Media, Quicktime). Producing devices which support multiple formats and technologies always will cost extra. There is also this complementarity between devices and content. A device manufacturer wants to build a device that can play a lot of content and content creators are interested to produce in a format for which there are many devices available.

6.1 Interoperability for DRM Systems

Achieving interoperability is one of the major reasons to create standards. A standard specifies technology for use in devices. If the devices are implemented according to the standard specification, all devices irrespective of the specific manufacturer are working more or less in the same way, or at least in a specified way. This implies that devices originating from different manufacturers can exchange data without interrupting the intended functionality offered by the device. If this sort of exchangeability is achieved, we call the individual devices "interoperable." Note that interoperability does not imply that the products of all manufacturers are identical. This would preclude competition, which is not the intention of any standard. However, there must be a minimum set of rules that every device is complying to, such that products originating from different companies can work together in a seamless fashion. That's what a user expects from her cell phone or TV set, or even from the paper she puts into a printer or copy machine; that is, irrespective of who has manufactured the phone, the user would like to be able to place or receive calls without even thinking of the type of telephone her communication partner on the other end is using.

End-to-end format, services, and device interoperability are desirable goals, both for end users and others involved in the digital content life cycle. Normative specifications for end-to-end interoperability are the province of various standards bodies - many such efforts are in progress at this time, e.g. Open Mobile Alliance [8] or MPEG-21 [2]. Degrees of end-to-end interoperability are possible within a particular industry segment, consumer demand and new business opportunities frequently introduce a requirement for interaction with systems built on different agreements and standards. Full interoperability can be addressed in several different ways, which we explore in the following sections [9].

6.1.1 Full Format Interoperability

Full format interoperability expects that the interchange representation of the digital content can be consistently processed based on agreement between all participants in the value chain. The audio CD and the DVD are good examples. All participants (creators, distributors, manufacturers, etc.) use the same data representation, encoding, protection scheme, trust management, key management, etc. Full format interoperability usually entails robustness criteria and a certification regime to establish trustworthiness and security of conformant implementations.

6.1.2 Connected Interoperability

Connected interoperability builds on the expectation that consumers will have online access and relies upon online services, some of them possibly transformative or capable of complex negotiation, to solve interoperability problems in a transparent way. While different parties may do things in different ways, translations or bridges exist between the ways different parties perform DRM functions, and mutually trusted parties can perform these translations transparently, e.g. translation of licenses, as long as devices are connected at least some of the time.

6.1.3 Configuration-Driven Interoperability

Configuration driven interoperability assumes that system components, possibly from different vendors can be downloaded and configured in real time at the consumer's device or software application. This allows consumer systems to effectively "acquire" functionality on demand in order to accommodate new formats, protocols, and so on. Ideally the consumer need not even be aware that the dynamic configuration is occurring. This amounts to the emulation of the behaviour of many software music players that can host downloadable compression codecs.

6.2 Standard Components for Full Format Interoperability

6.2.1 Transport Formats, Compression, and Bulk Encryption

Digital music and video require large amounts of data. For the foreseeable future, it will continue to require a noticeable amount of network bandwidth, storage space, and computing power to move, manipulate, or transform media content. An advantage of full format interoperability is to standardize a process that directly manipulates content bits. This includes transport (file) formats, compression (codec) formats, and bulk encryption of media bits for file download, Internet streaming, and broadband broadcast.

6.2.2 Content Key Distribution

The most important part of cryptographic systems is key management. The content is no more secure than are the content encryption keys. Any security analysis has to consider the possibility that clients will be compromised. The goal of key management is to limit the potential damage resulting from a security attack by limiting the value exposed to individual clients. One simple strategy is to encrypt a commercial movie with many different sets of content keys, so that if an attacker obtains keys to one copy of the movie, he cannot reliably redistribute keys to all circulating copies of the same movie. In addition to keeping content keys confidential, DRM clients must also worry about keeping identity credentials (e.g., private keys) secret.

6.2.3 Trust Management

No DRM system can operate without a means for establishing and verifing trust among the components. A hierarchical PKI model uses hierarchical certifications and anchors trust in a root certification authority. Public-key cryptography provides the technical means of verifying the integrity of certificates. Trust management decisions must be made on client devices and may be required more often than content access control decisions. Hence, the complexity of trust management operations is of concern. Public-key cryptography operations, especially producing digital signatures, are computationally expensive.

6.2.4 Languages for Expression of Rights

Content creators and consumers of content need to share a common license language for expressing the usage rules attached to content. As with trust management, the standardization of vocabulary and identifiers is probably more crucial than the choice of a specific language. Every DRM system in deployment has a means of expressing usage rules. The MPEG-21 Rights Expression Language [5]defines a vocabulary of media-related concepts and inherits by extension a larger vocabulary through the MPEG-21 Rights Data Dictionary [6]. There are many other rights expression formats in use.

7 What's the Role of Trusted Computing?

OpenTC [1] is a project funded by the European Community that will provide an open-source framework for establishing trusted application environments on free operating systems like Linux. In such a trusted environment, only certified, trustworthy applications are allowed to run. Trust in this environment is rooted on a Trusted Platform Module (TPM) [7], a hardware component that can securely store cryptographic keys and ensure integrity of the system. We aim to use such an environment for creating a DRM system which governs the use of all kinds of sensitive data, not just multimedia content [10]. An example for alternative uses of DRM is the medical sector, where patient records and related information have to be protected against unauthorised access. Without a trusted environment, attackers may enter a computer system e.g. by using a virus or exploiting a security vulnerability to obtain unauthorised access to stored information, including sensitive data. In a trusted system, sensitive information is protected by encryption. The corresponding keys are stored within the TPM and are bound to a specific platform state (This procedure is called "sealing" in the Trusted Computing Group nomenclature). Rogue software is never allowed to be executed in a trusted system and even if it were, it would alter the platform's state, thus disabling access to the "sealed" keys.

A trusted infrastructure on an open-source system may open the door for devising DRM systems providing two primary advantages: Transparency and interoperability. By introducing an open DRM core that is common to all applications, the DRM procedure becomes more transparent. This is in strong contrast to the current situation, where security is mainly based on obscurity, i.e. on keeping the function of the DRM system itself secret. This leads to proprietary applications to handle protected content and as a direct consequence thereof those applications preclude interoperability. Accordingly, many different systems and applications exist for performing the same task, each one having its own ways for managing content and licenses. In contrary to that, an open architecture facilitates interoperability, because the DRM core uses standardised technology for license management. Various elements of the MPEG-21 standard will be used to accomplish this mission [2]. Internally, the DRM core works with MPEG-21, so whenever licenses from external licensing domains are introduced to the system, e.g. licenses issued by OMA DRM [8] or Windows Media DRM, the DRM core translates them into an equivalent MPEG format so it can manage them. Such translations, although technically feasible, are facing trust problems. Since licenses are signed by the content owners or rights holders, a translated license must also be signed by a trustworthy entity. Such a signature is only possible when a trusted environment is present, like the one provided by OpenTC. The trusted environment is also beneficial in cases where content reencryption is needed.

MPEG-21 Rights Expression Language (REL) [5] is a language versatile enough to accommodate functionality from various other rights expression languages. Thus, translations to and from other languages are possible, as long as they are based on the same principles. Such translations are needed when content needs to be transferred to external devices for rendering. The procedure can be made transparent to the user, who does not have to deal with trust issues, as they are automatically taken care of by the DRM core.

8 A Concept for an Interoperable DRM System

We introduce a concept that is based on several services that we can expect from the OpenTC infrastructure: The TPM-Chip is the root of trust in the system and is used by OpenTC for building up a trusted environment for applications. Only certified applications are allowed to run in such a context and they can rely on the fact that the underlying operating system with its modules and drivers are trusted, too. We assume that all data within the secure environment is protected against attacks, so no special care or encryption in the user layer is necessary any more. The distributor of the operating system decides which program is secure and which not, and provides relevant certificates. These certificates may also contain information about the capabilities of the application or the level of security it needs to perform particular actions. Depending on this information, OpenTC can restrict access to sensitive information or specific hardware components of the system. Thus, uncertified applications, including viruses, manipulated hardware drivers and other malicious code cannot start in a secure environment. This protection is transparent to the user, as the OpenTC infrastructure takes care of it in the background without the need for user intervention. The following diagram in Fig. 4 shows our currently planned architecture with the above environment in mind.

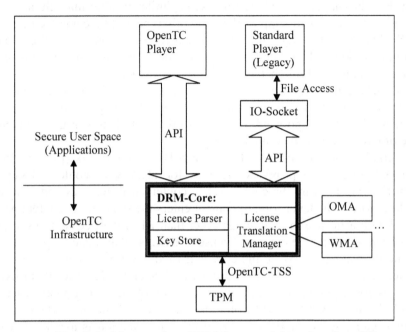

Fig. 4. Architecture for a DRM framework based on OpenTC

The central component of the system is the DRM-Core. Its tasks are to offer several services to the application layer regarding interpretation of licenses, as well as to provide the central key store for protected content. As it is a component used by several applications, it is placed within the OpenTC infrastructure. That way, it can be certified along with the system and be trusted by all applications. The Core consists of three basic parts: The license parser, the translation manager and the key store.

The License Parser offers services regarding verification and interpretation of licenses. These services are central to any DRM process and are accessed from the outside by an API, which includes all functions that are necessary for an application to access a protected file. An OpenTC-compatible player application can directly access the DRM-Core via the API to request access to protected content. The player has to provide its license, so the core can decide if the user has permission to access the data. If access is granted, the core returns the content key from the key store and the player can render the content. Legacy players, which cannot access the

API directly, are also supported by our architecture. Players of that kind are not aware of the DRM-Core, but are favoured by users for whatever reason. These cases are handled by an IO-Socket interface, which handles the license authentication and interpretation transparently to the application. For the player, the whole process is similar to a normal file access. The player only has to support the content's type and be connected to the IO-Socket through a plug-in. The player receives the unprotected content from the socket and can render it. The IO-socket in this case converts and forwards requests through the API to the DRM-Core. Since all applications, including the legacy ones, run in the secured environment, handing out the content key or the decrypted content itself is no problem, since it is guaranteed that the applications will not misuse it. This is a great advantage of having a trusted computing base.

Internally, the core uses MPEG-21 as a DRM framework ([3], [4], [5], [6]). MPEG-21 also provides facilities for identifying content. Unique identifiers are used by the core to relate content with licenses and keys in the key store. Whenever foreign content enters the system, i.e. content protected with a license in a language other than REL, the license translation subsystem converts the external license to REL, so that it can be processed by the license parser. Since the core is trusted, the translation can also be trusted. The license translator uses an extensible architecture which utilises plug-ins for different license formats. Our prototype will support at least OMA licenses, while other common ones, e.g. Windows Media and iTunes, can also be supported if respective information is available. The translation manager can be requested to export an MPEG license into any other supported format. The import/export functionality of the DRM-Core provides interoperability with other systems.

A particularly important component of the core is the key store. The key store contains the keys which were used to protect content in the system. The core ensures that a content key is given out only when a requested action is allowed by the license. The key store is organised as a table which contains keys and unique content identifiers. The same identifiers are used in the licenses to reference content. Respective technologies are part of the MPEG-21 standard [3]. The key store is implemented as an encrypted file, which is decrypted by the core when a secure environment is established. This is done with the help of the TPM, which seals the key store master key, so that it can only be accessed in a particular system integrity state. The core itself is thus only able to retrieve the master key when the system is secure.

9 Conclusion

We believe that by using the advantages of a trusted computing environment, we can develop a successful DRM-System that supports transparency, interoperability and hence is a basis for building fair DRM services.

Interoperability is a particularly important argument, as the incompatibility problems of existing DRM-Systems are widely known to the public. A system that is based on standardised open technology like MPEG fulfils the basic prerequisites for interoperability and compatibility with other systems. It can perform conversions between different formats and support numerous multimedia players as well as external devices.

Support of legacy software enables our DRM system to be integrated smoothly into an already existing system. By extending legacy players with a plug-in, they can also take advantage of the DRM-Core API and interpret content licenses.

Convenience is important in order for the system to be accepted by users. License management and interpretation, as well as content key management have to be transparent to the user. Since trustworthiness of the system is verified by the OpenTC infrastructure and declared to the DRM-Core, all license management procedures are hidden from the user by the DRM-Core and the player application.

Transparency is another important characteristic for wide acceptance. The whole system will be available as open-source. This does not mean that the system is less secure than other systems, because only certified DRM-Cores may be used. The advantage is that users can see exactly what happens with the licenses and the keys. The TPM-Chip just provides secure storage of the key store master key; all other functionality is in the DRM-Core and can be verified in the sources. It can even be extended by the open-source community if the need arises. The role of the community is especially important here, not only for acceptance, but also since no other DRM system supports open operating systems. Linux will thus be trusted by content providers to handle protected multimedia content in a similar way as other operating systems.

References

[1]   The OpenTC-Project Homepage: http://www.opentc.net/
[2]   MPEG: MPEG-21 Multimedia Framework Part 1: Vision, Technologies and Strategy. Reference: ISO/IEC TR 21000-1:2004. From ISO/IEC JTC 1.29.17 .11.

[3] MPEG: MPEG-21 Multimedia Framework Part 3: Digital Item Identification. Reference: ISO/IEC TR 21000-3:2003. From ISO/IEC JTC 1.29.17.03.

[4] MPEG: MPEG-21 Multimedia Framework Part 4: Intellectual Property Management and Protection Components. Reference: ISO/IEC TR 21000-4. From ISO/IEC JTC 1.29.17.04.

[5] MPEG: MPEG-21 Multimedia Framework Part 5: Rights Expression Language. Reference: ISO/IEC FDIS 21000-5:2004. From ISO/IEC JTC 1/SC 29/WG 11.

[6] MPEG: MPEG-21 Multimedia Framework Part 6: Rights Data Dictionary. Reference: ISO/IEC TR 21000-6:2004. From ISO/IEC JTC 1.29.17.06.

[7] Trusted Computing Group (2004) TCG Specification Architecture Overview. Trusted Computing Group, Incorporated. Revision 1.2.

[8] Open Mobile Alliance (2005) DRM Specification Candidate Version 2.0. http://www.openmobilealliance.org/release_program/drm_v2_0.html

[9] Koenen RH, Lacy J, Mackay M, Mitchell S (2004) The Long March to Interoperable Digital Rights Management. Proceedings of the IEEE, VOL. 92, NO. 6, June 2004, p.883-897.

[10] Schreiner F, Pramateftakis M, Welter O (2006) The role of Trusted Computing in Digital Rights Management within the OpenTC project. INDICARE Monitor (www.indicare.org), January 2006.

III IT Service Management

IT Service Management: Getting the View

Vitalian A. Danciu, Andreas Hanemann,
Martin Sailer, Heinz-Gerd Hegering

1 Introduction

The dictate of customer orientation has become ubiquitous with today's providers of connectivity and value-added services in the IT domain. Customers subscribe to services and are billed for service usage or the provisioning of customized services. Thus, customers' view on a provider's products is from a service perspective. To approach customer orientation, the providers must in consequence adopt a service-oriented view of their operations.

However practical the service concept may be to customers, services are not atomic entities. They are provided through collaboration of multiple resources managed by the provider. Such resources include hardware (computing, storage and network elements) as well as software components necessary to deliver the service. Conversely, the same resources are used to provide multiple kinds of services.

The management of IT resources, as well as systems and networks built from them, has been an important area of research in the past years. The concepts that have been developed in these disciplines (Hegering et al. 1999) have been implemented and allow a reasonably comfortable level of management for today's IT infrastructures. Service management, however, poses new challenges that are being addressed in current research efforts. Three important issues raised by the transition to service management are discussed in this work.

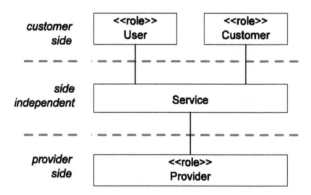

Fig. 1. The MNM Service Model – bird's eyeview

An important aspect that has to be considered in the context of service management – as opposed to resource management – is the interaction with customers. Fig. 1 shows a simplified version of the MNM Service Model (Garschhammer et al. 2001), which was developed in order to allow a consistent, formal representation of services. In its lower part the figure shows the provider side being responsible for provisioning the service and operating the infrastructure that supports it.

The service itself can be understood as a point of access for users, divided into a usage interface and a management interface for the *User* and *Customer* roles' use. Although we will focus on provider-side issues, messages from the customer side regarding the perceived status (e.g. malfunction, degradation) of a service play an important role. When a customer experiences problems with the service, the provider may be hard pressed to react quickly in order to honor the Service Level Agreements (SLA) in effect between customer and provider. A customer's report results in a service event for use in the provider side (see Section 3.1). It will not include the cause of the problem experienced or even the infrastructural components causing it. Remember, the customer only has knowledge of the service's interface – she is agnostic regarding its implementation. Hence, service events will only describe the effects of a (possible) problem in the provider's domain. From multiple descriptions of effects, the provider must infer the actual cause of the problem, identify malfunctioning or misconfigured resources and devise a problem solution. This process is by no means trivial. In large scale systems, its execution is impossible without appropriate tool support. The event correlation based approach discussed in Section 3.1 addresses the deduction of problem causes by means of user/customer feedback from a service management vantage point.

IT service management requires the assessment of dependencies of a service on specific resources, resource interdependencies as well as the mapping of resources on the services provided. Most information models and protocols currently employed to manage resources lack the means to express interdependencies among the managed entities in an explicit manner (e.g. McCloghrie et al. 1999; Case et al. 1996). Many state-of-the-art component-oriented management facilities are built upon this service agnostic foundation. In consequence, the rudimentary support they provide regarding the needs of the management of IT services relies on manual configuration and expert knowledge. Section 3.2 presents an approach to extending existing information models to represent services. The introduced concepts take into account (the issues of) interdependencies. Still, they allow continued use of the same, or similar, protocols and tools for the management of services as the ones currently employed in component and resource management.

Automation support for service management requires the acquisition of management data from the infrastructure (monitoring data) as well as other data related to a service and its customers. The concepts developed in the domain of resource monitoring allow the surveillance of the systems employed to provide a service, but without taking into account the requirements of service management as outlined above. However, attributes of services can be assembled from resource and network properties. Therefore, it makes sense to maintain the large, expensive base of deployed monitoring tools and provide a means to aggregate the disparate, resource-oriented data into service information. An architecture allowing the aggregation of resource monitoring data while reusing existing management tools as data sources is presented in Section 3.3.

In the next section, we describe a management scenario that highlights the issues mentioned above in an operational environment.

2 Web Hosting Scenario

The generic issues presented in the introduction are illustrated in this section by means of a management scenario. The simplified real-world case described originates in the academic domain and helps identify challenges to an IT service provider from the service management perspective. The challenges posed by the scenario are identified and serve as a starting point for the following sections of this work.

2.1 Scenario Description

An organization would like to have their web sites hosted by a specialized web hosting provider. There are various reasons for outsourcing of this service to an external provider. The organization may lack experience in running their own server and therefore would like to concentrate on designing the web site content. It may want to save costs in using an external provider as such a provider is able to share resources (servers, network connection) among customers. As a consequence, the provider can offer lower prices in comparison to the costs for a customer running its own server. In addition, provider offers on high availability solutions can be attractive for customers if the availability of the pages is critical for their relationship to their own customers.

In general, customers' quality demands for subscribed services are manifested in SLA guarantees. Example guarantees for the web hosting service are the availability of the service with respect to different time intervals (e.g., daily basis, per month), page access times, and time constraints on the management of the service. The latter ones can be response times for answering queries and constraints for problem escalation procedures.

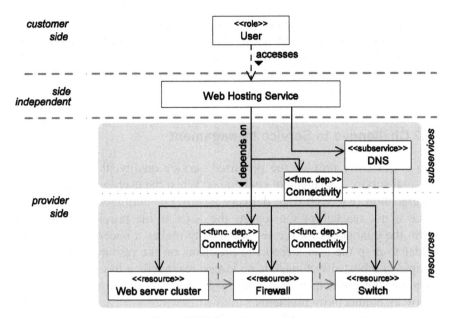

Fig. 2. Web hosting scenario

Our web hosting scenario is depicted in Fig. 2 and organized according to the MNM Service Model's distinction between customer, independent and provider sides of a service. The user, located on the customer side, accesses the web hosting service to view pages or to add, remove or update content. To implement the hosting, the provider uses a cluster of web servers to serve the customers' content, a firewall to limit access to the provider's network and a switch that connects the relevant resources in the provider domain. Besides managing these resources, the web hosting group uses the Domain Name System (DNS) service provided by another operations group within the provider's domain. Since the web hosting service relies on the DNS service, the latter is called a *subservice*.

The diagram's most important aspects are the interdependencies of resources and services. They are indicated by arrows pointing from the dependent entity to the entity being depended on. There are different kinds of dependencies which have to be taken into account. *Inter-service dependencies* exist between services and subservices. In this scenario, the web hosting service is dependent upon a DNS service which is responsible for the address resolution. Both services and subservices are dependent on resources like web servers, load balancers, and firewalls (*service-resource dependencies*). On the resource level, another kind of dependency exists which is primarily given by the network topology and devices (*inter-*

resource dependencies). In conclusion, the web hosting service relies on resources, subservices (black arrows), as well as on the interactions of these entities that are modeled as interdependencies in the diagram (gray arrows). Note that the seemingly simple service in our scenario is composed from four resources/subservices but exhibits ten dependencies of the types identified above.

2.2 Challenges to Service Management

To consistently provide the promised service quality, the provider faces several service management challenges. When the user experiences service degradation (e.g. web page delivery is slow) or malfunction (e.g. the service is not reachable) she reports the issue to the provider. Compliance with the guarantees for the service quality makes it necessary for the provider to map the user's report to problems on the resource level. For example, if a hosted web page is no longer reachable, it has to be determined whether the problem is caused by web servers, firewall configuration, or network connectivity problems.

Performing a manual diagnosis of the resources and their interdependencies is costly in terms of service down time. This results in financial costs, especially if contractual penalties apply. Worse, chronically slow response to customer complaints results in a loss of reputation in the marketplace for the provider in question. Therefore, it is desirable to automate the fault management for the services in order to support the time-critical process. A key challenge is to design a repository to store service management information which at present needs to be compiled from different sources. The provider has separate tools for server management, management of the network, and firewall configuration. In addition, the information displayed in Fig. 2, including the resources vital to the services and the dependencies among them, is typically managed using a separate tool, e.g. a CIM Object Manager (Distributed Management Task Force 2005). Considering the heterogeneous landscape of tools, it is difficult to maintain consistent service information in the management databases and correlate it with data gathered from management tools.

One possible approach to meeting this challenge is the design of completely new, service-oriented management tools that retain the functionality of existing, component-oriented tools and provide a service-oriented view of the provider's assets. The implementation of this approach would imply complete substitution of existing tools. These "legacy" tools, however, constitute an expensive installed base of software and hardware.

They are tied to management knowledge in that administrators are trained to execute management processes with the aid of the tools. A viable approach should therefore supply a means to continued use of most, if not all, existing components.

The desired service view should be provided in addition to – and not instead of – the component and networks oriented view on management issues.

3 Consolidating Service Information

In essence, a service view is produced by acquiring, filtering, aggregating and correlating resource-level data. Management facilities must therefore provide the corresponding functions. To allow integration (and thus continued use) of existing tools, these functions must be aligned along existing tool classes.

This section describes the refinement of low-level data into service specific information from a functional perspective, while taking into account information modeling and data flow issues.

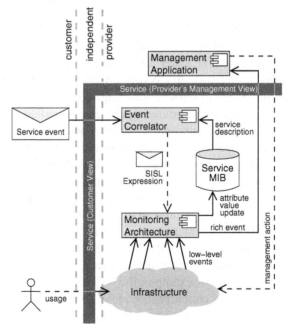

Fig. 3. Concept map

Fig. 3 gives an overview of the functional components aligned according to the Service Model described in the introduction (Fig. 1) and sketches data flow (solid lines) and actions (dashed lines).

Notifications of service failure (or quality degradation) originating with the customer (*service event*) can be correlated to identify resources potentially responsible for the malfunction (Section 3.1). To carry out this task, the *Event Correlator* component queries the *Service MIB* (Section 3.2) for service descriptions. A *monitoring architecture* is necessary for acquiring low-level data according to instructions given in a *SISL* document (Section 3.3). This data is further filtered and aggregated to produce data structures containing data pertaining to a service. Such data structures must be compliant to the information base defined for the service type at hand; they are used to update the attributes associated with monitored service instances or made available to management applications as *rich events*.

3.1 Service-Oriented Event Correlation

The scenario presented in Section 2 as well as the concept map show the need to match high-level customer reports pertaining to service quality degradations to the current situation on the resource level in order to identify malfunctioning resources. The methodology for matching these customer reports which is presented in the following is based on event correlation techniques (Hanemann and Sailer 2005). These techniques have been successfully applied to network and systems management for several years in order to correlate events to retrieve meaningful information.

The idea is to formalize customer reports into so called *service events* so that they can be processed automatically later on. The service events differ from events which are found on the resource level (*resource events*) in several aspects. While resource events are usually defined by vendors of network equipment, service events are defined according to service level agreements. They refer to degradations of the service quality with regard to quality of service (QoS) parameters (i.e. a service can be available, but with a poor quality) in contrast to usual binary states in the resource management (e.g. interface up/down). A consequence of the quality aspect consideration on the service level is that these aspects have to be mapped onto the resource level. For example, the CPU load of a server can be high due to a large number of concurrent requests to the server. From a pure resource fault management perspective this cannot be regarded as an error since the server is actually operational. However, the increased response time to requests can endanger the agreed service levels.

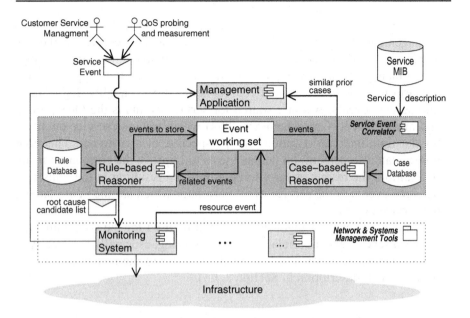

Fig. 4. Hybrid event correlation architecture

As a result of the examination of event correlation techniques (Hanemann and Sailer 2005) we have chosen a hybrid event correlation architecture (see Fig. 4). It consists of a rule-based reasoner and a case-based reasoner (compare Section 4.1). The idea behind this architecture is to combine the strengths of these approaches and to avoid their drawbacks.

Besides of the existence of efficient correlation algorithms, the flexible representation of knowledge in the rules has led to the choice of a rule-based reasoning module. The maintainability of the rules, which has been identified as a crucial issue for this technique, is ensured by the Service MIB that makes it possible to automatically derive the rules from the service modeling. As the provider needs current information regarding the offered services for the configuration management in any case the additional effort for the rule generation and maintenance is low. The automated derivation of the rules ensures that unintended rule interactions become less likely in comparison to encoding the rules by hand.

Due to the complexity of the service provisioning there are situations where the Service MIB and therefore the rules do not correctly reflect the current situation. As a consequence, a case-based reasoner is used to collect those events that cannot be covered by the rules. In these cases the root causes have to be found by the operation staff. It is often helpful to match the current event to prior cases in order to adapt a previous solution.

Events are received from different components. The Customer Service Management (Langer et al. 1998) is designed as an interface to the customers for the exchange of management information and to allow customers to manage their services in a predefined manner. It is applied in this scenario to transform customer reports about service quality degradations into service events. Another source for service events is the QoS probing and measurement (Garschhammer 2004) which tests the service quality in regular time intervals assuming the perspective of a customer. This component can also perform on demand tests to improve the correlation result. In addition, the resources have to be monitored resulting in the transfer of resource events to the service event correlator which are then correlated to the service events.

A standardized exchange format should be used for the communication between service event correlation and monitoring, especially for specifying what needs to be monitored and for the transfer of the resource candidate list (see SISL description in Section 3.3.3).

3.2 Service Management Information Base

The primary aim of the Service Management Information Base (*Service MIB*) is to provide management facilities with one single consistent representation of service management information. From a functional point of view, it therefore acts as a repository that can be queried for real-time service descriptions (Fig. 3). The Event Correlator component, for instance, relies on association information between services, subservices, and resources (e.g., Web Hosting Service depends on DNS service). In a broader sense, a Service MIB represents an accurate model of the IT services provided, including all information deemed important to carry out service management tasks.

Similar to models used in software engineering to describe computer programs, a representation of an IT resource relevant to management (*managed object*) necessitates a number of concepts: Firstly, an *Information Model* is required, which provides a formalism on how managed objects as well as relationships between managed objects are described. However, a model is of less long-term value if management data is represented in different ways – varying across different vendors, technologies, and product offerings (Black 1992). In order to achieve uniformity in the exchange of management information, the information model needs therefore to be complemented with standardized managed object definitions. Usually, these definitions contain generic management information, e.g., information that is common to a class of objects and not bound to a specific product.

In recognition of these facts, a number of management standards have been devised in the last decade (see detailed description in Section 4). These standards have been adopted by the vast majority of product vendors and thus significantly contributed to integrated network management efforts. However, they do not apply equally well to the area of service management (Sailer 2005). The reason for this is that the abstraction of a set of (physical) resources into a service needs to be described explicitly within the model. For instance, the knowledge that the connectivity of the Web Hosting service is dependent on the connection status of the switch and firewall components is vital to fault detection, but cannot be expressed with state-of-the-art information models. Specifically, current models do not reflect how resource information is linked to services.

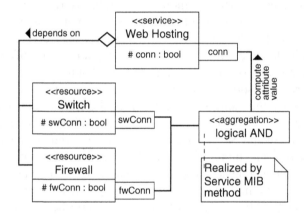

Fig. 5. Modeling of a service attribute (example)

To address these issues, we introduce aggregation methods into the service models. The goal is to augment current information models in order to support service characteristics. Fig. 5 shows a simplified UML class diagram of the Web Hosting service, which illustrates the following aspects:

- *Service-resource dependencies.* The knowledge that a service depends on a set of resources is expressed by the *depends on* relation (left-hand side of the figure). Modern information models usually incorporate means to express that kind of relationships, be it through association classes or table structures. However, they do not reflect *how* the service depends on the associated resources in terms of linking resource to service attributes.

- *Aggregation instructions.* Linkage of resource to service information is done through aggregation instructions (right-hand side of the figure). Aggregation instructions describe how service attributes are computed from a number of resource attributes; they are realized by Service MIB methods and designed in a way that allows for easy mapping to SISL expressions (see Section 3.3.3). The example shows an aggregation of the Web Hosting service's *conn* attribute from the *swConn* and *fwConn* attributes.

3.3 Technical Service View

To compose an integrated view of the services' state, the data gathered from system, network and application management tools needs to be combined in such a way that it reflects the service. Since the same data may be relevant to several services, a monitoring architecture needs to allow flexible configuration. This includes temporal parameters like different sampling intervals for the same data but for different services. Another requirement is the creation of data clusters, as monitoring different services may require data from intersecting sets of resources. Since new services may require new sources of data, monitoring must be easily extensible while retaining the same interfaces for configuration and data transport. Fig. 6 shows a layered architecture designed with the above requirements in mind (Danciu and Sailer 2005). The layers are arranged according to the process of refining monitoring data into service information. The lower layers are responsible to encapsulate a heterogeneous landscape of data sources, while the higher layers provide aggregated information to service management facilities. In the following, we describe the layers and components of the architecture in detail.

- *Resource layer and platform specific layer.* The lowest (resource) layer contains the data sources to be monitored. As suggested in the resource cloud, the data sources do not only differ in their set of attributes, but may include completely different types of objects. The multitude of management tools in the platform specific layer include integrated solutions, such as off-the-shelf management tools as well as scripts produced by in-house administrators. In any typical scenario, operators complement integrated solutions with their own tools.

- *Platform independent layer.* The first step towards a homogeneous service view is an architectural layer that hides the diversity of tools in the platform specific layer. In practice, this layer will consist of configurable adapters that interface tools in the platform specific layer or (not shown in the diagram) even query resources directly. The use of adapters allows the conversion of the monitoring data gathered into a common format, as well as the integration of heterogeneous data sources. The adapters acquire and retransmit data according to a configuration given to them via a uniform interface. Any new data source can be included by providing an adapter and a platform specific component (e.g. a management facility provided by a product vendor).

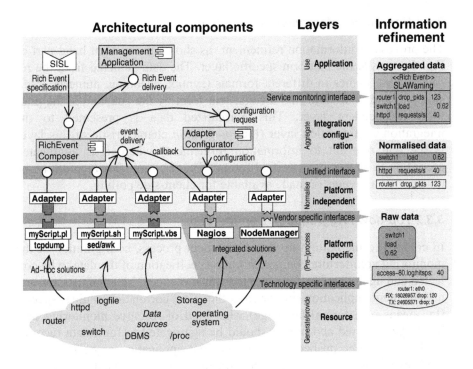

Fig. 6. Monitoring architecture for service data composition

- *Integration and configuration layer.* Adapter configuration is performed centrally in the integration/configuration layer. This layer is dominated by two components whose functional scope includes configuration and data composition. Both access the unified interface provided by the platform independent layer. The *Adapter Configurator* performs adapter setup in response to configuration requests. These requests originate at the *RichEvent Composer* in accordance with the requirements of a service monitoring task. The specification of these tasks is formulated in the specification language outlined later in this section.

- *Application layer.* After having been configured, the adapters relay data to the composer where it is aggregated into enriched events and made available to the management application. Though the architecture has been designed with service management in mind, it is suitable for policy based management approaches relying on rich event transport, as well as for Grid scenarios (Hollingsworth and Tierney 2003), where information from a multitude of heterogeneous data sources must be aggregated.

3.3.1 Bottom-up Information Refinement

The process of information refinement (as shown in the right hand part of Fig. 6) starts at the platform specific layer. The data gathered from the resource layer comes in different formats (syntax, encoding, numeric precision etc) and is brought into a consistent form by the adapters in the platform independent layer. This normalized data is presented to the integration/configuration layer (the *integration* characteristic of this layer is the one relevant to information refinement) where it is aggregated according to an a priori specified format. The resulting data records can be transported as events or made available for client-side polling.

3.3.2 Top-down Aggregation Configuration

In contrast to the bottom-up data refinement process, configuration of the monitoring architecture components and specification of the data to be collected and aggregated is done in a top-down manner. An administrator or a management application (in our case, the event correlation engine) specify (by means of a formal language) what kind of resource monitoring data has to be gathered and how it should be aggregated to form data records. Such data can be pushed to a management application as *rich events* or made available in other ways. When transmitted as rich events, the circumstances when an event is transmitted need to be formulated in a condition statement. These circumstances can be determined by a point in time, a number of collected samples, a sample value crossing a threshold, etc.

```
<aggregation id="webhostingConn">
    <description>...</description>
    <resources>
        <resource id="swConn">
            <source> switch </source>
            <sourceAttrib>connectivity </sourceAttrib>
            <interval> 10 </interval>
            <type> boolean </type>
        </resource>
        <resource>
        <resource id="fwConn">
            <source> firewall </source>
            <sourceAttrib>connectivity </sourceAttrib>
            <interval> 10 </interval>
            <type> boolean </type>
        </resource>
        <function id="swFwConn">
            <resourceRef> swConn </resourceRef>
            <resourceRef> fwConn </resourceRef>
            <method> AND </method>
            <parameters>
            <type> boolean </type>
        </function>
    </resources>
    <notifications>
        <condition id="timeout">
            timeout{600}
            ...
        </condition>
    </notifications>
</aggregation>
```

Fig. 7. Basic SISL example

3.3.3 SISL – A Language for Service Information Specification

The Service Information Specification Language (SISL) (Danciu and Sailer 2005) was devised to address the specification needs outlined above. It enables management applications to request aggregated information in a declarative manner, in that it allows combination of attribute sets with aggregation rules for management information. With SISL, rich events can be specified according to the dependencies between service information items. In consequence, the data records made available are constructed to correspond directly to service attributes (cp. Section 3.2).

SISL is a declarative, XML-based language suited for guiding the information refinement process described above. Language constructs can be categorized as follows:

- *Declarations of data sources and their attributes.* In SISL, data sources are represented as <resource> definitions. These definitions comprise the name of the data source (source) and the attributes to be monitored (sourceAttrib), along with a monitoring interval (interval) and the attributes' data type (type).
- *Aggregation instructions.* Basically, rich events are an aggregation of a number of (resource) attributes. Instructions on how this aggregation should be performed, are included in <function> definitions. Functions in that sense are made up of a number of references to resource attributes (resourceRef) and operations (method) to combine these attributes. At present, SISL supports arithmetical, logical as well as relational operations.
- *Conditions regarding emission of events.* In some cases, management applications may only want to receive events when certain conditions are fulfilled (e.g., load above threshold). This requirement is met with the <notifications> concept in SISL. It allows to define constraints for conditionally triggering rich events based on relational (*equals, greater-than*) as well as temporal (*timeout, counter*) expressions.
- *Declaration of the resulting data record format.* In general, rich events hold a number of monitoring samples originating from various data sources. SISL allows for flexible configuration of the amount of samples to be included in an event (<declaration> element).

Fig. 7 illustrates a basic example of SISL focused on the connectivity of the Web Hosting service described in Section 2. In the example, the monitored service is deemed to have proper connectivity if all connectivity-related resource attributes show supporting resources to function correctly. Correspondingly, the connectivity attributes of the firewall and switch component are included in the aggregation element. The resources are tested periodically (every 10 seconds) and an event is triggered in the case of failure (timeout).

4 Related Work

In this section, the state-of-the-art in the industry and academia with respect to the challenges identified in our scenario (compare Section 2) is juxtaposed to the ideas presented in this chapter. General overviews of management disciplines, SLA Management, and monitoring can be found in (Hegering et al. 1999; Lewis 1999).

4.1 Event Correlation

As mentioned in Section 3.1, event correlation techniques have proven to be useful for fault management in the area of network and systems management. Some details are given for rule-based and case-based reasoning in the following as these techniques have been selected for the service event correlator design. Other techniques of interest include the codebook approach (Kliger et al. 1995; Yemini et al. 1996) and model-based reasoning (Jakobson and Weissman 1993).

In rule-based reasoning (RBR, Jakobson and Weissman 1993; Lewis 1999) a set of rules is used to actually perform the correlation. The rules have the form *"conclusion if condition"*. The condition contains received events together with information about the state of the system, while the conclusion may consist of actions which lead to changes of the system and can be input to other rules.

The rules in an RBR system are more or less human readable, so that their effect is supposed to be intuitive. Fast algorithms like the RETE algorithm (Forgy 1982) exist to actually perform the correlation. In practice, the rule sets may become quite large which may lead to unintended rule interactions and makes it difficult to maintain the system. In addition, the system fails if an unknown situation occurs which has not been covered by the rules so far.

In contrast to other techniques the case-based reasoning approach (CBR, Lewis 1993, 1999) needs no prior knowledge about the infrastructure. It contains a database of cases which have occurred before, together with the identified root causes. While the first root causes have to be identified by hand, an automated matching to prior cases is performed in later stages. Therefore, the learning ability of this approach is an important advantage of this approach, although the correlation to the case database is less efficient than other techniques.

4.2 Information Modeling

In the following, several information models are discussed with respect to their suitability for modeling service management information. The Common Information Model (Distributed Management Task Force 2005) introduced by the Distributed Management Task Force is an object-oriented information model that aims at providing a common way to represent information about networks and systems as well as services. The CIM Core Model contains the specification of the class *service*, which acts as a superclass from which specific service classes (e.g. print service) can be derived. Additionally, dependencies between services and other CIM elements (e.g., *ServiceAffectsElement*) are expressed by association classes. However, only few service attributes have been defined so far for the basic service class as well as associations pertaining to that class.

The Internet Information Model (IIM, McCloghrie et al. 1999) designed by the Internet Engineering Task Force revolves traditionally around the Simple Network Management Protocol (SNMP, Case et al. 1996). This is a read/write, state based protocol for altering variables in a management information base (MIB) and is used by the vast majority of commercial products. Unlike more elaborate information models, the IIM offers neither object-oriented modeling features, nor does it support modeling of services in an explicit manner. However, isolated attempts have been made to model single service classes (Hazewinkel et al. 1999).

As part of the New Generation Operations Systems and Software (NGOSS) program the TeleManagement Forum released a Shared Information/Data (SID) model (TeleManagementForum 2003). It employs an object-oriented modeling approach and constitutes a framework for defining service management information from a business-oriented point of view. The use of object-oriented design techniques places it in the mainstream of modern design concepts, and allows for reuse of existing modeling tools. SID offers the most promising modeling framework, but is currently in an early development stage.

4.3 Commercial Tools

Starting from its traditional network management solutions HP has started to address service monitoring with its product *Service Navigator*. This product allows a provider to see dependencies in the service provisioning in a graphical manner. In Microsoft Windows environments it is also possible to extract the dependencies automatically from the operating system. The *Business Cockpit* tool gives an overview of the current compliance to SLA guarantees, while the *Event Correlation Services (ECS)* tool offers an event correlation on the resource level.

HP's ECS is rule-based similar to other tools like *IBM Tivoli's Enterprise Console* (TEC). Exemptions with respect to the correlation technology are *Smarts* (codebook approach) and Aprisma's *SpectroRX* (case-based). In general, the event correlation which can be found in the industry can be classified as resource-oriented in our terms (compare Netcool04).

Mercury Interactive provides an application called *dashboard* which gives an overview about the fulfillment of SLAs. In addition, Mercury has analyzed a set of application protocols like SAP communication in order to be able to install virtual customers. These virtual customers perform typical user interaction with the application server and therefore check its proper operation from an external perspective.

In summary, the tool support is focused on specific aspects of service management without offering an integrated solution.

5 Conclusion

As IT services become commodities, providers are faced with new, greater management challenges. Customer demands paired with the need for cost efficient operations impose requirements that service providers are compelled to meet.

Providers need to react quickly to customer service requests and fulfill Service Level Agreements. To achieve these business goals, they require a base of management tools that integrate the interaction with customers and the management of infrastructure at an operational level.

In this chapter, we presented an approach to correlation of customer notices into statements regarding managed infrastructure entities. With the aid of service oriented event correlation techniques failure or degradation of services can be attributed to single infrastructure elements, thus speeding the identification and resolution of service problems.

To facilitate reasoning based on service events, a formal description of the services provided to customers is necessary. A suitable representation of services is provided by the Service Management Information Base (Service MIB). Services are represented as aggregations of information pertaining to infrastructure elements as well as information from (e.g. customer) management databases.

These higher-order management concepts must be projected onto a technical management layer. For this purpose, we have proposed a dynamically configurable monitoring architecture. The monitoring framework employed is capable of providing monitoring data in accordance to specifications given in the Service Information Specification Language (SISL).

In this chapter, the presentation of concepts has been organized in a top-down manner, initiated by customer actions. However, problems originate with the infrastructure and may sometimes be more quickly detected on a technical, operational level – before the customer becomes aware of a problem at all. For this reason, future work will address the integration of service impact analysis and recovery (Hanemann et al. 2005) into the developed framework. Service impact analysis aims at determining the impact of one or more resource failures onto the offered services and the corresponding customer SLAs. The analysis results serve as a decision aid to select suitable recovery measures.

Acknowledgment

The authors wish to thank the members of the Munich Network Management (MNM) Team for helpful discussions and valuable comments on previous versions of this paper. The MNM Team directed by Prof. Dr. Heinz-Gerd Hegering is a group of researchers of the University of Munich, the Munich University of Technology, the University of the Federal Armed Forces Munich, and the Leibniz Supercomputing Center of the Bavarian Academy of Sciences. Their web–server is located at http://www.mnm-team.org.

References

Black U (1992) Network Management Standards -The OSI, SNMP and CMOL Protocols. McGraw-Hill, 1992
Case J, McCloghrie K, Rose M, and Waldbusser S (1996). RFC 1902: Structure of management information for version 2 of the simple network management protocol (snmpv2). RFC, IETF, January 1996. URL ftp://ftp.isi.edu/in-notes/rfc1902.txt.
Danciu V, Sailer M (2005) A monitoring architecture supporting service management data composition. In Proceedings of the 12th Annual Workshop of HP OpenView University Association, number 972–9171–48–3, pp 393–396, Porto, Portugal, July 2005. HP
Distributed Management Task Force (DMTF) (2005) Common Information Model (CIM) Version 2.9. Specification, Distributed Management Task Force, June 2005
Forgy C (1982) Rete: A fast algorithm for the many pattern/many object pattern match problem. Artifical Intelligence Journal, 19(1):17–37
Garschhammer M (2004) Dienstguetebehandlung im Dienstlebenszyklus: von der formalen Spezifikation zur rechnergestützten Umsetzung -in German. PhD thesis, University of Munich, Department of Computer Science, August 2004.

Garschhammer M, Hauck R, Kempter B, Radisic I, Roelle H, Schmidt H (2001) The mnm service model -refined views on generic service management. Journal of Communications and Networks, 3(4), November 2001.

Hanemann A, Sailer M (2005) Towards a framework for service-oriented event correlation. In Proceedings of the International Conference on Service Assurance with Partial and Intermittent Resources (SAPIR 2005), Lisbon, Portugal, July 2005. IARIA/IEEE

Hanemann A, Sailer M, Schmitz D (2005) A framework for failure impact analysis and recovery with respect to service level agreements. In Proceedings of the IEEE International Conference on Services Computing (SCC 2005), Orlando, Florida, USA, July 2005. IEEE.

Hazewinkel H, Kalbfleisch C, Schoenwaelder J (1999) RFC 2594: Definitions of managed objects for WWW services. RFC, IETF, May 1999. URL ftp://ftp. isi. edu/in-notes/rfc2594.txt

Hegering H-G, Abeck S, Neumair B (1999) Integrated Management of Networked Systems -Concepts, Architectures and their Operational Application. Morgan Kaufmann Publishers, 1999

Hollingsworth J, Tierney, B (2003) Instrumentation and monitoring. In Ian Foster and Carl Kesselman, editors, The Grid: Blueprint for a New Computing Infrastructure. Morgan Kaufmann

Jakobson G, Weissman M (1993) Alarm correlation. IEEE Network, 7(6), November 1993.

Kliger S, Yemini S, Yemini Y, Ohsie D, Stolfo S. (1995) A coding approach to event correlation. In Proceedings of the Fourth IFIP/IEEE International Symposium on Integrated Network Management, pp 266–277, Santa Barbara, California, USA, May 1995. IFIP/IEEE.

Langer M, Loidl S, Nerb M (1998) Customer service management: A more transparent view to your subscribed services. In Proceedings of the 9th IFIP/IEEE International Workshop on Distributed Systems: Operations & Management (DSOM 98), pp 195–206, Newark, DE, USA, October 1998. IFIP/IEEE.

Lewis L (1993) A case-based reasoning approach for the resolution of faults in communication networks. In Proceedings of the Third IFIP/IEEE International Symposium on Integrated Net-work Management, pages 671–682, San Francisco, California, USA, April 1993. IFIP/IEEE.

Lewis L (1999) Service Level Management for Enterprise Networks. Artech House, Inc., 1999.

McCloghrie K, Perkins D, Schoenwaelder J. (1999) RFC 2578: Structure of management information version 2 (smiv2). RFC, IETF, April 1999. URL ftp:// ftp.isi.edu/in-notes/rfc2578.txt.

Mercury. Mercury interactive. http://www.mercury.com.

Netcool04 (2004). Managing today's mission-critical infrastructures: Discovery, collection, correlation, and resolution with the netcool suite. http://www. micromuse.com/downloads/pdflit/wps/Muse_Discovery_Correlation_Resolution-_Jan04.pdf, January 2004.

OpenView. HP OpenView. http://www.managementsoftware.hp.com/

Sailer M (2005) Towards a Service Management Information Base. In: IBM PhD Student Symposium at ICSOC05, Amsterdam, Netherlands, December 2005

TEC. IBM Tivoli Enterprise Console. http://www-306.ibm.com/software /tivoli/ products/enterprise-console/.

TeleManagementForum (2003) Shared Information/Data (SID) Model Concepts, Principles, and Domains. Technical Report GB 922 Member Evaluation Version 3.1, July 2003.

Yemini S, Kliger, Mozes E, Yemini Y, Ohsie D (1996) High speed and robust event correlation. IEEE Communications Magazine, 34(5), May 1996

When Infrastructure Management Just Won't Do: The Trend Towards Organizational IT Service Management

Michael Brenner, Markus Garschhammer, Heinz-Gerd Hegering

1 The Road Towards IT Service Management

Originally, research in the still comparatively young discipline of IT management revolved around solving the technical issues that are brought on by the complexity, heterogeneity and distribution of IT infrastructure components in typical IT provider scenarios. Consequently, up to the mid-1980s advancements have been mainly limited to the field of network and system management, addressing technical integration issues. While the resulting management systems have grown significantly in complexity, the focus of IT management has until recently stayed on the technology-oriented view of the IT organization (ITO).

However, in practice there is often quite some disparity between the ITO-view on the health and performance of its infrastructure and the user's view of the reliability and quality of the services offered by the ITO. Various initiatives in *Quality of Service* (QoS) management have attempted bridging this gap, defining QoS-parameters in a service- or user-oriented manner and mapping these to the parameters of technical infrastructures. Even though in practice, especially in IP-networks, many issues remain to be addressed, research QoS-management has brought forward many successful concepts for solving quality issues for standardized telecommunications services (e.g. telephony, video-conferencing). Most representative of these projects is probably *Asynchronous Transfer Mode* (ATM), a network technology that enables for its network connections the guarantee of meeting target values of basic QoS-parameters (e.g. delay, jitter, throughput) which can be mapped to user-oriented QoS (e.g. perceived voice quality, video quality).

In corporate scenarios however, the focus is more on complex *enterprise services* (e.g. e-business portals, enterprise resource planning, customer relationship management services), than on communication and multimedia services. For these services, performance is not as big an issue as availability ("Availability matters above everything else" (Lee and Ben-Natan 2002)). Yet, for these services, the situation has not improved in an analogous manner. On the contrary, the decentralization of IT in the 1980s and 1990s, followed by the demands for integrating IT systems with those of other departments, customers and suppliers at the height of the e-business phase in the late 1990s and early 2000s, has brought an unprecedented complexity and often unreliability to these services – which at the same time have become more and more business-critical. Due to the enormous heterogeneity of the underlying software and hardware infrastructure, a comprehensive technological solution, based on standardized management interfaces, to the problems of enterprise services, seems to be far off in the future.

This situation is not unlike the one in the early days of *Software Engineering*, when there was widespread dissatisfaction of customers with the often unsuccessful outcome of large software development projects. The answer of the Software Engineering concept was to not rely solely on supplying the programmer with advanced languages and productivity tools, but to also adopt and adapt engineering and project management methods for managing large development projects. The current shift in *IT Service Management* (ITSM) is quite similar: Here it is mostly corporation's discontent with their internal IT provisioning, concerning a perceived lack of alignment to business goals and unsatisfactory transparency of costs and results, that drives the rising interest in organizational ITSM aspects.

The following section will further motivate the need of organizational IT service management. Section 3 presents a comprehensive taxonomy for standards and approaches in the area of IT service management together with an outline of the most common standards. Section 4 concludes with a short summary and an outlook on further research issues.

2 Why Infrastructure Management Just Won't Do

The in current practice and theory undisputed key to better alignment between business needs and IT efforts is *Service Level Management* (SLM) - the conclusion and management of Service Level Agreements comprising guarantees of meaningful service levels. The following paragraphs will define important SLM terms and argue, based on an exemplary discussion of the QoS-parameter availability, why service level compliance necessitates the consideration of organizational management aspects.

SLM tries to achieve more customer-oriented IT service provisioning through negotiating, concluding, then continuously monitoring and adapting Service Level Agreements between the IT organization and its customers (Hegering et al. 1999; CCTA 2000; Lewis 1999). A SLA specifies the conditions of how an IT service is to be provided. In corporate scenarios, this IT service is usually requested by the customer organization to support one or more of its business processes (see Fig. 1). The customer organization is primarily interested in the performance of its business process, which is measured by *Key Performance Indicators* (KPI). KPI is a term used to describe key figures and ratios relevant to a business process - e.g. lead time (or cycle time), i.e. the average time needed to complete a process instance, from its triggering event to conclusion. The IT organization's focus is however usually not on the performance of its customer's business process, but on managing its own infrastructure through controlling the quality-relevant parameters of its infrastructure components, i.e. the *Quality of Device* (QoD) parameters (Dreo Rodosek 2002).

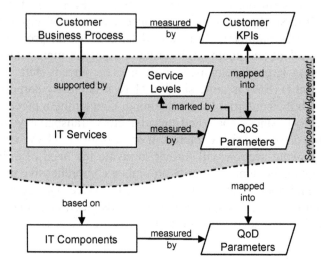

Fig. 1. Basic SLM concepts (based on Lewis 1999)

It should be noted, that for every quality aspect there are usually two fundamental types of performance parameters, serving different purposes: real-time status parameters and parameters encapsulating longer-term characteristics. For example for the aspect *availability*, a parameter can refer to the current *operational status* of a component ("up" or "down"), or to the likelihood of it being available over a prolonged time interval, i.e. to its *reliability* (e.g. measured in *mean time between failures*). In the context of Service Level Management, we usually refer to the latter *time-integrated* parameters.

A SLA contains a description of the service and a definition of its functionality. Especially in corporate scenarios, where often many applications and IT systems have been custom-developed over the years by dedicated internal system development organizations, the basic functionality of a service is, most of the time, relatively easily agreed upon. At the core of a SLA however, and usually posing the harder problems, is the definition of non-functional quality goals or *service levels* (see also Brenner et al. 2006). Even before agreeing on a quality goal for an IT service, it is first necessary to agree on how the quality of the service can be measured. This is the problem of defining and measuring QoS parameters: They should be meaningful for the performance of the customer's business process, i.e.

every QoS parameter should have influence on at least one KPI of a customer's business process, otherwise its usefulness is questionable. If on the other hand poor IT performance influences customer-KPIs detrimentally, then this should be traceable by a QoS parameter.

Specifying QoS parameters in the conclusion of a SLA requires a fair amount of effort and willingness to compromise of both parties involved: Neither the mapping of customer KPIs to QoS parameters, mainly the responsibility of the customer, nor the mapping of QoS parameters to component parameters, a task required by the IT provider, is trivial. When parameter definitions are agreed upon, service levels can be defined by marked ranges of QoS parameters (see again Fig. 1). For instance, a service level "gold" might define the acceptable range of the QoS parameter *availability* "greater than or equal 99.9%".

Of all QoS parameters, *availability* is in practice (Lee and Ben-Natan 2002) and principle (an unavailable service cannot be attributed any other quality) the most fundamental and important one for enterprise services. For an IT organization to guarantee service levels, especially if the SLA specifies penalties for noncompliance, it must be able to predict what service levels are achievable at what cost with reasonable precision. Traditionally, IT organizations have focused on improving availability through adapting their technical infrastructure, e.g. by using more reliable components or building more fault-tolerant systems e.g. using automatic failover mechanisms.

Consequently, predicting achievable service levels means mapping QoD parameters to QoS parameters, a task for which e.g. automation through the use of a *quality management application* integrated into a *service management platform* has been proposed (Dreo Rodosek 2002).

Management of just technical aspects, as might be suggested by Fig. 1, is not sufficient for guaranteeing availability-related service levels though. Contributing to the calculation of overall service availability are not only technical factors, but also organizational conditions - we will see that the picture of service level management in Fig. 1 is still missing an essential part.

The common definition of availability is based on the two fundamental parameters *mean time between failures* (MTBF) and *mean time to repair* (MTTR). Assuming continuous service time (i.e. no scheduled downtime) and MTBF being large compared to MTTR one comes to the familiar formula (see e.g. OSI 1997):

$$availability = \frac{MTBF - MTTR}{MTBF} \qquad (1)$$

For underlining the fact that MTBF and MTTR contribute to availability in equal measure, this can also be expressed as:

$$availability = 1 - \frac{MTTR}{MTBF} \tag{2}$$

For instance, halving MTTR will improve overall availability to the same extent as doubling MTBF. A prediction of achievable availability targets and the costs involved in achieving them, necessary for negotiating SLAs, must therefore take both parameters into account. Even though mainly influenced by infrastructure improvements, technical measures are often not the most efficient way (Scott 1999) to improve MTBF. But it is MTTR that is almost exclusively dependent on non-technical factors.

Fig. 2 illustrates the parameters that time to repair (or downtime) is composed of: The detection time, i.e. the time until a service failure (or service incident) is registered, might be shortened by technical measures like the use of monitoring tools (although in practice many incidents are still first reported by users to the service desk).

The activities for incident resolution, however, to the largest part involve human intervention and their durations are dependent on the effectiveness of the collaboration of the IT support staff.

This means for achieving service level compliance, it is essential to manage these collaborative activities, i.e. the IT service management processes. The (averaged) parameters contributing to downtime, like response time, repair time, etc., are essential for the calculation of achievable availability-related service levels.

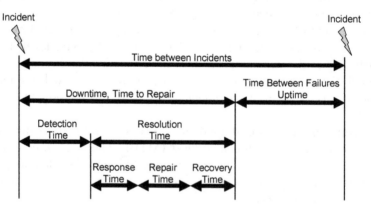

Fig. 2. Time parameters influencing availability

They constitute some of the central ITSM-KPIs of the IT organization's processes, which (expanding on the concepts depicted in Fig. 1) we must include into the scope of service level management, as illustrated in Fig. 3.

Efficient achievement of availability-related service levels cannot be done without organizational IT service management, nevertheless organizational ITSM does not supplant technological service management, rather complements it. For instance, when deciding how to cost-effectively improve availability, organizational and technological measures must be weighed against one another.

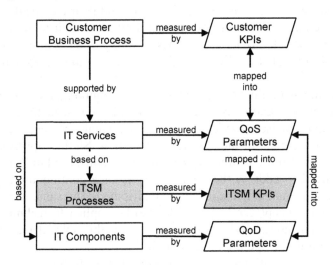

Fig. 3. Mapping of ITSM KPIs to QoS Parameters

IT service management must hence be based upon two pillars of equal importance: a technological approach - and an organizational approach, based on principles of *Business Process Management* (BPM). So BPM, a concept which has thrived since the late 1980s thanks to advancements in information technology, now is being applied to IT itself.

The adoption of several BPM or TQM (Total Quality Management) related concepts, often in an adapted form, has been proposed for IT service management. Also new, specialized frameworks and collections of knowledge have been developed. Combined with the existing and continuously evolving standards for infrastructure-oriented IT management, this results in a large, hard-to-overview number of approaches and methods related to IT service management. The following section therefore will give an overview of the most common standards related IT service management and, while many standards address several aspects of ITSM, provide a simple taxonomy for classifying them by their main focus.

3 Survey of ITSM-related Standards and Methods

Of the many methods and standard references in works on IT service management, some address mainly technical issues, others put more weight on organizational aspects. But this is not the only fundamental distinguishing characteristic: All methods implicitly or explicitly address some phase in the life cycle of a management solution in more detail than the other ones.

This section will introduce a simple, generic life cycle model of management solutions and place existing methods and standards into a taxonomy based on the defined life cycle phases and their technical or organizational orientation. Most methods either do declare their relative position to only a few selected other approaches or, more often than not, not for any. When performed, the alignment is often done rather informally (eTOM 2004b).

So while it might be difficult to exactly pinpoint the position of approaches in this taxonomy, even the approximate placement yields a much clearer and concise overview on the fundamental differences between the variety of methods in their overall orientation. Similar approaches to organize the quagmire of frameworks are for instance used in (Sheard 2001).

The need to address the distinct phases of a continuous improvement life cycle in process management is undisputed. The same continuous improvement concept can in principle also be applied to technical management - even though little guidance exists on this subject matter which is usually left to the operations team to decide on.

There is a multitude of models for phases of process management, which are usually arranged in a continuous improvement wheel or a life cycle (see e.g. Neumann et al. 2003; Borghoff and Schlichter 2000; CCTA 2000). Most specify between four and six phases, but many more could theoretically be identified, since the focus of the models varies considerably: One phase in a specific model might map to two or more phases in another cycle, or not be present at all. For instance, the Deming Wheel (CCTA 2000) does not explicitly include process execution.

A simplified, generic model limited to three basic life cycle phases is depicted in Fig. 4.

During the *Design* phase an aspect of the management solution (e.g. process definition, traffic shaping policies, event correlation rules) is specified, if necessary implemented (not represented in this model by a dedicated phase) and then carried out in the *Execution* phase. During process execution, relevant performance parameters are monitored and subsequently combined and summarized into performance indicators, representing the quality of the management solution (e.g. process cycle time, aggregate traffic throughput, success rate of event correlation).

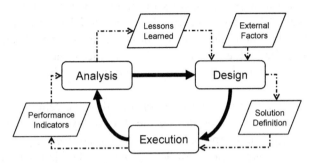

Fig. 4. Generic management solution cycle

These are then the basis of *Analysis*. Results of the analysis, e.g. evaluation to what extend the last change in management solution definition has been beneficial for the effectiveness and efficiency of the overall management effort are then, possibly together with changes in external factors, the basis for adjusting the solution design.

The basic classification scheme for ITSM-related methods and standards depicted in Fig. 5 shows how some of the methods most often quoted in the context of IT service management relate to one another in terms of their main guidance focus.

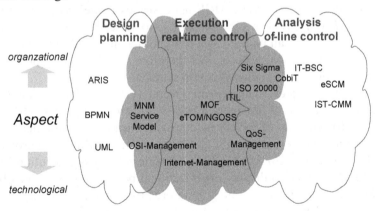

Fig. 5. Main focus points of ITSM-related standards

The lower an approach is positioned, the more technological its orientation, the more it is concerned with managing IT infrastructure by technical means. Accordingly a higher position indicates a more organizational approach to IT management.

Life cycle phases are shown in Fig.5 as differently colored, partly overlapping areas. Most of methods putting most weight on *Design* give guidance on how to model solutions, e.g. specify modeling notations and rules. Also abstract design guidance, like collections of generic BPM principles might be located here. The main addressee of these methods is the designer of a management solution, albeit in many circumstances the design will be partly or completely done by the same personal that later has to use or execute the solution.

Approaches concentrating on *Execution* mostly give relatively specific guidance on what is to be done during the day-to-day management operations. This guidance predetermines a lot of design choices, e.g. by providing frameworks, templates, protocol definitions etc. Guidance in this field could in principle be to a large part described using the standards located in the *Design* area, though in practice this is unfortunately seldom done.

Methods for *Analysis* are concerned mostly getting an aggregate, comprehensive view of the state of management operations, evaluating the performance of the management solution itself and thus laying the basis for future improvements.

The remainder of this section will give an outline of the methods and approaches depicted in Fig. 5 and motivate their position in the taxonomy proposed above.

ARIS (Scheer 1997) is a semi-formal technique and toolset for modeling business processes. In the context of ITSM, ARIS can be used for the design of management processes. ARIS uses various model types, most notably *Event-driven Process Chains* (EPC), to describe processes. Even though ARIS models can be used as a basis for technical designs, it clearly focuses on organizational aspects. We therefore position this approach in the upper left corner of our classification scheme.

Recently, the Object Management Group (OMG) released the final adopted specification of *Business Process Modeling Notation (BPMN)* (BPMN 2006). The aim of *BPMN* is to provide means to comprehensively specify business processes using a graphical notation. OMG also provides a standard mapping of *BPMN* to *BPEL* (Business Process Execution Language). *BPMN* is able to display organizational boundaries as well as fine grained process activities thus integrating organizational as well as technological aspects. The notation is used for the design of business processes. Accordingly, *BPMN* is displayed in the middle of the design area to indicate its integrating approach.

The *Unified Modeling Language* UML (Rumbaugh et al. 1998) has been developed to offer multiple means to support the technical design of applications. Organizational aspects are somewhat reflected in use case diagrams, but the main focus of UML lies on technical design of object oriented models. As a modeling technique UML obviously is suitable for the design of technical management processes as well as applications. As the modeling focus is rather technological than organizational driven, UML is positioned in the lower part of design area in our scheme.

The *MNM-Service-Model* (Garschhammer et al. 2002) was developed to clearly depict the differences between service provisioning and service management and to delimit responsibilities in provider chains. The model may be used to analyze the design of a service (chain) in its operation. The model therefore is positioned in the overlapping area between design and execution phase in our model. As the model integrates technical as well as organizational aspects it is positioned right in the middle of our scheme to indicate its integrating focus.

Concepts of *OSI Management* (OSI 1992) are often referenced in the area of management. Implementations of the OSI Management Standards however have never been widespread, despite their generally excellent conceptual quality. The standards give design as well as implementation guidelines and therefore could be used in the design as well as in the execution phase of our life cycle. *OSI Management* is based on "classical" device and component management. Even though its concepts may be used to describe more organizational focused concepts we position *OSI Management* in its original sense as a technical approach to service management.

Of all the standardization efforts for IT Service Management, the *IT Infrastructure Library* (ITIL) (Rudd 2004) has recently enjoyed the biggest popularity in Europe and is - at least there - now indeed a de-facto standard. The release of ISO 20000 (ISO 2005), which is based on the *ITIL-*aligned BS15000 by the *British Standards Institution* (BSI) (Dugmore 2004), will probably bring even wider adoption of *ITIL* in the industry.

ITIL's focus is on coordinating the collaboration of IT personnel on not completely pre-determinable tasks. *ITIL* therefore gives primarily guidance on processes for planning, supporting and controlling operational activities and infrastructure changes. Even though the processes outlined in ITIL need to be adapted to be applied in real world scenarios, it gives rather comprehensive guidance on objectives, activities and artifacts. While by supplying basic *Key Performance Indicators* (KPI) for every process it also provides some controlling advice, and also includes a brief introduction to modeling, these areas are clearly not its main focus. Accordingly we position *ITIL* as framework to support IT service management processes in their execution phase, though rather on the right rim as it stresses the need for continuous improvement through process analysis. While some basic technical aspects of supporting management systems are discussed, the core of ITIL is its technology-agnostic business process guidance, thus warranting its organizationally oriented position.

ISO 20000 (see ISO 2005) enables the certification of IT organizations (similar to ISO 9000). While the purpose of ISO 20000 is evaluating ITIL-aligned management solutions, its auditing is based on a different kind of analysis than the one described for the *Analysis* life cycle phase discussed above. An ISO 20000 audit verifies that all necessary prerequisites for quality-oriented IT service management, like well defined and documented procedures and responsibilities, are in place. ISO 20000 stresses the need for process analysis and prominently features the Deming cycle. However, in an audit, rather than evaluating actual KPI values and triggering a continuous improvement cycle, the continuous improvement process itself is evaluated. Since it is stressing continuous improvement and Service Level Management, i.e. alignment to customer (business) needs, it is therefore placed slightly higher and more into the *Analysis* area than ITIL.

Microsoft Operations Framework (MOF) (MOF 2004) is based on ITIL, but is not committed to being technology-independent. MOF extends the ITIL process framework in its *Process Model* mainly by technology-specific operations processes. It also adds a *Risk Discipline* and a *Team Model*. MOF is rather well documented and for many processes contains somewhat more detailed process definitions than ITIL. It also proclaims itself to contain "prescriptive guidance", rather than ITIL's "descriptive guidance", thus putting less weight on adaption and continuous improvement of the management solution (albeit it stresses the continuous improvement of the service solution). Consequently it is linked to the execution phase of our life cycle. As it is somewhat more technology oriented than ITIL, MOF is positioned slightly lower in the center of the *Execution* area.

The *enhanced Telecom Operations Map* (eTOM) (eTOM 2004a) defines all process elements necessary for service provisioning, for each of which however it describes only the "what", not the "how". Thus, it does (at least yet) not provide ready-made internal or cross organizational workflows or interfaces. But the eTOM can lend a common structure to organization-specific workflows, significantly facilitate communications with customers and suppliers, and provide a basis for process automation efforts like the NGOSS initiative (NGOSS 2004), of which the eTOM forms an integral part. We see the NGOSS/eTOM approach supporting the (automated) execution of service management and provisioning processes and position these in the center of the *Execution* area.

Together with SNMP (simple network management protocol) *Internet-Management* (Case et al. 1990) became widespread in the area of systems management. The approach of Internet Management is to keep things as simple as possible. The approach could be seen as adapted but light weight *OSI Management* with the prominent SNMP as the main but only contribution. Internet Management is clearly an approach to handle systems in operation and is therefore positioned at the bottom of the *Execution* area.

Six Sigma (Pande and Holpp 2001) is an approach in the (total) quality management domain. It was developed to analyze existing and already implemented processes in order to define corresponding KPIs to build the basis for an impartial process analysis. Its major objective is to distinctively document every step of this analysis to ensure sound and unquestionable results. As this approach provides an assessment of the quality of existing processes it is positioned in the upper segment of our scheme, indication its relation to organizational aspects. *Six Sigma* is shown in the overlapping area of *Execution* and *Analysis* to reflect its design to analyze implemented processes.

QoS Management as shown in our scheme is to understand as a concept with no corresponding standards. We see this concept as management strictly aligned to ensure the required quality of a technical service with QoS parameters bound to the quality of devices. As described in (Dreo Rodosek 2002) this approach spans the execution and the analysis phase of a service and its management solution. *QoS Management* is conducted on a very technical basis, the devices, but is aiming on more organizationally related optimization. Accordingly, *QoS Management* is positioned in the lower third of the overlapping between the *Execution* and the *Analysis* area of our scheme.

The objective of *CobIT* (see CobIT 2005) is to enforce IT governance. The framework provides means to ensure the alignment of IT and core business processes. It mainly focuses on analyzing existing IT processes and gathering information about their alignment to business objectives. Thus, it is more concerned with organizational than technical aspects. As it analyzes established processes in operation we position it in the upper segment of the *Analysis* area, in the vicinity of the *Execution* area to reflect this close relation.

The management concept *Balanced Score Card* (BSC) can be adapted to IT as well to build an *IT-BSC* (von Grembergen 2000). This approach uses a performance measurement system integrating various aspects of processes from costs to customer satisfaction. Measures are bound among each user to reflect complex relationships between performance indicators in an enterprise. The *IT-BSC* is a comprehensive method to analyze in detail how business objectives are reflected in processes. As the *IT-BSC* only is a special form of the enclosing management concept *Balanced Score Card* it is positioned in our scheme as a high level analyzing technique.

An approach to assess a provider's capabilities to provide IT service and to show rooms for improvement is the *IT Services Capability Maturity Model* ITS-CMM (Clerc et al. 2004). Maturity is measured on a five level scale (note that unlike CMMI, ITS-CMM does as yet not support the continuous capability level representation). Each level represents a set of standard processes an enterprise has to implement to achieve this level. As the levels are clearly defined, it is obvious which processes have to be implemented next to reach a higher level. Thus, *ITS-CMM* provides assessment and guidance for improvement as well. As these guidelines are a direct outcome of the levels defined we see *ITS-CMM* as an analyzing technique concerned with processes. It is therefore positioned right in the middle of the *Analysis* area indicating that it is neither strictly technically nor strictly organizationally oriented.

The scheme we present here and the positioning of each standard is consciously fuzzy to ease its understanding and given a comprehensive overview. As can easily be seen, there is no standard spanning all life cycle phases but there are some approaches integrating organizational aspects as well as technological ones. Most standards focus on the execution phase of the life cycle and there are surprisingly few methods usable in the design phase.

One research issue therefore is the integration of different approaches to build up a chain of methodologies deployable over the whole life cycle without the need to use different models or description techniques in each life cycle phase. This integration could be driven by providing tools to support design and analysis for execution centric approaches like ITIL, eTOM or MOF. The issue is already covered in some approaches eTOM, for example, offers an addendum describing its relation to ITIL, but most approaches do not discuss this mapping issue at all. Another development will possibly be the extension of design techniques to deliver fine grained refinements which could be used straight forward to implement the execution phase. Summed up, the continuous improvement cycle deployed to service management poses a load of new research issues mainly resulting from the need for integration of many aspects mostly very different in their kind.

4 Conclusion

Management of IT systems and infrastructures faces a shift towards organizational management as technical potentials are fairly utilized. Consequently, standards for IT service management available today cover organizational as well as technical aspects. As the idea of continuous improvement gains increasing importance in IT service management, solutions and the standards they are based on have to be seen in close relation to the whole improvement life cycle.

The presented taxonomy classifies existing standards and approaches in the area of IT service management relying on two fundamental characteristics: the life cycle phase an approach addresses primarily, and whether it is more technically or organizationally focused. We use this taxonomy to illustrate the relations between the various standards.

Our survey showed a variety of standards deployable in specific segments of our taxonomy. However integral approaches (e.g. that cover the whole life cycle) are still missing. Further research will therefore focus on the integration of existing approaches to build a life cycle and aspect (technological or organizational) spanning set of standards and related tools.

References

Brenner M, Garschhammer M, Nickl F (2006) Requirements Engineering und IT Service Management – Ansatzpunkte einer integrierten Sichtweise, Proc. Modellierung 2006 (MOD'06), GI Lect. Notes Informatics (To be published)

Borghoff UM, Schlichter JH (2000) Computer-Supported Cooperative Work. Springer

BPMN (2006) Business Process Modeling Notation (3 1.0) OMG Final Adopted Specification, February, http://www.3.org/Documents/OMG%20Final% 20 Adopted %203%201-0%20Spec%2006-02-01.pdf

Case JD, Fedor M, Schoffstall ML, Davin C (1990) RFC 1157: Simple Net-work Management Protocol (SNMP), IETF, ftp://ftp.isi.edu/in-notes/rfc1157.txt

CCTA (ed) (2000) Service Support. The Stationary Office

Clerc V, Niessink F, Bon Jv (2004), IT Service CMM, A Pocket Guide, van Haren Publishing

CobIT (2005) IT Governance Institute: CobIT 4.0, http://www.isaca.org/bookstore

Dreo Rodosek G (2002) "A Framework for IT Service Management," Habilitation

Dugmore J (2004) "BS15000: past, present and future," Servicetalk, vol. 04, Apr. 2004. [Online]. Available: http://www.bsi-global.com/ICT/april-04.pdf

eTOM (2004a) enhanced Telecom Operations Map – GB921 (2004) Telemanagement-Forum, Nov. 2004, release 4.5.

eTOM (2004b) enhanced Telecom Operations Map – The Business Process Framework – eTOM-ITIL Application Note – Using eTOM to model the ITIL Processes - GB921L (Version 4.0 für Member Vote), Telemanagement-Forum, , Februar 2004, http://www.tmforum.org/

Garschhammer M, Hauck R, Hegering H-G, Kempter B, Radisic I, Roelle H, Schmidt H (2002) A Case–Driven Methodology for Applying theMNM Service Model. In: R. Stadler und M. Ulema (Editors): Proceedings of the 8th International IFIP/IEEE Network Operations and Management Symposium (NOMS 2002), Seiten 697–710, Florence, Italy, IFIP/IEEE, IEEE Publishing, http://www.mnm-team.org/php-bin/pub/show_pub.php?key=ghhk02

Grembergen Wv (2000), The Balanced Scorecard and IT Governance, Information Systems Control Journal, Volume 2

Hegering H-G, Abeck S, and Neumair B (1999) Integrated Management of Networked Systems — Concepts, Architectures and their Operational Application. Morgan Kaufmann Publishers, Jan. 1999.

ISO (2005) ISO/IEC 20000-1:2005 – Information Technology - Service Management - Part 1: Specification, ISO/IEC, Dec. 2005.

Lee JJ, Ben-Natan R (2002) Integrating Service Level Agreements – Optimizing Your OSS for SLA Delivery. Wiley

Lewis L (1999) Service Level Management for Enterprise Networks. Artech House

MOF (2004) Microsoft Cooperation: MOF Executive Overview, April 2004. http://www.microsoft.com/technet/itsolutions/techguide/mof/mofeo.mspx.

NGOSS (2004) The NGOSS Technology-Neutral Architecture – TMF053, Tele-management-Forum, Feb. 2004, release 4.0.

Neumann S, Probst C, Wernsmann C (2003) "Continuous process management," In: Becker J, Kugeler M, Rosemann M (eds) Process Management, Springer

OSI (1992) Information Technology -- Open Systems Interconnection -- Systems Management Overview, iso 10040, ISO-IEC

OSI (1997) "OSI Networking and System Aspects – Quality of Service," ITU-T, Recommendation X.641, Dec. 1997.

Pande, Holpp (2001) What Is Six Sigma?, McGraw-Hill

Rudd C (2004) An Introductory Overview of ITIL, itSMF. July 2004, http://www.itsmf.com/publications/ITIL%20Overview.pdf

Rumbaugh J, Jacobson I, Booch G (1998) Unified Modeling Language - Reference Manual. Addison–Wesley

Scheer, A-W (1997) Wirtschaftsinformatik: Referenzmodelle für industrielle Geschäftsprozesse. Springer, 7 Auflage, 1997. ISBN3-540-62967-X

Scott D (1999) Making Smart Investments to Reduce Unplanned Downtime, Gartner, Mar. 1999.

Sheard SA (2001) Evolution of the Framework's Quagmire. IEEE Computer 34(7): pp 96-98

IT Service Management Across Organizational Boundaries

Nils gentschen Felde, Heinz-Gerd Hegering, Michael Schiffers

1 Introduction

While network and system management have a long research tradition (Sloman 1994; Hegering et al. 1999) and are well reflected in the industry (Hewlett-Packard 2006; IBM 2006; BMC 2006; Computer Associates 2006), the advent of Service-Oriented Architectures (SOA) (Birman and Ritsko 2005) led to a significant paradigm shift from classical device-oriented IT-management to a more service-oriented approach. The reasons for this shift are manifold and are discussed in more detail in an accompanying paper (Brenner et al. 2006): it is first a consequence of the liberalization efforts witnessed in telecommunication markets and the technical convergence of computer networks and telecommunication systems (see e.g., Kaaranen et al. 2001; Kyun Kim and Prasad 2006). Second, the constantly growing specialization of today's enterprises is leading to dynamic collaboration patterns of inherently competitive organizations. For these collaborations to succeed, however, it is no more sufficient to provide a dependable infrastructure. Instead, members increasingly depend on guarantees regarding the qualities of the services they are relying on. Third, globalization effects require enterprises to permanently "re-adjust" themselves to their core competencies, as the ongoing discussions on business process re-engineering and process optimization show. Consequently, we are observing increasing efforts in outsourcing complete (or parts of) IT processes (Beaumont and Khan 2005) pushing the need of adequate customer service management concepts to the fore (Langer 2001; Nerb 2001).

As has been shown in (Dreo Rodosek 2002), IT service management extends the traditional device management in several aspects. Device-oriented management focuses on the management of *individual resources* (e.g., network devices, end systems or applications), service management emphasizes on *IT services* such as Web services, Email services or Grid services instead. Consequently, device-oriented management answers questions of availability and reliability of single devices or of server load balancing. IT-service management, however, addresses issues of managing resources with respect to the delivered services according to management policies and Service Level Agreements (SLA) between the involved parties.

The emphasis is thus on the detection of dependencies between services (see Fig. 1), on the adequate treatment of service quality issues, on the adaptation of IT infrastructures, on the federation of services, on service deployment, on the virtualization of services, and on the dynamic and distributed service provisioning [1].

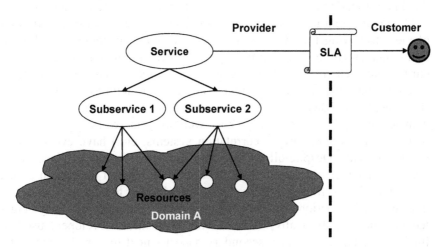

Fig. 1. Service dependencies

Whereas device-oriented management is driven almost exclusively by a provider's objectives, service management strengthens the customer's role. For example, the notion of quality in device-oriented management scenarios is provider-centric as it refers to the utilization of resources by observing Management Information Base (MIB) variables (e.g., CPU load, storage utilization, software versions) of a particular device or component. The Quality-of-Service (QoS) level, however, is individually negotiated between a provider and her customers and is manifested in SLAs.

Service management within a single domain or organization is difficult enough; service management across organizational boundaries complicates the discussion further. Providers may genuinely cooperate or they may compete. In competing cases, providers may offer equivalent or similar services, calling for a notion of service similarity and for adequate metrics to decide which one to select. There may be varying understandings of service attributes, QoS-parameters, usage metering, or dependability characteristics between different Service Providers, requiring a semantically sound treatment of service descriptions. Successful service provisioning (i.e., realizing a service upon a given infrastructure (Dreo Rodosek 2002))

---

[1] Note the n:m relationships between services, resources, and providers: one service may be provisioned upon several resources and one resource may contribute to several services. One service may be provided by several providers while one provider may offer several services.

requires adherence to both local and global policies which, however, may change over time. Mechanisms to detect these changes and to resolve potential conflicts with existing contracts and obligations are mandatory.

IT-management has traditionally been discussed from a functional point of view following the FCAPS dimensions (fault management, configuration management, accounting management, performance management, security management), or resource-wise (network management, systems management, database management, etc.), or sometimes vendor-related (HP Openview, IBM Tivoli, Oracle database systems, etc.). Standards for management (SNMP, CIM, etc.) as well as frameworks (policy-based management systems, event correlation systems, etc.) have evolved in a similar manner. Despite all the standards and frameworks in place, however, IT management is still a complex problem. Part of the reason is that the standards and frameworks were developed either to address a subset of management functionality/resources or were targeted at early-stage-technologies. Additionally, systems and application developers used to think of manageability as a secondary aspect - next to core functionality. Although adequate standards for IT service management are just evolving from traditional management concepts, most of them are still in their infancy. For example, service instrumentation technologies offered today, are still on a very basic level and the management view remains incomplete. It lacks critical information on the state of services while they are executing and on the messages that are travelling between various endpoints.

To overcome these difficulties a Web Services based approach to service management seems promising. One reason is that existing management standards (such as SNMP, CIM) are too low level to allow flexible, coordinated interaction patterns for the management of inter-organizational services. Such flexibility, however, is required for service partners to interface with management applications for, e.g., inter-organizational resource monitoring in Grids, identity management in federated environments, or the formation of groups of collaborating resources across organizations. Although there exists a variety of distributed software platforms that could be useful to implement management applications, Web services technologies are maturing as the likely future platform for management services, for the same reason that other distributed applications use Web services to achieve platform independence and interoperability by exposing interfaces and hide implementations (OASIS 2005).

The intention of this paper is not to provide a comprehensive tutorial on multi-institutional IT service management. Instead, we want to exemplarily explore some of the challenges associated with this topic in more detail: the monitoring of resources across organizational boundaries, the cooperative management of identities in federated environments, and the management of Virtual Organizations in Grids.

The remainder of the paper is structured as follows: section 2 introduces a scenario of dynamic Grids dedicated to crisis and disaster management. This scenario will serve as a reference model for subsequent sections as it exemplifies typical issues in service management across organizational boundaries. Section 3 addresses issues of orchestrating, monitoring and provisioning of services by closer looking at Federated Identity Management, Grid monitoring, and management aspects of Virtual Organizations in Grids. Section 4 discusses a proposal for a management framework based on Web Services technologies. Finally, section 5 shortly summarizes this paper.

2 The EmerGrid Scenario

To further outline the complexity of IT service management across organizational boundaries and to provide a reference example for subsequent discussions, we introduce the scenario of a fictitious Grid-based Emergency handling and crisis management (EmerGrid). We first give a very short introduction to Virtual Organizations in Grids. We then describe the scenario in more detail and discuss some of the implications for inter-organizational IT service management.

2.1 Virtual Organizations in Grids

Grid computing is an emerging computing paradigm which addresses the problem of coordinated resource sharing and problem solving in dynamic, multi-institutional Virtual Organizations (Foster et al. 2001). Technically, Grids provide an infrastructure for e.g., high performance computing and massive data handling by connecting a variety of heterogeneous resources (such as computing elements or storage elements) via high bandwidth networks. Although these resources are 'owned' by autonomous organizations, they may be 'delegated' by their owners to several, even overlapping, Virtual Organizations (VO) according to various policies (see Fig. 2).

Such an ownership/delegation pattern does not only cause unprecedented technical problems, as the literature on Grid Computing shows (Foster and Kesselman 2004), it also implies non-trivial organizational challenges. In order to solve these, Grids separate the traditionally fixed connections between resources and services and between services and Service Providers. Core concepts Grids strictly adhere to are thus 'virtualization', 'orchestration', and 'federation'. The creation of VOs, e.g., requires a homogenized view (i.e., virtualization) on heterogeneous resources, their coordination (i.e., orchestration) into objective-driven workflows, and the cooperation (i.e., federation) of the respective Service Providers for the duration of a VO.

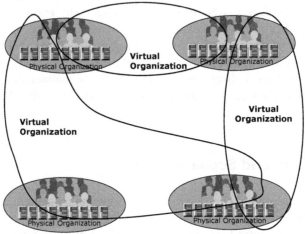

Fig. 2. VO concept

It should be noted, though, that resources are not limited to physical ones (e.g., Storage Area Networks), they may also include logical ones (e.g., simulations packages), and even human ones (e.g., especially skilled personnel).

Service management relates to VOs in two ways: service management within organizations in order to support multiple VOs, and service management within an already established VO to provide correct services to its members. In both cases, although at different levels, service management not only has to enforce a set of policies as far as group membership, resource access, accounting, etc. are concerned, it will also be more and more decentralized and subject to virtualization efforts.

2.2 Scenario Description

EmerGrid (see Fig. 3) describes an as yet fictive crisis management scenario addressing the correct and effective management of diverse crisis and disaster situations. EmerGrid has been inspired by the FireGrid scenario Berry et al. 2005), the Next Generation Grid Disaster scenario (NGG2 2004), and by the health care scenario described in (Hegering et al. 2003).

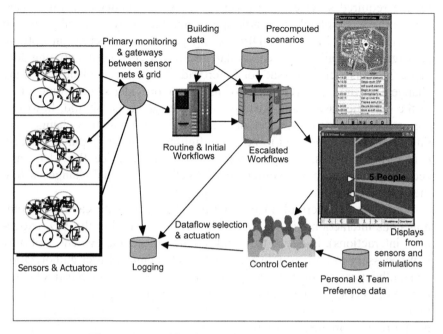

Fig. 3. EmerGrid (adopted from (Berry et al. 2005))

A critical analysis of disasters such as the World Trade Centre collapse, the fires at the Mont Blanc tunnel, the Christmas Tsunami wave, the New Orleans Katrina flood, mass panic situations, or disastrous traffic accidents have revealed many mistaken decisions which have been attributed to a lack of information about the conditions within a fire or a flood and the imminent real world effects of the phenomenon. Grids offer a promising opportunity to significantly improve controlled interventions in such emergency cases by synchronizing on-the-spot data (typically read from sensors) with data base contents and high performance computing facilities for, e.g., simulating the behaviour of tunnel constructions under sudden exposure to explosives with their (sometimes unknown) chemical profiles (Berry et al. 2005).

In case of emergent crisis events [2] the crisis response teams will spontaneously form a Virtual Organization within EmerGrid (EmerGrid-VO), either instigated by a distinguished principal or automatically. Unfortunately, however, it is a priori not known which Service Providers, resource owners, users, and administrators need to contribute to an EmerGrid-VO. Consequently, there may be several Service Providers who are able to of-

---

[2] or planned training manoeuvres

fer the required services in principal, others only under constraints, and again others completely unconditioned since they may be legally obliged to participate in EmerGrid. Discovering providers, selecting an optimal package from available, often similar, service offers, and negotiating adequate SLAs is a crucial issue for EmerGrid. As the service landscape may change over time, EmerGrid has to ensure any provider's commitment to – in the extreme case – long-lasting stable engagements. Should, however, the quality of a set of services or their providers' reputation change over time, EmerGrid-VOs need to be re-configured on-the-fly replacing poorly performing services, dropping contract breaking Service Providers, and accommodating to new requirements reflecting situational changes within the crisis event.

Whenever members of an EmerGrid-VO interact with each other (endogenous interactions) or interact with entities external to the VO (exogenous interactions), issues of trust and reputation become evident. Not only is it necessary to both establish and monitor schemes of user authorization and authentication during the whole lifetime of an EmerGrid-VO, the choice of Service Providers to whom tasks may be assigned to, needs to be re-assured permanently as well. EmerGrid therefore incorporates a trust monitoring component that will gather information from several reputation sources in order to establish a meaningful trust assertion for a given set of Service Providers. A provider's reputation level may be obtained either directly from known trusted evaluations in the past, from reputation brokers, from generally accepted escrow holders, or from genuinely trustable governmental authorities.

Assume now that a critical service in EmerGrid apparently fails. In this case a typical management task will be to track down the root causes to the erroneous resources via the service chains involved (Hanemann et al. 2005). For EmerGrid's survivability (Rowanhill 2004) it is essential that this analysis is eventually assisted by appropriate tools and that adequate counter measures are initiated quickly.

2.3 Multi-Institutional Service Management

Analyzing the EmerGrid scenario reveals some basic characteristics of multi-organizational services that make them especially challenging to manage. Per constructionem, EmerGrid services belonging to different domains, need to cooperate. A good portion of the EmerGrid management challenges stems from the many different view points. For instance, a local IT manager would be interested in managing the services in her domain. Her vantage point is thus the services on "her machines". Another perspective is that of the process manager in EmerGrid who is interested in a successful orchestration of adequate (sub-) services to drive the rescue process to completion. This will involve workflows across management domains, maybe across enterprises, or possibly across organizations not even involved in EmerGrid. A business manager, though, may be interested in the service agreements and the penalties possibly due when her local business processes experience unannounced suspensions in case of EmerGrid priority interrupts.

A critical challenge in EmerGrid is the strong push to have all relevant services discoverable, either at design time or at run time. Technically, EmerGrid's service endpoints [3] must be discovered at run time, but the discovery mechanism is not limited to a single domain anymore. As the resources and services may be unknown in sudden events, EmerGrid may contain a resource broker and appropriate directory services which have to ensure that provided services are protected with the correct type of security capsules. Authorization and authentication of users seems trivial and is in principle well-understood in single domains. Multiple domains and aiming at a Single Sign On (SSO) functionality, however, pose the necessity to deploy concepts of Federated Identity Management (FIM) and Trust Management (see section 3.1). Determining who is making use of which provided services when, in which context, and how the services are performing in a wider sense is the task of service monitoring (see section 3.2). Setting up the organizational context in such a way that the required services are provisionable and manageable while at the same time obeying policies and sticking to enforceable service agreements is guided by the management of an organization's life cycle. In section 3.3 we will investigate this issue in a bit more detail for dynamic VOs in Grids.

3 Orchestration, Monitoring, and Provisioning of Services

3.1 Identity Management in Federated Environments

An essential part of service provisioning across organizational boundaries is the setup, configuration, maintenance and deletion of user accounts in the general context of Identity & Access Management (I&AM) (for this section we mainly follow (Hommel and Reiser 2005; Hommel 2005,

---

[3] An endpoint indicates a specific location for accessing a service using a specific protocol and data format.

2005a; Hommel and Schiffers 2006). To facilitate cross-organizational identity data exchange early attempts to grant "foreign" services access to "private" data quickly turned out to be too tedious and to suffer from bad scalability. Having to set up accounts for users from other organizations and getting applications to work with different schemas leads to a massive administrative overhead and is impractical when more than a handful of organizations is involved (Hommel and Reiser 2005). Classically, a central identity repository provides the user data required for authentication, authorization and accounting, as well as for service personalization. I&AM systems are therefore fed by an organization's Human Resource Management Systems (e.g., SAP, Oracle) and Customer Relationship Management databases (e.g., Siebel, Peoplesoft). Per constructionem, they thus contain sensitive data, which must be protected due to privacy and governance aspects. However, in an increasing number of scenarios (see EmerGrid in section 2), cross-organizational identity data transfer is required. If, for example, IT services are outsourced to third parties, identity data are required for personalized service provisioning and billing.

Several standards like the OASIS Security Assertion Markup Language (SAML (OASIS 2005a)), the Liberty Alliance specifications (Liberty 2006), and the Web Services Federation Language (WS-Federation, (IBM 2003)) have been proposed to provide methods for Service Providers to securely retrieve information concerning a user from the user's so-called Identity Provider, an important new role in the context of identity management. The application of these standards to inter-domain service provisioning is known as Federated Identity Management (FIM).

SAML is based upon the eXtensible Markup Language (XML) and works with assertions. Currently, assertions for *authentication, authorization* and *attributes* are defined. SAML messages are transmitted using the Simple Object Access Protocol (SOAP) over HTTP and can be used by every standard web browser. Further, SAML can be extended, e.g. using the eXtensible Access Control Markup Language (XACML) (Moses 2005) in order to realize finer granularities of access control, a critical requirement from Grid computing scenarios like EmerGrid.

In the Liberty Alliance Project about 150 global organizations are working together with the objective to develop an open standard for FIM. The architecture proposed consists of three blocks: The Identity Federation Framework (ID–FF), the Services Interface Specifications (ID–SIS) and the Web Services Framework (ID–WSF). In the first block, the Liberty Alliance defines how data is to be exchanged between Identity- and Service Providers using the SAML assertion format. The second part defines the personal and the employee profiles, which include basic information about the user for the use within FIM scenarios. Finally, ID-WSF describes the

SOAP bindings, a discovery service, an authentication service and an interaction service. These services are thought for user interaction in order to provide additional information possibly needed for a certain transaction.

The efforts around the Web Services Federation (WS-Federation) Language are lead by IBM. The language fits into a series of Web Services standards and is another building block of the Web Services Security (WS-Security) framework[4]. WS-Security allows different sites to establish a trust relationship and to federate among each other. Further, it enables the brokering of, for example, trust and authentication. To do so, a WS-Federation member retrieves a so-called "security token" from its Identity Provider. She may subsequently use this token to gain access to resources belonging to an arbitrary Service Provider as long as she is authorized. As may be derived from Fig. 4, FIM generically requires a concept of orchestration for the different user provisioning services.

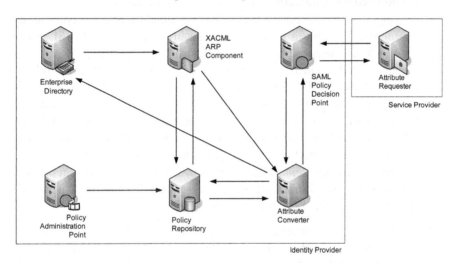

Fig. 4. Identity management orchestration (Hommel 2005)

Whereas service composition refers to the creation of complex services from usually smaller, simpler ones, *orchestration* denotes the description of the sequence of all activities that make up the compound service. Note that compound services are not limited to a single organization; instead the service domain (Tan et al. 2004) may extend across one or more organizations. Also, service compositions do not necessarily mean hierarchical compositions ("a service consists of sub-services"); they may also denote a

---

[4] A good graphical overview of the Web Services standards is given in
www.innoq.com/ soa/ ws-standards/poster/Web_Services_Standards_09_2005.pdf

service chain ("service A followed by service B followed by service C") (Nerb 2001). Synonymous terms for orchestration are choreography, flow composition, and workflow. Services orchestration thus covers the management of the transactions between the individual services, including any necessary error handling, as well as the description of the overall process.

Although a tremendous step towards orchestrating user provisioning services, existing FIM approaches all lack several important properties and functionalities for a smooth orchestration of services across organizational boundaries (Hommel 2005):

- *Limitation to specific technologies:* Today none of the FIM approaches can be applied to scenarios beyond Web Services.
- *Lacking orchestration support:* Although user information is provided by the user's Identity Provider, Service Providers requesting the data are not notified automatically in case of attribute changes.
- *Missing federated security and privacy control:* While the communication channels within a federation are secured properly, all FIM approaches lack a *common* public key infrastructure. Additionally, an interorganizational security model for the correlation of security relevant events is missing. The support of Attribute Release Policies (ARP), i.e., the specification of which user information may be disseminated to whom under which conditions, is only available for specific implementations. Shibboleth (Shibboleth 2006) is such an implementation. However, it uses a proprietary format with limited expressiveness.
- *Limited syntax and semantics of attributes:* No syntax and semantics for the exchange of arbitrary attributes are specified. Only the Liberty Alliance tries to define a set of attributes within its ID-SIS.

To overcome these limitations extensions to the standard SAML architecture have been suggested (Hommel 2005a; Hommel and Schiffers 2006). In addition, XACML (Moses 2005) constructs have been proposed for the specification of access policies to identity information. An implementation of these components extensions to Shibboleth is underway (see also (Hommel and Schiffers 2006) for an application to user provisioning in Grids).

3.2 Service Monitoring Across Organizations

As service orientation becomes critical to business operations, the task of managing such service landscapes will increasingly be imperative to the success of business operations. A key concept in this context is that of service *manageability*. Manageability is defined as a set of capabilities for discovering the existence, availability, health, performance, and usage, as well as the control and configuration of a service within a service-oriented architecture. Service manageability is a prerequisite for service monitoring. Within Grid scenarios monitoring of resources, data, jobs and applications across organizational boundaries is indispensable. Using an adequate Grid-wide monitoring architecture, information not only about single devices or resources but also about more complex objects like Grid services is gathered. The information is then fed into service management applications for FCAPS handling and more business driven tasks such as billing processes. A major challenge arising from the EmerGrid scenario with respect to multi-domain monitoring is the heterogeneity of underlying resources and services while covering a multiple of independent organizations with differing business perspectives and various management policies. Beside these organizational problems several technical challenges have to be faced and solved. Due to the lack of early standards in Grid Computing, a variety of Grid monitoring frameworks has been proposed and developed.

The Global Grid Forum (GGF) (GGF 2006) specifies a generic "Grid Monitoring Architecture" (GMA) (Tierney et al. 2000) the role model of which is shown in Fig. 5. It consists of information providing entities, the *producers*, the *consumers*, and a *directory service*. Consumers are Grid management components using the information provided by the producers. They may retrieve a list of the currently available producers along with their corresponding capabilities from the directory service and register directly with the producers that satisfy their needs. The producer will provide monitoring data to its registered consumers in either push or pull mode. The GMA specification does not imply any interfaces or implementation details so that compliant monitoring frameworks need not necessarily be compatible among each others.

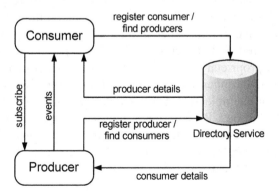

Fig. 5. GMA roles (Tierney et al. 2000)

In the Grid context, there exist several GMA compliant monitoring tools. The most known ones are the MDS (Monitoring and Discovery System) services within the Globus Toolkit (GT) (Foster 2005), the Unicore (UNiform Interface to COmputing REsources) (Unicore 2006) monitoring components, the R-GMA (Relational Grid Monitoring Architecture) (Cooke et al. 2004) which provides the monitoring capabilities of the Grid middleware gLite (EGEE 2006), GridICE (the Eyes of the Grid) (Aiftimiei et al. 2006), the OCM-G/G-PM (Grid-enabled OMIS-compliant Monitor / Grid-enabled Performance Measurement Tool) (Bali et al. 2004), GridRM (A Resource Monitoring Architecture for the Grid) (Baker and Smith 2004), and MonaLisa (Monitoring Agents using a Large Integrated Services Architecture) (Legrand at al. 2004). In the following we will shortly present the first three monitoring frameworks, namely MDS, the Unicore monitoring components and R-GMA, as they are widely spread in the Grid community and follow promising monitoring approaches.

The *Monitoring and Discovery System* (MDS) is developed by the Globus Alliance and provides the monitoring framework for the Globus Toolkit. The MDS is a GMA compliant implementation and addresses two major aspects – monitoring and discovering resources and services in the Grid. It implements a Web Services interface for arbitrary information providing entities and transfers the information using an appropriate XML schema. The current version 4 of MDS supports query, subscription and notification protocols. Further, it is build using the Web Services Resource Framework (WSRF) specification (Czajkowski et al. 2005) in order to satisfy interoperability and extensibility requirements.

Unicore provides a Grid middleware which includes several monitoring capabilities. Besides submitting a job to the Grid, Unicore supports the controlling and monitoring of jobs and therefore, a graphical user interface is included. All the information necessary for the monitoring and controlling of tasks is maintained by Unicore servers. They are responsible for the communication between the different sites based on the "Unicore Protocol Layer" (UPL) that, among other things, handles security aspects such as authentication and SSL (Secure Socket Layer) secured communication. The UPL is a proprietary protocol and thus implies a major disadvantage of Unicore and its inherited monitoring framework. No widely accepted standard, as for example Web Services, is supported so that any extension of Unicore has to be UPL compliant. Consequently, achieving an interoperability of Unicore with respect to other Grid monitoring tools is difficult. Currently, there are some projects on the way to address these issues (GRIP GRIP 2006), Unicore/GS (John Brooke 2005).

The *Relational Grid Monitoring Architecture* (R-GMA) (Cooke et al. 2004) is an extension to the GMA standard and introduces the concept of the republisher. The role model is illustrated in Fig. 6.

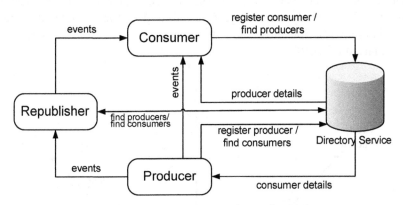

Fig. 6. R-GMA roles (Cooke et al. 2004)

It implements a "producer", a "consumer" and a "directory service" as demanded by the GMA and depicted on the right hand side of Fig. 6. The R-GMA "republisher" provides the capability of forwarding the information gathered by the producers to the consumers. Additionally, the monitoring information can be passed to other consumers which have subscribed to the producers and do not directly belong to the R-GMA. Thus, the monitoring information is made available to applications that are not part of the R-GMA model in order to support the extensibility and interoperability of this approach.

3.3 Dynamic Virtual Organizations in Grids

As the EmerGrid scenario shows, in service-oriented environments the lifetime of services typically exceeds that of resources in a transparent fashion. For example, users of a file storage service will not notice whether their data is being migrated to new hardware, no matter whether a broken hard drive is being replaced or a new file server with higher capacity is added to the service.

From a management perspective, the life cycles of services and resources are, however, quite similar and can be broken down into phases such as planning, building, operating, changing and withdrawing. Yet, service management has developed with a focus on managing a single organization's services. However, for many applications (like EmerGrid), services need to be composed from multiple organization's resources. In

Grids these composed services are provided by Virtual Organizations (VO) to their members. Thus, VOs do not "own" any resources or services. Availability in this context is defined by dependability metrics, capacity criteria, and sets of economic criteria. A special problem arises when considering VOs as dynamic objects exhibiting a life cycle and dynamic membership relationships: How to manage the creation, operation, and termination of VOs?

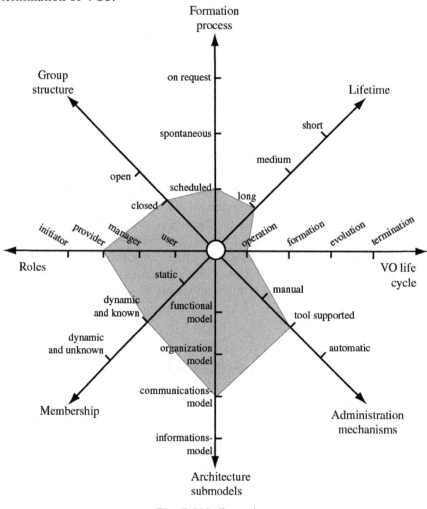

Fig. 7. VO dimensions

Historically, management methods and tools for resource, service and VO management have developed independent of each other. Thus, real world Grid projects suffer from interoperability issues due to extreme heterogeneity that has to be dealt with by the Grid middleware. As a consequence, today's middleware solutions handle both resource and service management in a centralized fashion, i.e., the participating organizations are not in control anymore about who is using their resources for which purposes. While this may be adequate for organizations, which provide dedicated resources to Grid projects, it bypasses their local resource and access management. This situation is, in general, unacceptable for organizations which provide resources for multiple Grids and local services like depicted in the EmerGrid scenario.

Managing VOs in Grids thus necessitates coping with several layers of entities: resources, services, organizations, and the VOs themselves. While resource management has been studied thoroughly, managing a VO's life cycle and its dynamic membership relations has not been investigated in sufficient depth yet. Although a critical requirement in emerging Grids (see the EmerGrid scenario in section 2), it is still unclear what exactly is needed for dynamically setting up and closing down Virtual Organizations. Some dimensions of the VO-management task are depicted in Fig. 7 where the marked area around the origin indicates the topics covered by existing approaches.

As per today, VO-management services in Grids and federations have not been addressed adequately. Although there are some promising attempts to provide solutions to the VO-formation problem (see the Conoise-G project in (Patel et al. 2005)) they lack the generality and do cover only parts of the classification in Fig. 8. Once a VO is established, the operation management needs to handle the dynamics within the VO. Among other things (e.g., workflow management), this requires adequate mechanisms for a thorough membership management across organizations. Existing solutions are the Virtual Organization Membership Service (VOMS) (VOMS 2006), PERMIS (PERMIS 2006), and Shibboleth (Shibboleth 2006) with its Globus Toolkit integration GridShib (Barton et al. 2006). VOMS mainly consists of four parts:

- The *User Server* which handles per VO requests from a client and returns the information requested about a user,
- a *User Client* that contacts the User Server and authenticates a user by presenting the user's certificate (typically an X.509 certificate) and obtains a list of groups, roles and capabilities of the user,
- the *Administration Client* used for administration purposes like e.g. adding users, creating new groups or changing roles of users,
- and the *Administration Server* for accepting requests from clients and keeping the database up to date.

VOMS may be used with the Globus Toolkit Grid middleware and thus performs the relevant management actions within the Grid. PERMIS implements a role based access control mechanism.

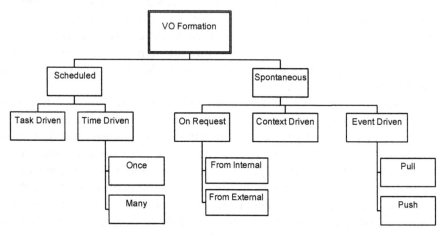

Fig. 8. VO formation

PERMIS can also be deployed upon a Globus Toolkit driven Grid infrastructure and represents an alternative to VOMS. In contrast to VOMS PERMIS is capable of using properly formatted policy files in order to make decisions based on the given policies. PERMIS is able to perform both access control to services and resources in federated environments and managing policies and role assignments. Shibboleth is capable of providing a Single Sign On (SSO) in inter-organizational environments. It deploys an attribute-based authorization while respecting the user's privacy. Shibboleth is based on the OASIS SAML standard. As stated before, SAML defines web browser profiles which are used for the two main functionalities of Shibboleth: the Identity Provider and the Service Provider. The Identity Provider creates, maintains and manages the user's identity, while the Service Provider performs the access control to resources and services.

GridShib is an implementation of Shibboleth for Grids. The package mainly consists of two plug-ins – one for Shibboleth and one for the Globus Toolkit. With these plug-ins Service Provides may securely request user attributes from a Shibboleth Identity Provider using mechanisms of the Globus Toolkit.

Comparing both VOMS and Shibboleth we see a lot of matches such that the support of multiple VOs and their appropriateness for dynamically creating VOs. Their main differences are to be found in operational issues.

VOMS lacks high dependability conformances as the central VOMS server may be a single point of failure, Shibboleth needs to cross VO borders when authorizing users as the user's attributes are administered in her home domain which may not belong to the Grid VO[5].

Once the objectives of the VO are satisfied the purpose of the VO has become obsolete and it can be terminated. This may happen either on demand or scheduled. In either case, the respective termination service needs to release reserved and allocated resources and to adjust audit records. Which information belongs to who after a VO's death is depending on bilateral SLAs and global policies. In the EmerGrid scenario this may be a critical issue. Generic solutions to the VO management problem are under investigation (see Hommel and Schiffers 2006).

4 A Framework for Inter-Organizational Service Management Based on Web Services Standards

As pointed out earlier, highly dynamic, large-scale, and multiorganizational environments pose new organizational and technical challenges but lack an integrated management solution. The main reasons for this deficiency are the decentralized control and the implied necessity of communication between system administrators and users, affiliated with a variety of independent organizations and domains: different sites imply different institutional goals and often "strong personalities" to be integrated. Every site needs to remain autonomous as far as the operating procedures and policies are concerned.

In order to face these challenges a unified architecture amended by components for inter-organizational monitoring, orchestration, accounting and billing is needed, as the EmerGrid scenario in section 2 implies. Recently a framework based on Web Services technologies has been proposed as a promising approach for overcoming these difficulties.

Traditionally, the Web Services have been considered permanent, meaning their lifetime is essentially infinite and the clients do not have to worry about when a service comes into existence or when it goes away. This means there is no standard way of notifying clients of life cycle events such as creation, upgrade, and destruction. Real IT resources, however, are commissioned and decommissioned on a per need basis. Hence, their Web Service representations have to reflect this.

---

[5] Further evaluation criteria may be found under http://www.d-drid.de/fileadmin/ dgrid_document/Dokumente/VOMS-Thesenpapier.pdf

4.1 The Web Services Management Standards Stack

Although initially separated, Grid services and Web Services have converged recently in the WSRF (Web Services Resource Framework). This was accomplished by defining precise methods to deal with service states and service lifetimes. WSRF is a set of five different, but interlocking, specifications. Additionally, a set of new specifications called WSN (Web Services Notification) (OASIS 2005b) has been defined to support the publish/subscribe pattern of message exchange.

The development of WSRF and WSN has been instigated by both the desire to look at Grid services as normal Web Services and by the need to create a Web Service infrastructure layer that can be used by other specifications. Such a specification is the Web Services Distributed Management specification (WSDM). WSDM contains two parts: the management using Web Services (MUWS) (OASIS 2005d) and the management of Web Services (MOWS) (OASIS 2005c).

MUWS uses WSRF to expose resource states and life cycle information and it uses WSN for asynchronous notifications. Furthermore, MUWS defines a number of IT management specific resource properties and topics that can be used for exposing a manageability interface.

The difficulty with MUWS is its limited view point. Whereas other approaches like the Java Management Extension (JMX) (Sun Microsystems 2006) and the Common Information Model (CIM) (DMTF 2006) individually define complete management technology stacks, MUWS is concerned with "what goes on the wire". The expectation is that one would be able to use MUWS along with pieces of other standards like Web-Based Enterprise Management (WBEM) to create complete management solutions. An example would be to expose a CIM-specified model through MUWS mechanisms. This discussion should, however, not imply that any CIM model or JMX-instrumented system could automatically be exposed using MUWS techniques without loss of information or capability. CIM models, for example, are object-oriented, and these model objects do not always map well to services, the unit of management in MUWS. For more information on this research issues see (Sailer 2005).

4.2 Web Services Management Framework

Recently the Web Services Management Framework (WSMF) (Catania et al. 2003) has been proposed for addressing the management of IT resources (including Web Services and Grid services) *using* Web Services. The specification thus comprises both MUWS and MOWS. As any other management solution, multi-institutional service management using WSMF must address the fundamental management questions (Hegering et al. 1999): What are the managed objects (i.e., which resources have to be managed)? What are their interfaces? How does management information get exchanged (i.e., which operations and notification protocols are needed)? The following discussions are mainly based on (Catania et al. 2003).

4.2.1 Web Services as Managed Objects

Generally, a managed object provides management capabilities by implementing appropriate management interfaces. In WSMF the management interfaces are described using the standard Web Services Description Language (WSDL). Hence, the managed objects themselves are Web Services, not resources. A manager uses WSMF concepts to manage all the resources of a management domain in a uniform way (note that such a domain can cover several organizations).

The management capabilities described by WSDL documents include a number of functions required for the management of services (Hegering et al. 1999; Dreo Rodosek 2002): the discovery of management WSDL documents, the discovery of the relations and event notifications of the managed objects, the registrations and the retrieval of event notifications, the monitoring, auditing, and controlling of various aspects of the managed objects. Managed objects may be implemented as part of the managed resources directly or provided in a separate layer. Managed objects may expose a variety of other (non Web Services related) management interfaces to support those management capabilities which are appropriate for the underlying resource.

4.2.2 Interfaces and Interface Collections

Interfaces are defined as descriptions of a set of related management capabilities of managed objects. Managed objects implement interfaces to provide management capabilities for the managed resources that they represent. WSMF allows management interfaces to be grouped into collections of interfaces to describe a group of management capabilities yielding classes of managed objects. Interfaces can be extended to define additional capabilities. WSMF provides a base interface collection that describes a set of management capabilities common to all managed objects. The base interface collection contains the set of properties representing information about a managed object as attributes, the set of functions that can be provided to support the management of a managed object as operations and the set of events and state changes that can be reported by a managed object as notification types. WSMF has defined six categories of operations based on the FCAPS-categories defined by OSI (see e.g., Hegering et al. 1999). The categories are: monitoring, discovery, control, performance, configuration, and security.

WSMF allows the separation of features of a single managed object into multiple management interfaces. This has several advantages: First, it allows a managed object to provide management capabilities incrementally by supporting one interface initially and extending this support gradually if needed. Second, management interfaces allow resource owners to selectively decide what management information should be provided to what manager role by exposing selective interfaces. This allows a managed object to expose all management interfaces to an administrator, and a restricted subset to all other users.

4.2.3 Events and Notifications

An event subsystem is an integral part of any management solution. However, currently there is no widely adopted Web Services-based standard for such a subsystem. WSMF has defined its own Web Services-based event subsystem to better meet this requirement. A detailed and formal description of this subsystem can be found in the WS-Events specification (Catania et al. 2003a).

WS-Events define operations to subscribe for event notifications and the notification syntax and processing rules to inform one or more subscribers that an event has occurred. An event is a state change in a managed resource or processing of a request by the managed resource that can be communicated through a notification. There are two modes to get these notifications: a push mode and a pull mode. In the push mode, when an event occurs, the managed object sends a notification to the subscribers to inform them of a state change. In the pull mode, the subscriber issues calls to the managed object to request all the notifications that happened since the last pull call.

For efficiency and scalability reasons, WSMF supports bulk subscription and notification operations. In the push mode, the management client can subscribe to more than one notification type in a single subscribe call. In the pull model, notifications from more than one type can be retrieved through a single call.

The tradeoffs between both usage modes are important to consider. The push mode tends to be more networks intensive while the pull model may require more computation and memory resources at the managed object. Also, the pull mode makes it possible to apply WSMF to scenarios where the managed object may not be able to establish connection with the subscriber, a scenario not untypical for EmerGrid (see section 2).

The operations for the push and pull modes are grouped in two different interfaces. In both modes, a subscribe call is used to register an interest for one or more event types. In the push version, an extra call-back URL is needed to identify the endpoint that will receive the notifications. For scalability reasons, any subscription has an associated expiration time.

In WSMF, it is up to the subscriber to ensure the renewal of subscriptions before they expire. A successful subscription call returns a unique SubscriptionId. The SubscriptionId acts as a handle and is passed as a parameter for all other notifications. For more information on WSMF we refer to (Catania et al. 2003) and related documentation.

5 Summary

In this paper we have addressed aspects of IT-service management across organizational boundaries. Starting from a complex scenario we have identified several issues to be tackled when successfully managing IT-services in such environments. We have especially discussed the necessity of adequate security concepts to ensure that service provisioning is protected by appropriate security capsules. We saw that authorization and authentication of users, although well understood in single domains, in multiple domains when aiming at SSO functionality, poses unprecedented challenges in deploying FIM-concepts and Trust Management. FIM also served as an example for an orchestration of services across organizations. Determining who is making use of which provided services when, in which context, and how the services are performing in a wider sense is the task of service monitoring which we discussed for Grid environments. Provisioning services requires an organizational context. Setting up this context in such a way that the required services are provisionable and manageable while at the same time bound to policies and enforceable service agreements is guided by the management of an organization's life cycle. We addressed some of the challenges related to the management of dynamic VOs as they appear in Grids. Finally, we shortly presented the Web Service Management Framework (WSMF). Although this framework is still in its infancy, it represents a promising approach for managing IT-service across organizational boundaries.

Service management across organizational boundaries is a hot research topic. Most of the concepts are still under discussion or are just being implemented prototypically. Consequently, we were only able to scratch the surface in selected areas which, however, are critical as they build the cornerstones of a new service-oriented IT paradigm.

Abbreviations

ARP	Attribute Release Policies
CIM	Common Information Model
CSM	Customer Service Management
FCAPS	Fault Management, Configuration Management, Accounting Management, Performance Management, Security Management
FIM	Federated Identity Management
GGF	Global Grid Forum
GMA	Grid Monitoring Architecture
GridICE	the Eyes of the Grid
GridRM	A Resource Monitoring Architecture for the Grid
GT	Globus Toolkit
I & AM	Identity and Access Management
ID-FF	Identity Federation Framework
ID-SIS	Services Interface Specifications
ID-WSF	Web Services Framework
MDS	Monitoring and Discovery System
MIB	Management Information Base
MonaLisa	Monitoring Agents using a Large Integrated Services Architecture
MOWS	Management Of Web Services
MUWS	Management Using Web Services
OASIS	Organization for the Advancement of Structured Information Standards
OCM-G/G-PM	Grid-enabled OMIS-compliant Monitor / Grid-enabled Performance Measurement Tool
ODP	Open Distributed Processing
OGSA	Open Grid Services Architecture
PERMIS	Privilege and Role Management Infrastructure Standards Validation
QoS	Quality of Service

R-GMA   Relational Grid Monitoring Architecture

SAML   Security Assertion Markup Language

SLA   Service Level Agreement

SNMP   Simple Network Management Protocol

SOA   Service-Oriented Architecture

SOAP   Simple Object Access Protocol

SSO   Single Sign On

Unicore   UNiform Interface to COmputing REsources

UPL   Unicore Protocol Layer

VO   Virtual Organization

VOMS   Virtual Organization Membership Service

WS   Web Services

WSDM   Web Services Distributed Management

WSMF   Web Services Management Framework

WSRF   Web Services Resource Framework

XACML   eXtensible Access Control Markup Language

XML   eXtensible Markup Language

References

Aiftimiei C, Andreozzi S, Cuscela G, De Bortoli N, Donvito G, Fantinel S, Fattibene E, Misurelli G, Pierro A, Rubini GL, Tortone G (2006) GridICE: Requirements, Architecture and Experience of a Monitoring Tool for Grid Systems. In: Proceedings of the International Conference on Computing in High Energy and Nuclear Physics (CHEP2006), Mumbai, India. February 2006

Baker MA, Smith G (2004) Ubiquitous Grid Resource Monitoring. In: Proceedings of the Third UK e-Science Programme All Hands Meeting (AHM2004), Nottingham, UK, April 2004

Bali B, Bubak M, Funika W, Szepieniec T, Wismüller R, Radecki M (2004) Monitoring Grid Applications with Grid-Enabled OMIS Monitor. In: Proceedings of the First European Across Grids Conference, Springer LNCS, Volume 2970, Santiago de Compostela, Spain, February

Barton T, Basney J, Freeman T, Scavo T, Siebenlist F, Von Welch, Ananthakrishnan R, Baker B, Goode M, Keahey K (2006) Identity Federation and Attribute-based Authorization Through the Globus Toolkit, Shibboleth, Gridshib, and MyProxy. In: Proceedings of the 5th Annual PKI R&D Workshop, April 2006 (To appear).

Beaumont N, Khan Z (2005) A Taxonomy of Refereed Outsourcing Literature, Working Paper 22/05 of the Monash University, Department of Management, Melbourne/Australia,

Berry D, Usmani A, Torero J, Tate A, McLaughlin S, Potter S, Trew A, Baxter R, Bull M, Atkinson M (2005) FireGrid: Integrated Emergency Response and Fire Safety Engineering for the Future Built Environment. In: Proceedings of the UK e-Science All Hands Meeting (AHM 2005)

Birman A, Ritsko JJ (2005.) Service-Oriented Architecture, IBM Systems Journal, Volume 44, Number 4,

BMC (2006) BMC Software; Online Resource http://www.bmc.com/, last checked 6.3.2006

Brenner M, Garschhammer M, Hegering H-G (2006) When Infrastructure Management Just Won't Do: The Trend towards Organizational IT-Service Management. In: Kern E-M, Hegering H-G, Brügge B (eds) Managing Development and Application of Digital Technologies, Springer Berlin, Heidelberg, New York, pp 131-146

Catania N, Kumar P, Murray B, Pourhedari H, Vambenepe W, Wurster K (2003) Web Services Management Framework, Version 2.0, http://devresource.hp.com/drc/specifications/wsmf/WSMF-Overview.jsp

Catania N, Kumar P, Murray B, Pourhedari H, Vambenepe W, Wurster K (2003a) Web Services Events (WS-Events) Version 2.0,
http://devresource.hp.com/drc/specifications/wsmf/WS-Events.pdf

Computer Associates (2006) CA Software; Online Resource http://www.ca.com/, last checked 6.3.2006

Cooke AW, Gray AJG, Nutt W, Magowan J, Oevers M, Taylor P, Cordenonsi R, Byrom R, Cornwall L, Djaoui A, Field L, Fisher SM, Hicks S, Leake J, Middleton R, Wilson A, Zhu X, Podhorszki N, Coghlan B, Kenny S, Orsquo Callaghan D, Ryan J (2004) The Relational Grid Monitoring Architecture: Mediating Information About the Grid., Journal of Grid Computing, 2(4):323–339, December 2004

Czajkowski K, Ferguson D, Foster I, Frey J, Graham S, Sedukhin I, Snelling D, Tuecke S, Vambenenepe W (2005) The WS-Resource Framework, Jan 2005

DMTF (2006) Common Information Model, http://www.dmtf.org/standards/cim/

Dreo Rodosek G (2002) A Framework for IT Service Management; Habilitation, Ludwig Maximilian University Munich

EGEE (2006) gLite: Lightweight Middleware for Grid Computing; Online Resource http://glite.web.cern.ch/glite/, last checked 6.3.2006

Foster I (2005) Globus Toolkit Version 4: Software for Service-Oriented Systems; Proceedings of the IFIP International Conference on Network and Parallel Computing, Springer LNCS, Volume 3779

Foster I, Kesselman C (2004) The Grid 2; Morgan Kaufmann Publishers

Foster I, Kesselman C, Tuecke St (2001) The Anatomy of the Grid: Enabling Scalable Virtual Organizations; International Journal of High Performance Computing Applications, Volume 15, Number 3, 2001, pp 200-222

Garschhammer M (2004) Dienstgütebehandlung im Dienstlebenszyklus – von der formalen Spezifikation zur rechnergestützten Umsetzung (in German); Dissertation, Ludwig Maximilian University Munich

GGF (2006) Global Grid Forum, History and Background; Homepage of the Global Grid Forum; http://www.ggf.org/L_About/hist&back.htm

GRIP (2006) The Grid Interoperability Project (GRIP); http://www.grid-interoperability.org

Hanemann A, Sailer M, Schmitz D (2005) Towards a Framework for IT Service Fault Management. In: Proceedings of the European University Information Systems Conference (EUNIS 2005), Manchester, England

Hegering H-G, Abeck S, Neumair B (1999) Integrated Management of Networked Systems - Concepts, Architectures and their Operational Application; Morgan Kaufmann Publishers

Hegering H-G, Küpper A, Linnhoff-Popien C, Reiser H: Management Challenges of Context-Aware Services in Ubiquitous Environments. In:Proceedings of the 14th IFIP/IEEE Workshop on Distributed Systems: Operations and Management (DSCOM 2003); Heidelberg, Germany

Hewlett-Packard (2006) HP OpenView Management Software; Online Resource http://www.managementsoftware.hp.com/, last checked 6.3.2006

Hommel W (2005) An Architecture for Privacy–Aware Inter–Domain Identity Management. In: Proceedings of the 16th IFIP/IEEE International Workshop on Distributed Systems: Operations and Management (DSOM 2005), Barcelona, Spain, October, 2005

Hommel W (2005a) Using XACML for Privacy Control in SAML–based Identity Federations. In: Proceedings of the, 9th IFIP TC–6 TC–11 Conference on Communications and Multimedia Security (CMS 2005), September 2005

Hommel W, Reiser H (2005) Federated Identity Management: Shortcomings of existing standards. In: Proceeding of the 9th IFIP/IEEE International Symposium on Integrated Network Management (IM 2005), Nice, France

Hommel W, Schiffers M (2006) Supporting Virtual Organization Life Cycle Management by Dynamic Federated User Provisioning. Submitted to 13th Workshop of the HP OpenView University Association (HP-OVUA), Nice/France, 2006

IBM (2003) Web Services Federation Language, http://www-128.ibm.com/developerworks/library/specification/ws-fed/, July 2003

IBM (2006) IBM Tivoli Software; Online Resource http://www-306.ibm.com/software/tivoli/, last checked 6.3.2006

Brooke J (2005) The John Brooke University of Manchester: Unicore-UniGrids: Activities and Strategies for Open Source Grids; GridCoord Workshop "The use of open middlewares for Grids"; October 12th 2005, Sophia Antipolis, France

Kaaranen H, Ahtiainen A, Laitinen L, Naghian S, Niemi V (2001) UMTS Networks; John Wiley and Sons Ltd.

Kyun KY, Prasad R (2006) 4G Roadmap and Emerging Communication Technologies; Artech House Publishers

Langer M (2001) Konzeption und Anwendung einer Customer Service Management Architektur (in German); Dissertation, Technical University Munich

Legrand IC, Newman HB, Voicu R, Cirstoiu C, Grigoras C, Toarta M, Dobre C (2004) MonALISA: An Agent based, Dynamic Service System to Monitor, Control and Optimize Grid based Applications. In: Proceedings of the International Conference on Computing in High Energy and Nuclear Physics (CHEP2004), Interlaken, Switzerland, September 2004

Liberty (2006) The Liberty Alliance Project, http://www.projectliberty.org

Moses T (2005) OASIS eXtensible Access Control Markup Language 2.0, Core Specification; OASIS XACML Technical Committee Standard

Nerb M (2001) Customer Service Management als Basis für interorganisationales Dienstmanagement (in German); Dissertation, Technical University Munich

NGG2 Expert Group (2004) Next Generation Grid 2: Requirements and Options for European Grids Research 2005-2010 and Beyond; Final Report

OASIS (2005) An Introduction to WSDM; Committee Draft 1

OASIS (2005a) Security Assertion Markup Language (SAML) v2.0, http://docs.oasis-open.org/security/saml/v2.0/saml-2.0-os.zip, March 2005

OASIS (2005b) Web Services Base Notification 1.3 (WS-BaseNotification) Public Review Draft 02, 28 November 2005

OASIS (2005c) Web Services Distributed Management: MOWS Primer; Working Draft 6, Dec. 2005

OASIS (2005d) Web Services Distributed Management: MUWS Primer; Working Draft 21, Dec. 2005

Patel J, Teacy WTL, Jennings NR, Luck M, Chalmers St, Oren N, Norman TJ, Preece A, Gray PMD., Shercliff G, Stockreisser PJ., Shao J, Gray WA, Fiddian NJ, Thompson S (2005) Agent-Based Virtual Organisations for the Grid. In: Proceedings of the Fourth International Joint Conference on Autonomous Agents and Multiagent Systems (AAMAS '05); ACM Press, New York

PERMIS (2006) The Privilege and Role Management Infrastructure Standards Validation, http://sec.isi.salford.ac.uk/permis/

Rowanhill JC (2004) Survivability Management Architecture for Very Large Distributed Systems; Dissertation, School of Engineering and Applied Science of the University of Virginia, USA

Sailer M (2005) Towards a Service Management Information Base. In: Proceedings of the IBM PhD Student Symposium at ICSOC05, Amsterdam, Netherlands, December, 2005.

Shibboleth (2006) The Shibboleth Project, http://shibboleth.internet2.edu/, 2006

Sloman M (1994.) Network and Distributed Systems Management; Addison-Wesley Publishing Company

Sun Microsystems (2006) Java Management Extensions; http://java.sun.com/products/JavaManagement/

Tan Y.-S., Vellanki V., Xing J., Topol B., Dudley G. (2004) Service Domains; IBM Systems Journal, Vol 43, No 4, 2004

Tierney B, Aydt R, Gunter D, Smith W, Swany M, Taylor V, Wolski R (2000) A Grid Monitoring Architecture, The Global Grid Forum Performance Working Group, March 2000, http://www.gridforum.org/documents/GFD.7.pdf.

Unicore Forum (2006) What is Unicore?; Homepage of the Unicore Forum;
    http://www.unicore.org/unicore.htm
VOMS (2006) The Virtual Organization Membership Service, http://infnforge.
    cnaf.infn.it/projects/voms, 2006

Acknowledgement

The authors wish to thank the members of the Munich Network Management (MNM) Team for helpful discussions and valuable comments on previous versions of this contribution. The MNM Team, directed by Prof. Dr. Heinz-Gerd Hegering, is a group of researchers of the Ludwig Maximilian University of Munich, the Munich University of Technology, the University of the Federal Armed Forces Munich, and the Leibniz Supercomputing Center of the Bavarian Academy of Sciences. The team's webserver is located at http://www.mnm-team.org.

IV Future Communication Networks

Trends in Telecommunication Networking

Jörg Eberspächer

1 Introduction

Despite the Ups and Downs in the IT and communication markets the network technologies are evolving rapidly. Driving forces are, on the one hand, the continuous progress in microelectronics, optoelectronics and software technology, in emerging network architectures, algorithms and protocols. On the other hand requires the strong market competition the manufacturers and operators to look for new or improved cost-efficient technologies for their products. Last but not least the development is driven by new applications. In the following contribution important networking trends are described.

2 Innovation Across All Layers – the Key Trends

2.1 The Network Traffic Is Continuously Increasing!

The worldwide network traffic is rapidly increasing every year. According to investigations by, among others, the U.S. market research firm IDC, the Internet traffic volume shows a persistent exponential growth over the last 30 years, and it is predicted to continue to grow similarly in the foreseeable future. This is in contrast to the stagnating voice traffic. The aggregated user data rate will, by the end of the decade, exceed one petabit per second (= 1 Pbit/s = 1 million Gbit/s!). The traffic growth is based on different factors. Due to the fast technical evolution the networked PC became the key component for business and private communication. New network technologies enabled inexpensive high volume data communications. Based on the "open platform" of the Internet a big variety of network applications like E-mail, WWW, E-Commerce, Electronic Banking, Audio and Video Streaming and File sharing have evolved and were filling the "network pipes". At present the Web and the popular file sharing have the largest share. Hence we can see in networking a clear technology-application spiral effect which was reinforced by the deregulation of the telecommunication markets in the 1990s.

2.2 The Network Capacity Is Continuously Increasing!

The continuous growth of traffic together with high expectations into the network business have, in the last years, led to a substantial upgrading of the network capacities, both in the long-distance network ("backbone ", "core network") and in the access network. This became possible by the continuous technical advances in optical transmission over silica fiber. Today one fiber can carry, in commercial systems, hundreds of optical channels, each with a bit rate of up to 10 Gbit/s over hundreds of kilometres, by using the novel wavelength division multiplex technique (WDM), (Fig. 1). This corresponds - assuming a channel bit rate of 10 Gbit/s - to a total capacity of one fiber of around 2 Tbit/s. And this is not the end. 100 Tbit/s can be reached. On the horizon are also „pure" photonic networks with switching of data packet in the optical domain (Jourdan et al. 2001).

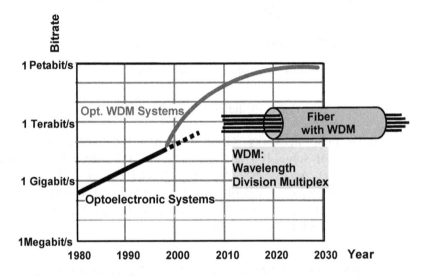

Fig. 1. Evolution of transmission rates

The situation is changing also in the access network where are currently the bottlenecks. The break-through was the development of the Digital Subscriber Line DSL which brings 10 Mbit/s and more to the customer via conventional twisted-pair copper lines. On short distances of a few hundred meters bit rates of up to 100 Mbit/s are possible. However, in the long run optical fiber is the only medium, which allows to eliminate the capacity bottleneck in the "last mile" (Fig. 2).

What about wireless access? Wireline networks will, in the foreseeable future, offer higher transmission capacities than wireless networks. However, the progress in wireless technologies is astonishing. Wireless Local Area Networks (WLAN) are making progress towards higher transmission rates. Today's systems according to the standards IEEE 802.11x offer bit rates of 10 ... 50 Mbit/s (IEEE 2006). Research for Gigabit WLAN is under way (Eberts 2005).

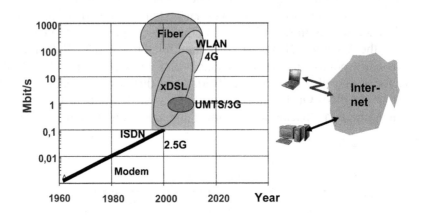

Fig. 2. Evolution of access networks

The cellular radio networks (GSM, UMTS/3G) deliver comparatively small bit rates of some 100 kbit/s. Upgrades to 2 Mbit/s (High Speed Downlink Packet Access HSDPA, High Speed Uplink Packet Access HSUPA) are in preparation (Holma and Toskala 2006). Research on the next generation of wireless networks promises to bring a big leap forward towards 100 Mbit/s (see section 2.6).

2.3 Ethernet Everywhere: The LAN-WAN Convergence

The success of the Internet is, among others, due to the relatively simple Ethernet technology used in Local Area Networks (LAN). However, the Ethernet technology has changed dramatically since the beginnings 30 years ago. The bit rates were increased from 10 Mbit/s (in a shared bus network) to 1 Gbit/s today, point-to-point, not shared. Standards for 10 Gbit/s (10GbE) are under work, and instead of shared bus systems switched Ethernet is primarily used. Now Ethernet is entering the access network as Ethernet First Mile (EFM) and the metro area as Metro Ethernet (Eth 2006). The recent trend is carrier-grade Ethernet for the core, i.e. the extension of the Ethernet into the core transport network, where bit rates of 100Gbit/s are planned (Meddeb 2005; Schmid-Egger et al. 2006). This means that in near time we will have a homogenous infrastructure based on different types of Ethernet (over copper cable, fiber or radio) replacing the traditional SDH and ATM infrastructure (Fig. 3).

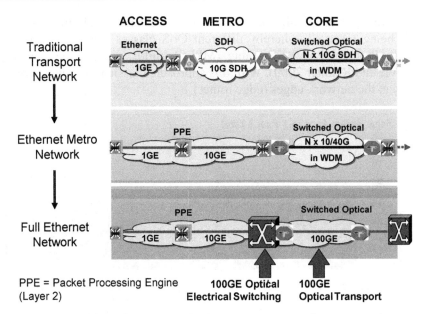

Fig. 3. Ethernet for transport in the access, metro and core network

2.4 IP Everywhere: the Dream of the Next Generation Network (NGN) with QoS

The Internet is based on the protocol architecture TCP/IP (transmission control/Internet Protocol), which, practically, consists of more than 100 protocols. The strength of the "platform" TCP/IP lies in the well standardized and up to now sufficiently simple network architecture, optimized for data communication. The weakness of the TCP/IP architecture is up to now the missing end-to-end quality of service (QoS). Relatively high and temporally varying packet losses (Fig. 4) are typical for the Internet as well as fluctuating delays. Low delay and low packet loss is however necessary for all kinds of real time traffic (e.g. telephony). Since some years research is ongoing on new and better "QoS-aware" Internet protocols. Besides the increase of the transmission rates special QoS protocols and techniques for resource management (RM) were developed (Eberspächer and Glasmann 2005). Nearly all of them are based on the notion of "connections" or "flows", taken from the classical network technologies like Asynchronous Transfer Mode ATM and ISDN. By using special signalling protocols, based on the SIP (Session Initiation Protocol) protocol, Connection Acceptance Control (CAC) methods and resource management functions along predefined or data paths network resources (capacity and buffer memory) are being reserved, whereby different QoS classes can be realized. The Multi Protocol Label Switching (MPLS) builds, e.g. on these concepts (Davie and Rekhter 2000). With this approach, classical IP routers are used only at the network edges (edge router).

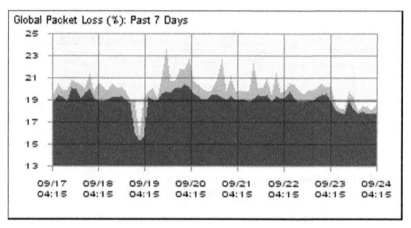

Fig. 4. Packet loss in the Internet. Typical measurements taken over one week.
Source: http://www.internettrafficreport.com/main.htm

The IP network is evolving to the "Next Generation Network" NGN, which is a QoS-enabled "universal" network (NGN 2005, NGN 2006).

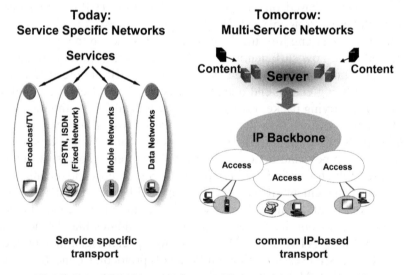

Fig. 5. Transition from service-specific to multi-service networks

By this we are moving from service-specific networks to multi-service networks based on an IP backbone (Fig. 5) where all kinds of services are supported: realtime like Voice-over-IP (Eberspächer and Picot 2005) and video and non-realtime. The long-predicted "convergence" of networks becomes now reality.

2.5 Reliability, Availability, Manageability

Although the IP technology is rather robust against network faults, there are some serious drawbacks. The fault recovery times of today's IP networks are too high for high-speed networks and "mission critical" applications, many seconds instead of some milliseconds or even microseconds. To improve the situation, IP networks with mechanisms for fast fault recognition and localization are needed and techniques for automatic switching of alternative routes, to which, in an emergency case, paths can be switched over in milliseconds. A big variety of options are being developed and investigated, in all relevant protocol layers, from the IP layer down to the physical layer. The goal is to create a network infrastructure ("lower layers") with carrier-grade availability, a high degree of flexibility and easy manageability. The latter is very important for the cost-efficient operation of the network infrastructure. New architectures for dynamic control of Multilayer Transport Networks like the Automatic Switched Optical Network ASON (Fig. 6) or the Generalized Multi Protocol Label Switching GMPLS will allow the fast provisioning of paths and alternative routes in the network (Tomic et al. 2004).

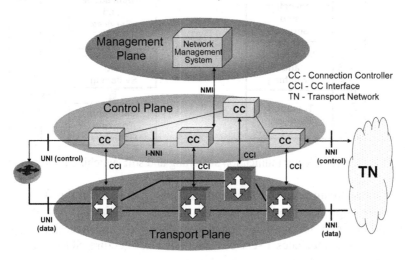

Fig. 6. Automatic switched Optical Network ASON

It is done via a control plane similar to the techniques used in classical switching networks. Via the user network interface (UNI) the higher layers can establish flexibly paths and connections in the transport plane. The vision is the almost complete automation of the operational processes, to save costs and to speed-up the service deployment.

2.6 Open, Programmable and Anyway Secure Networks

The trend to "open systems", originating from the Internet, is a key to the further network evolution. The convergence of telecommunication and computing can be seen in the soft switch architecture (Fig. 7). The conventional "hardware switches", which are based on manufacturer-specific switching platforms, are replaced by high performance and high-available standard computer platforms and equipped with open interfaces, on which third parties can establish innovative services. The challenges with the openness of the systems are the security threads and the reliability and compatibility issues.

The next step is to introduce open source switching products; some are already on the market (e.g. the Asterisk PBX). A completely new approach is formed by the active and programmable networks. In these networks, software functions can be loaded - on demand - from special service data bases (repositories) onto special programmable network nodes (Campbell et al. 1999).

Classical Telco System   Soft Switching Architecture

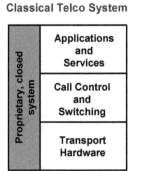 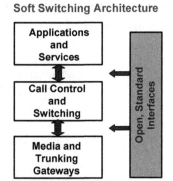

Fig. 7. Classical telecommunication switching and soft switching architecture

User data streams can then be modified and operated "on the fly" (Fig. 8). Another approach are Web services (Ferris and Farrell 2003) whereby clearly defined services are located in the Web and accessible through standardized interfaces (Service Oriented Architecture SOA (Perrey and Lycett 2003).

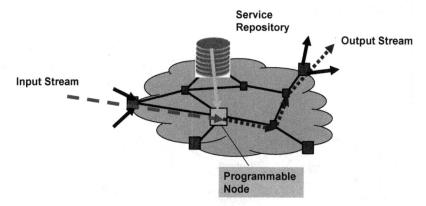

Fig. 8. Programmable networks

Generally, it is not clear today, which role the classical network carriers will play in the future: Do they participate in the value chain or do they serve only as bit pipe operators? Unclear is also, how to ensure information and communication security in a time, where the society is more than ever dependent on an intact network infrastructure. Threats are everywhere: From the terminals over the transmission lines and soft switches to the data bases and information servers (FK 2005). The "open" networks show many open flanks for unwanted intruders who threaten data integrity and personal and business information. Today a rich spectrum of security mechanisms is available. But on the one hand these are not always used and on the other hand the threats are growing permanently or are changing themselves. Conclusion: the competition between the aggressors and the defenders of the information and communication security will never stop!

2.7 Ubiquitous Mobility

After the great success story of the mobile telephony with today over 1.5 billion users world-wide the data applications are gaining momentum. Mobile communication evolves towards the "Mobile Internet" (Fig. 9). Packet switching is being introduced also in the cellular radio networks, beginning with the General Packet Radio Service GPRS in GSM and in the next phase with the packet services in third generation networks (UMTS, 3G).

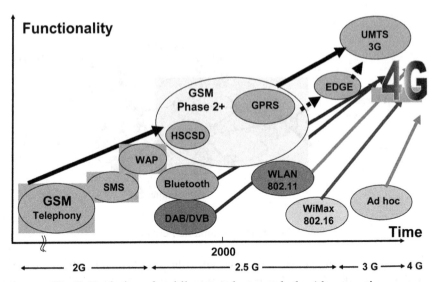

Fig. 9. Evolution of mobile networks towards the 4th generation
(Mobile internet)

An important role will play the IP Multimedia subsystem IMS which brings the IP technology to 3G. It supports QoS IP-based real time and multimedia communication and their control (Poikselka et al. 2005). However: the convergence towards a homogenous "universal" mobile network is farer than ever. In contrast, the number of system technologies is currently increasing. Depending on the degree of mobility and the required bit rate, depending on the application scenario, depending on the cost requirements, different wireless systems will be used (Fig. 10): Bluetooth and similar systems for short range communication (< 10 meters), DECT and WLAN for inhouse use and in hot spots and the cellular networks for global coverage and high mobility. Clearly, we see a strong competition in each field when the mobile networks are evolving "beyond 3G" towards the 4th generation (4G, (WWRF 2006)).

The newest wireless technology coming on the market is WiMAX (Worldwide Interoperability for Microwave Access) according to IEEE 802.16 with a reach of over 10 km, so it may be an interesting approach for covering the last mile, especially in rural areas, where it may be an alternative for DSL (wireless DSL). In future, WiMAX which builds on the newest communication technologies, may even threaten 3G.

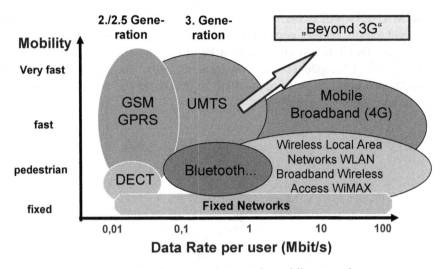

Fig. 10. Mobility versus data rate in mobile networks

From the users' perspective, the location based and personal services may be of some attractiveness. Important issues are here methods to deliver the positioning and location information across all the different network technologies (Zündt et al. 2006) and to enhance the location services by using the context the user is currently in. For the realization of such and other innovative functions in the networks a set of software-based auxiliary functions are needed (middleware).

2.8 Self Organization: Ad Hoc and Peer to Peer

Since several years, one trend in communication systems is to introduce more self organization thus going away from classical centralized network and service control.

In the mobile world, the technology of Mobile Ad Hoc networks (MANET) has gained much attention. These infrastructureless, self organizing networks are working in unlicensed frequency bands and use operational principles completely different from conventional networks (Toh 2002). Particularly in the multi-hop form the Ad Hoc networks can be used both for intercommunication in small mobile communities as well as for the coverage extension of cellular networks (Fig. 11). Routing, reliability and security of such networks are still the subject of worldwide research. Taking into account the high interest in Ubiquitous Computing (as predicted by Marc Weiser in 1993 (Weiser 1993)) and in wireless communication between devices of any kind (machine-to-machine communication) the MANETs will experience a big upswing in the next years. Examples are vehicle-to-vehicle communication and the promising fields of sensor networks (Karl and Willig 2005), a key to "Ambient Intelligence" (Tafazolli 2005; Eberspächer and von Reden 2006). The wireless mesh networks also build on self organization to overcome the intricate procedures of today's network deployment.

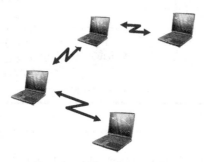

Fig. 11. Ad hoc networking

Another self organizing technology is Peer-to-Peer networking (P2P). P2P means the direct communication between the millions of autonomous computers ("peers") in the Internet without making use of centralized services except the pure bit transport across the IP infrastructure (Steinmetz and Wehrle 2005). In a P2P network, the end systems act, at the same time, as clients and as servers, hence are called servents.

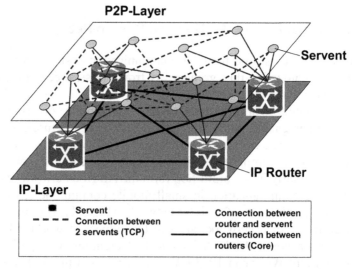

Fig. 12. Peer-to-peer networking

The new P2P paradigm has stimulated a number of new services and applications. File sharing is the most prominent of them. Fig. 12 shows the basic architecture of such a computer network consisting of a IP-based transport layer and the P2P virtual overlay network. Today the portion of the P2P traffic in the Internet amounts to over 50%, primarily caused by music and video file sharing. But P2P has far more potential. With P2P we can configure flexibly overlay networks, which allow efficient searching of any kind, the formation of grid computer clusters and many kinds of conventional communication services, but not centrally controlled. Last but not least, it can also be combined with Ad Hoc networking. Clearly, P2P is beginning to revolutionize the net world!

2.9 User Orientation

From the view of the users, most important is the improvement of the user friendliness of the systems. The Web browser was a good start. Beyond that numerous techniques for "human machine interaction" were developed and investigated e.g. speech recognition, handwriting recognition, gesture recognition, finger print sensors, intelligent software agents, smart cards, or eyeglasses with displays. The rising complexity of the systems and their functional enrichment makes it indispensable to involve the end user into the definition and design of functions, devices and systems. This is not trivial however, since new developments will often be technology-driven, so that the customer hears usually relatively late from the upcoming innovations. The early involvement of the user is even more difficult since the users often cannot imagine the real potential of new services and functions. Fast providing of prototypes is therefore a key to today's product development.

3 Summary and Outlook

The evolution of telecommunications is rapidly advancing. New technologies foster new applications and vice versa. The up to now diverse networks are converging towards an all-IP network. On the other hand, the variety of access technologies is even more increasing, and will bring us quicker than expected to the final goal: A world where communication is possible everywhere, every time and with everybody, and to affordable costs.

References

Campbell, AT et al. (1999) A survey of programmable networks. Comput. Commun. Rev. 29 (No 2). pp. 7–23

Davie B, Rekhter Y (2000) MPLS. San Francisco: Morgan Kaufman Publishers

Eberspächer J, v. Reden W (2006): Umhegt oder abhängig? Der Mensch in einer digitalen Umgebung. Berlin: Springer

Eberspächer J, Picot A. (2005) Voice over IP. Bonn: Hüthig

Eberspächer J, Glasmann J (2005): QoS-Architekturen und Resource Management im Intranet. (Real-Time Enterprise in der Praxis). Berlin, Springer, pp 187-213

Eberts, J. et al. (2005) Paving the Way for Gigabit Networking. IEEE Communications Magazine. 43 (4): 27 – 30

Eth (2006) http://www.metroethernetforum.org/

Ferris C, Farrell J. (2003): What are Web Services? Communications of the ACM 46 (No 6), p. 31

FK (2005) Feldafinger Kreis: http://www.feldafinger-kreis.de

Foster I, Kesselman C (1998) The Grid: blueprint for a new computing infrastructure. San Francisco: Morgan Kaufmann Publishers

Holma H, Toskala A (2006) HSDPA/HSUPA for UMTS High Speed Radio Access for Mobile Communications. Chichester, Wiley

IEEE (2006) http://grouper.ieee.org/groups/802/11/

Jourdan A et al. (2001) The Perspective of Optical Packet, Switching in IP-Dominant Backbone and Metropolitan Networks. IEEE Communications Magazine. March 2001. pp. 136-141

Karl H, Willig A (2005): Protocols and Architectures for Wireless Sensor Networks. Chichester: Wiley

Meddeb A (2005) Why Ethernet WAN Transport? IEEE Communications Magazine Nov. 2005, S. 136-141

NGN (2005) http://www.comsoc.org/ci1/Public/2005/oct/current.html

NGN (2006) http://de.wikipedia.org/wiki/Next_Generation_Network

Perrey R, Lycett, M (2003) Service-Oriented Architecture. Applications and the Internet Workshops, 2003. Proceedings. 2003 Symposium on. Pp. 116 – 119

Poikselka M, Mayer G, Khartabil H (2005) The IMS. Chichester, Wiley

Schmid-Egger A, Kirstädter A, Eberspächer J (2006) Ethernet in the backbone: An approach to cost-efficient core networks In: Kern E-M, Hegering H-G, Brügge B (eds) Managing Development and Application of Digital Technologies, Berlin, Springer, pp 195-210

Steinmetz R, Wehrle K (2005) Peer-to-Peer Systems and Applications. Berlin: Springer

Tafazolli R (2005) Technologies for the Wireless Future. Chichester: Wiley

Toh CK (2002) Ad Hoc Mobile Wireless Networks. Upper Saddle River: Prentice Hall

Tomic S et al. (2004) ASON and GMPLS—Overview and Comparison. Photonic Network Communications 7 No.2: p. 111 – 130

Weiser M (1993) Some Computer Science Issues in Ubiquitous Computing.
    Comm. ACM 36 (No. 7). pp. 75-84
WWRF (2006) http://www.wireless-world-research.org
Zündt M et al. (2006) LACBA – A Location-Aware Community-Based Architec-
    ture for Realizing Seamless Adaptive Location-Based Services. To appear in:
    Proc. 12th European Wireless Conference. Athens 2006

Ethernet in the Backbone: An Approach to Cost-efficient Core Networks

Arno Schmid-Egger, Andreas Kirstädter, Jörg Eberspächer

1 Introduction

Backbone networks represent the top of the network hierarchy of carrier networks. They connect networks of different cities, regions, countries or continents, and usually comprise SONET/SDH or Packet-over-SONET (PoS) technology. The complexity of these technologies imposes substantial financial burdens on network operators, both in the area of Capital Expenditures (CAPEX) and Operational Expenditures (OPEX).

The Ethernet protocol is a possible enabler of more cost-efficient backbone networks, as it is characterized by simplicity, flexibility, interoperability and low costs. While Ethernet is traditionally a Local Area Network (LAN) technology, continuous developments already enabled its deployment in Metropolitan Area Networks (MANs). Recent research and standardization efforts aim at speeding up Ethernet to 100Gbps, resolving scalability issues and supplying Ethernet with carrier-grade features. For this reason, Ethernet might in the near future become an attractive choice and serious competitor in the market of backbone networks.

The first part of this paper elaborates on requirements and possible architectures of carrier-grade Ethernet-based core networks. Current and future standards in the areas of Quality-of-Service, resilience, network management, and scalability that introduce carrier-grade features into Ethernet will be outlined. Different network architectures and related introduction strategies will also be explained briefly.

The second part of this paper examines the economical performance of Ethernet networks in comparison to SONET/SDH-based network architectures. Both CAPEX and OPEX are considered in hands-on business cases, and the results indicate that Ethernet backbone networks have a high cost advantage in both cost categories.

2 Outline of Carrier-Grade 100G-Ethernet Backbone Networks

Fig. 1 shows two possible protocol stacks of future 100G-Ethernet backbone networks: Protocol stack (1) depicts core network transport via native Ethernet that uses MAC-in-MAC encapsulation [1]. Alternatively, (2) represents a MPLS-based backbone network that uses Ethernet for layer-2 transmission between the MPLS nodes [2]. Both architectures require a control plane to provide for network-wide functionality of signaling, traffic engineering, quality-of-service and protection, established e.g. via Generalized-MPLS (GMPLS) [3].

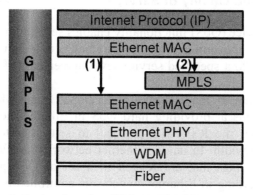

Fig. 1. Protocol stacks of Ethernet backbone networks

The mapping of protocol functionality to the requirements of core networks is shown in Fig. 2 for both native Ethernet (1) and MPLS Ethernet (2) backbone network architectures. Functionality that is provided or controlled by GMPLS is also included in the illustration.

	provide high bandwidth	QoS Features	Resilience Mechanisms	OAM Features
IP		DiffServ	Rerouting	Ping etc.
1) native Ethernet		BW reservation (GMPLS) + Eth priorities	VLAN prot sw or RSVP-TE fast reroute	IEEE 802.1ag Connectivity Fault Mngt
2) MPLS Ethernet		BW reservation (GMPLS) + LSP priorities	LSP prot. sw or RSVP-TE fast reroute	Fault detection of nodes and paths
Ethernet PHY	100Gbps			
WDM	DWDM		standby channels	
Fiber	bundles		redundant fiber deployment	

Fig. 2. Protocol layer functionality in Ethernet core networks

In the following, the main enablers of carrier-grade Ethernet backbone networks are shortly introduced.

2.1 End-to-End Quality of Service

Quality of Service (QoS) functionality enables service providers to guarantee and enforce transmission quality parameters (e.g. bandwidth, jitter, delay) according to a specified service-level agreement (SLA) with the customer.

A QoS framework that is currently developed by the Metro Ethernet Forum (MEF) aims at providing hard QoS in Ethernet networks [4]. This framework uses the RSVP-TE protocol to setup end-to-end paths with dedicated bandwidth. In native Ethernet networks, traffic is labeled with Service-VLAN tags that are related to a set of QoS parameters. QoS-conform forwarding in Ethernet switches is controlled by GMPLS [5]. In MPLS Ethernet networks, MPLS packets are labeled with MPLS tags and forwarded along the specific Label Switched Paths. A connection acceptance control (CAC), which is also operated by GMPLS, guarantees that the required bandwidth is available along the requested path.

The MEF's definition of generic service-level parameters enables a high flexibility in SLA definitions: The Committed Information Rate (CIR) determines the minimum amount of bandwidth available to the customer, while the Excess Information Rate (EIR) provides additional bandwidth during low network load periods. Maximum burst sizes corresponding to the CIR and EIR are defined accordingly.

For more details on enabling hard QoS in Ethernet networks, see [4], [6], and [7].

2.2 Resilience Mechanisms

The proposed new restoration mechanism of Ethernet, the Rapid Spanning Tree Protocol [8], scales badly with increasing network dimensions, as its convergence time depends on the number of network nodes. For this reason, GMPLS will be used to manage protection of links and paths in carrier-grade Ethernet networks.

For both native Ethernet and MPLS Ethernet networks, GMPLS can pre-provision backup paths and switch over in the case of failure. In native Ethernet networks, multiple spanning trees are set up to accommodate different traffic flows. Every spanning tree corresponds to a certain service-VLAN tag. In the failure case, the connection is switched over to a different S-VLAN that uses a redundant path but connects the same set of nodes. In MPLS Ethernet networks, the GMPLS control plane redirects traffic of affected LSPs to backup LSPs.

Additionally, Link Aggregation Groups [8] may be set up in both scenarios to provide protection for individual links.

Restoration mechanisms like RSVP-TE Fast Reroute might also be used if the protection requirements are less severe. For example, the GMPLS control plane might pre-establish backup paths for premium traffic but envision slower restoration mechanisms for best-effort traffic.

Additional, generic resilience concepts have been developed by the MEF in their protection framework [9] in order to enable interoperability between future Ethernet devices of different vendors.

2.3 Operations Administration & Maintenance

Enhanced OAM functionality is another cornerstone of carrier networks, providing failure detection, localization and performance monitoring.

The IEEE 802.1ag standard extension, named Connectivity Fault Management, defines essential fault management functionality like loopback continuity check and traceroute. Together, this set of functions will finally introduce path discovery and verification as well as fault detection and isolation into Ethernet. Furthermore, an OAM framework set up by the MEF focuses on providing SLA measurements (connectivity, latency, loss, jitter) for Ethernet networks [10].

2.4 Core Network Scalability

With its origin in the LAN, Ethernet meets several scalability issues on its progress into Wide Area Networks.

Address space limitations will be resolved with the upcoming IEEE Provider Backbone Bridge standard [11], which enables the provider to encapsulate customer Ethernet frames into a second Ethernet header ("MAC-in-MAC"). Besides an immense reduction of the size of forwarding tables in provider equipment, Ethernet services can be provided across the networks of different carriers.

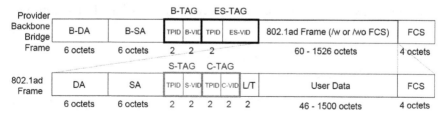

Fig. 3. Provider backbone bridge frame format [11]

In MPLS Ethernet networks, address space is not critical, since MPLS labels are used for switching. These labels have a length of 20bit and enable up to a million of LSPs per link, as they are only locally significant.

The spanning tree protocol (STP) presents another bottleneck of Ethernet, as it enables only tree topologies whereas backbone networks typically have meshed or ring topologies. A successor to the STP that enables new topologies and permits loops would be the most desirable solution. Alternatively, a set of VLANs could be established across the backbone network in a way that all links are covered by one or more VLANs. However, this latter solution comes along with increased management complexity.

Another area of work is the maximum Ethernet frame size of 1500 Byte, which generates processing overhead especially with increasing transmission speeds. The standardization of "Jumbo frames" that contain 9000 Byte or more of user data is another desirable feature of a new Ethernet standard [12].

As node distances are usually in the area of a few hundred kilometers or even more, the transmission distance of Ethernet signals is another topic that has to be considered carefully upon the deployment of Ethernet in backbone networks. Current 10G Ethernet hardware provides link ranges of 70-80km, but with the speeding up of Ethernet to 100Gbit/s, new challenges arise: Second degree (slope) chromatic dispersion has to be exactly compensated, birefringency effects become grave, and the signal-to-noise ratio of 100Gbit/s signals is generally lower as fewer photons are transmitted per optical impulse. Although several experiments and field trials of the past (e.g. that of Siemens, British Telecom, and the University of Eindhoven in the EU IST project FASHION with 160Gbit/s signals over 275km standard single-mode fiber [13]) showed that long-distance transmissions of high-speed signals are definitely feasible, the complexity and costs of the required optical equipment is currently still at a very high level. On the other hand, the effort spent on extending the signal reach of Ethernet signals is rewarded by equipment savings.

Fig. 4 illustrates the possible port count savings in an Ethernet core network where optical grooming can be applied up to the maximum transmission distance avoiding unnecessary electrical processing of transit traffic.

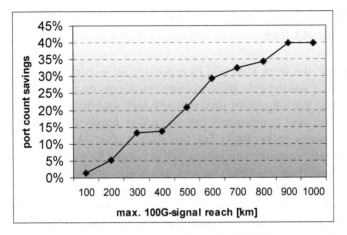

Fig. 4. Port count savings in grooming-enabled Ethernet networks

These results were derived for a native Ethernet network following the topology of a generic German backbone, which was also used during the CAPEX and OPEX analyses below [14].

Fig. 5. Reference network topology

The IEEE usually defines a broad set of physical Ethernet interfaces. Thus, besides a single 100G-Ethernet signal, a multiplexing of lower bit-rate optical signals into a 100G signal is also conceivable (e.g. 10x10G or 4x25G). Although the maximum transmission range of these multiplexed signals would certainly be longer than that of a pure 100G-signal the multiplexing requires additional costly WDM equipment and the signal would occupy several wavelength channels on the fiber.

3 CAPEX Comparison of Different Backbone Network Architectures

In general, the term CAPEX incorporates all expenditures related to the purchase of equipment, infrastructure, buildings or furniture. As we want to compare the impact of different network architectures on CAPEX, we will neglect cost components that are not or barely affected by the choice of the network technology. For this reason, the CAPEX calculation only considers the costs for equipment that is related to the network architecture choice, including switches, routers, line cards and optical modules, while the costs of WDM-equipment and fiber are not included.

In order to calculate the total CAPEX of a specific network architecture, future traffic loads, network device counts and network device prices have to be estimated. The German reference network above was used for the physical topology of the considered backbone and corresponding traffic matrices were extrapolated to determine future link loads. According to predictions by TeleGeography [15], the traffic is assumed to grow ho-mogenously at a rate of 40% per annum. A shortest-path routing algorithm is applied to determine the single link loads.

From the link loads, the number of switches, routers and line card ports can be obtained for any different network architecture. In the SONET/SDH business cases, this device count includes equipment needed for upgrading the existing network in order to accommodate additional traffic (incre-mental CAPEX scenario). In the Ethernet business cases, the migration from SONET/SDH had to be respected with the consequence that the ma-jority of components have to be acquired at the point of migration and only a few IP routers can be reused (green field / migration CAPEX scenario).

Future equipment prices are extrapolated following a careful analysis of market data, past price developments, and price relations between Ethernet and SONET/SDH. The prices of switches and routers in basic configura-tion (chassis, power supply, backplane, route processor, and switching fab-ric) are assumed to remain constant. For line cards that make up the largest cost component, a price extrapolation is indispensable, as they experience immense price reductions over time.

Fig. 6 shows the past development of the prices for 10G Ethernet and Gi-gabit Ethernet bandwidth in the form of average prices for 10G port capac-ity (1 x 10GE port or 10 x GbE ports). Evaluated were press releases and official price lists ([16] – [24]) for high-end modular switches with long-reach (10km) optical modules of the following companies: Cisco, Entera-sys, Extreme Networks, Force10, Foundry Networks, and Riverstone Net-works.

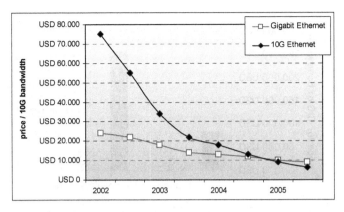

Fig. 6. Past price development for Ethernet bandwidth (10G port capacity)

As a next step, the price development dynamics of 10GE and GbE were used to estimate future prices for GbE, 10GE, and finally 100GE after its market entry (Fig. 7). The market entry of 100GE is expected for the year 2009, as a standardization typically needs 3 years and is expected to start in this year (2006).

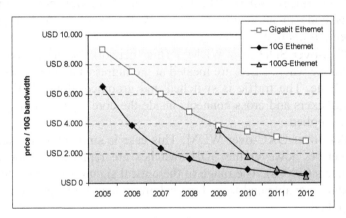

Fig. 7. Future price development of Ethernet bandwidth

For SDH and POS line cards, price extrapolations proved to be more difficult than for Ethernet as less market data is publicly available. Therefore, the methodology used to predict future SDH and POS port prices was to consider the current price ratios compared to Ethernet bandwidth and assume that this price ratio remains constant. The prices of POS, SDH, and Ethernet interfaces for routers and switches are illustrated in Fig. 8 for different optics [21].

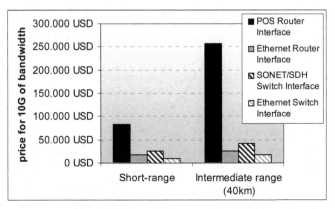

Fig. 8. Price comparison of router and switch interfaces

The following generic network architectures were considered in the subsequent business cases:

- IP/POS-over-WDM: The backbone consists of Label Edge Routers (LERs) and Label Switch Routers (LSRs), which are all equipped with POS interfaces. SONET/SDH is only used for transporting the IP packets node to node, directly over WDM or fiber. A 1+1 protection scheme is applied.

- IP/POS-over-SDH-over-WDM: This network scenario considers a backbone where LERs are located at the ingress and egress points of the backbone. The traffic is switched and groomed along SDH add-drop-multiplexers and cross-connects inside the core. A 1+1 protection scheme is applied.

- IP/POS-over-OXC-over-WDM: This case is similar to the previous architecture, however the SDH switches are replaced by optical cross-connects (OXCs). The range of the optical signal is assumed to be large enough to enable end-to-end optical grooming. A 1+1 protection scheme is applied.

- IP/MPLS-over-Ethernet-over-WDM: The backbone consists of LERs at the edge and MPLS-enabled Ethernet switches in the core of the backbone. This architecture corresponds to a MPLS Ethernet architecture as outlined in section 2 (Fig. 1). A 1:1 protection scheme is applied, i.e. all capacity is overprovisioned by 100%.

- Ethernet-over-WDM: The core and outer core are a native Ethernet network with Ethernet switches both at edge and core. A few LERs are deployed to handle a small share of traffic that requires IP routing (share assumed to be 30%), however Ethernet traffic does not have to traverse

LERs at the ingress and egress points of the backbone. 1:1 protection is applied.

- Ethernet-over-WDM with service-level protection: The network architecture is identical to the one before except that only premium traffic is protected against failure (share of premium traffic set to 30%).

Fig. 9 illustrates the accumulated CAPEX results for the years 2009 to 2012. The CAPEX is split up into components belonging to the IP layer (LERs, LSRs and interfaces) and components belonging to the transport layer (e.g. Ethernet switches and interfaces).

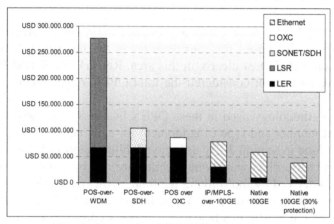

Fig. 9. Accumulated CAPEX comparison

The cost component of LERs is high for all SDH-related infrastructures due to the high prices of POS interfaces. On the transport layer, a pure POS-over-WDM network causes the most costs as only expensive router interfaces are used. POS-over-SDH architectures prove to be much cheaper as the SDH network employs SDH switches and interfaces instead of expensive LSR equipment for core switching. A POS-over-OXC network has an even better CAPEX performance due to lower switch and optical transceiver prices of OXC hardware.

Without exception the Ethernet business cases perform all better than SDH architectures. The MPLS Ethernet business case is the most expensive among the possible Ethernet architectures, as a considerable amount of CAPEX is related to LERs and corresponding interfaces. A native 100G-Ethernet network enables higher savings in the LER category. With native 100G-Ethernet networks that employ a service-level differentiated protection scheme, the CAPEX can be reduced even further.

If we consider the CAPEX performance of the different business cases over time, the Ethernet business cases show high initial CAPEX of 100GE networks (new technology) in comparison to SDH network architectures (incremental approach). However, from the year 2009 on the incremental CAPEX of Ethernet networks decrease to a level well below SDH network CAPEX and on an extended timeframe the CAPEX advantage of Ethernet would even increase.

4 OPEX Comparison of Different Backbone Network Architectures

While OPEX of network operators include many more categories, the repair process is chosen for consideration as the impact of 100G-Ethernet can be predicted most clearly in this area. Remark: As WDM failures and fiber breaks are not considered the total OPEX repair process values are very low.

The methodology used in these OPEX business cases was to determine the total number and type of equipment for each network architecture and year as done in section 3. By using availability figures [25] the average repair time for a given backbone architecture can be estimated. The related costs are derived by multiplying the total repair time with the average salary of a field or point-of-presence technician. The general scenario and assumptions are mostly identical to the CAPEX consideration. Fig. 10 shows the results of the repair process OPEX, accumulated over the years 2009 to 2012.

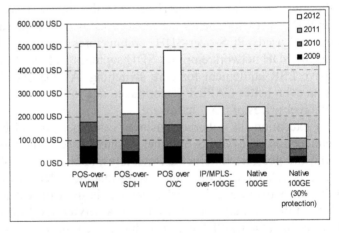

Fig. 10. OPEX repair process comparison

Again, Ethernet networks are more economical than SDH architectures, which is mostly due to the reduced device count enabled by 100G-Ethernet: Compared to the 40Gbit/s POS/SDH interfaces, Ethernet networks require less switches and line cards due to the higher port bandwidth of 100Gbit/s. The possibility of applying a service-level protection scheme can further reduce overprovisioning and the related OPEX.

While the OPEX of the repair process is very low for Ethernet, further OPEX savings may be enabled via the provisioning of Ethernet services in comparison to legacy services like e.g. leased line or Frame Relay. A study conducted by the MEF indicates total OPEX savings of around 20% in affected areas [26]. Thus, the OPEX advantage of Ethernet is not only limited to a small share of OPEX but Ethernet architectures enable considerable savings in a wide range of OPEX areas.

5 Conclusion

Ethernet evolved from LAN into Metro areas covering speeds from 10 Mbps up to 10 Gbps and the next generation Ethernet speed of 100Gbps will be the enabler of Ethernet-based pure packet core networks. Carrier-gradeness of Ethernet-based packet architectures is the major point. A careful analysis of the required protocol features like network resilience, QoS, and OAM shows many redundancies within the layers of today's network architectures that have to be resolved shaping a new end-to-end Ethernet layer with the required scalability.

A CAPEX and OPEX analysis demonstrates a considerable cost advantage of 100G-Ethernet in comparison to SDH-based solutions. The superior CAPEX performance results from a huge cost advantage of Ethernet devices and their fast price decline. The reduced switch and line card count in 100G-Ethernet networks and the efficient economics of Ethernet services are responsible for a superior OPEX performance.

Therefore, it can be said that Ethernet has a promising future in core networks, not just as link technology supporting an upper routing layer, but as a complete, cost-effective, and service-oriented infrastructure layer in the area of core networks. The industry-wide efforts to cover remaining challenges also confirm this outlook.

Acknowledgement

The authors thank all people contributing to this study for their friendly support, especially Monica Jäger from T-Systems and Andreas Iselt, Sandrine Pasqualini, and Harald Rohde from Siemens Corporate Technology.

References

[1]   IEEE, Provider Backbone Bridges, [Online]. Available: http://www.ieee802. org/1/pages/802.1ah.html

[2]   IETF, MPLS Label Stack Encoding, (RFC 3032) [Online]. Available: http:// www.ietf.org/rfc/rfc3032.txt

[3]   IEC, Generalized Multiprotocol Label Switching (GMPLS) [Online]. Available: http://www.iec.org/online/tutorials/gmpls/

[4]   Khandekar S Developing A QoS Framework For Metro Ethernet Networks To Effectively Support Carrier-Class SLAs, [Online]. Available: http://www. metroethernetforum.org/Presentations/IIR_DevelopingQoSFramework.pdf

[5]   Papadimitriou D, Choi, J, A Framework for Generalized MPLS (GMPLS) Ethernet, IETF Internet Draft [Online]. Available: http://www.ietf.org/inter-net-drafts/draft-papadimitriou-ccamp-gmpls-ethernet-framework-00.txt

[6]   Atrica Corp., Delivering Hard QoS in Carrier Ethernet Networks, [Online]. Available:http://www.atrica.com/body/products/whitepapers/Delivering_ Hard_QoS_in_Carrier_Ethernet_Networks_v12.pdf

[7]   MEF, Bandwidth Profiles for Ethernet Services [Online]. Available: http: //www.metroethernetforum.org/PDFs/WhitePapers/Bandwidth-Profiles-for-Ethernet-Services.pdf

[8]   IEEE, Media Access Control (MAC) Bridges, [Online]. Available: http:// standards.ieee.org/getieee802/download/802.1D-2004.pdf

[9]   MEF, Requirements and Framework for Ethernet Service Protection in Metro Ethernet Networks, [Online]. Available: http://www.metroether-netforum.org/PDFs/Standards/MEF2.pdf

[10] Squire M, Metro Ethernet Forum OAM, [Online]. Available: http://www. metroethernetforum.org/presentations/MEF%20OAM%202003-12-01.pdf

[11] Suzuki M, Bottorff P, Chen M, Addressing Issues of Provider Backbone Bridges, [Online]. Available: http://www.ieee802.org/1/files/public/docs 2004/ah-suzuki-addressing-issues-1104-01.pdf

[12] Small Tree Communications, The Importance of Jumbo Frames in Gigabit and 10-Gigabit Networks, [Online]. Available: http://www.small-tree.com/ jumbo_white_paper.pdf

[13] Lehmann G et al., An 160Gbit/s Network Field Trial Report, [Online]. Available: https://medicongress.be/UploadBroad/Session%2002/ Presenta-tion%2002- 04.pdf

[14] Schupke DA, Jäger M, Hülsermann R (2003) Comparison of Resilience Mechanisms for Dynamic Services in Intelligent Optical Networks, Fourth International Workshop on the Design of Reliable Communication Networks (DRCN), Banff, Alberta, Canada

[15] TeleGeography, Global Internet Geography, [Online]. Available: http://www.telegeography.com/products/gig/

[16] NetworkWorld, 10G or not 10G?, [Online]. Available: http://www.network-world. com/news/2002/120210gig.html

[17] LightReading, Force10 Slashes 10-GigE Pricing, [Online]. Available: http://www.lightreading.com/document.asp?site=lightreading&doc_id=27068

[18] Foundry Networks, Press release, [Online]. Available: http://www.foundry-net. com/about/newsevents/releases/pr1_28_03.html

[19] Zach Fierstadt, 10G Matures, [Online]. Available: http://www.arnnet.com.au/index.php/id;2086580617;fp;256;fpid;319049444

[20] Foundry Networks, Press release, [Online]. Available: http://www.hbi.de/clients/Foundry_Networks/pms04/09_02/Modules090204.php

[21] Cisco, Global Pricelist (February 2005), [Online]. Available: http://shop.muk.com.ua/cisco_price/index.html

[22] Foundry Networks, Press release, [Online]. Available: http://www.hbi.de/clients/Foundry_Networks/pms05/18_05/Portpreise_Draft2.php

[23] NetworkWorld, Force10 aims high with 10G switch, [Online]. Available: http://www.networkworld.com/news/2002/0830force10.html

[24] NetworkWorld, Bronx hospital leaps to 10G [Online]. Available: http://www.extremenetworks.com/aboutus/pressroom/news/NetWorld_Bronx10Gig.pdf

[25] NOBEL Project, Availability Model and OPEX related parameters, to be published

[26] MEF, Service Provider Study: Operating Expenditures [Online]. Available for MEF members: http://www.metroethernetforum.org

V Mobile Services

A Generic User Innovation Toolkit Architecture for Mobile Service Creation

Bernhard Kirchmair

1 Introduction

With the deregulation of the telecommunication industry in the 1990s, with ever more companies providing digital services[1] in the domain of mobile services, with key technologies maturing (and, thus, getting easier to access and utilize), and with users getting more sensitive towards new technologies and services, the respective market environment has become highly competitive (Magnusson et al. 2003). While there were only little incentives for companies to develop novel end user telecommunication services as industry still consisted of monopolies and faced regulation, innovation as an important key to sustainable competitiveness is again in focus. Innovation facilitates differentiation and differentiation is considered to lead to competitive advantage (Porter 1998). However, in order to reveal the full potential of new capabilities derived from technical possibilities in the domain of mobile services, industry has to discover which services are wanted and needed by current and future users. Users may face needs for services that are currently not provided, but could be easily made possible by utilizing yet available technology in the right way. In this context, the imperative of innovation applies in particular. Considering today's market characteristics, the incentive to develop innovative value-adding services that meet user needs accurately is extraordinary high.

Toolkits for user innovation are a novel approach for commercializing on customer creativity and innovativeness (von Hippel 1999; von Hippel and Katz 2002). The main rationale is that a considerably large share of customers is eager to actively participate in new product development and innovation processes to get products that meet their needs perfectly (von Hippel 2005). As user needs are likely to be heterogeneous, chances are high that resulting products are quite innovative (Thomke and von Hippel 2002). So far, this approach has mainly been applied to the development of material products such as custom food, industrial chips, surgical instruments and mountain bikes (Lüthje 2000, 2003; Lüthje et al. 2003; Magnusson et al. 2003). The application of the toolkit for user innovation approach to the development of intangible products, particularly digital services, seems to be very promising. Digital services that are developed following the toolkit approach may fulfil user requirements more accurately (increasing customer satisfaction and minimizing risk), are expected to be more innovative (rising its potential for market success), and may be cheaper and faster to realize (shortening time-to-market) (Kirchmair 2005).

---

[1] Digital services are defined as services realized by software and are provided through electronic means (Kirchmair 2005).

This article proposes a *conceptual toolkit* architecture for mobile service creation that may serve as the basis for a future full-scale implementation. In the following, the domain of mobile services is introduced in more detail.

2 The Domain of Mobile Communication

A service domain is determined by a certain class of digital services and can be characterized by applying a system model approach[2] (Lupp and Gerstheimer 2001). A system model characterizing a service domain, and related digital services respectively, denotes two main aspects: *possibilities* and *requirements*. Former can be regarded as capturing technological elements of a domain in terms of what is technically feasible. Latter can be regarded as capturing economic elements in terms of user needs and usability. Requirements for a service's functionality, behavior, and capabilities are determined by users. The process of capturing user needs is mainly a social and analytical task. A realization of the services wanted has to occur through technological means, however.

The present technological possibility system of the domain of mobile services includes the following five dimensions[3]:

- The dimension of *communication* relates to communication parameters, i.e. what types of mobile communication are possible at all (e.g. unidirectional, bidirectional, synchronous, asynchronous, etc.) and at which speed and what time communication can be practiced.
- The *data* dimension relates to the types of data that can be transmitted (e.g. audio, video, images, etc.).
- The dimension of *location* which relates to technological possibilities for including a user's location into mobile communication processes.
- The dimension of *personalization* captures technological possibilities for adapting the process of mobile communication to preferences and needs of individual users.
- The *interaction* dimension relates to the interface between users and the mobile communication system, i.e. input and output interfaces. Each single dimension covers different aspects of domain-related technolo-

---

[2] A system model is an abstraction and simplification of the modeled entity and shows the relevant aspects for a clearly defined problem (Churchman et al. 1957).

[3] Dimension are adapted from (Lupp and Gerstheimer 2001).

gies. Linking these dimensions and bringing them into relation spans the domain's technological possibility space.

From a user's point of view, mobile services can be characterized by aspects of their usage, and service-related needs respectively. The requirement system consists of the six dimensions of *user, place, time, process, intention,* and *condition*.

These dimensions completely describe any domain-related user need. A need as an abstract concept always relates to a user who experiences this need. The first dimension describes this user. Moreover, a need is linked to a certain place and time, i.e. at which location and when the need comes up. The process dimension characterizes a service's functionality. The intention captures the goal a user wants to achieve with a service. Finally, the condition dimension specifies any restrictions on a service's usage or capabilities.

An arbitrary example for how a user need can be captured by these dimensions could be a wanderer (user) in the Tuscany (place) who wants to get notified about upcoming thunderstorms (process) immediately (time), to be able to start searching for a shelter in time (intention). But the notification shall only occur if the likelihood for a thunderstorm rises above a certain user-defined level (condition).

The integration of both systems, the technological-oriented possibility system and the user-oriented requirement system, results in a comprehensive characterization of the domain of mobile services. This system of mobile communication is visualized in Fig. 1.

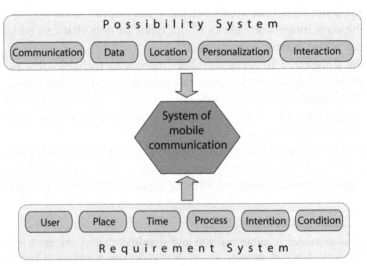

Fig. 1: The system of mobile communication

3 A Toolkit Architecture for Mobile Service Creation

In the following, a conceptual toolkit architecture for mobile service creation is introduced. First, an overview is given of the requirements the architecture is based on. Then the architecture is briefly described, before its components and utilized key technologies are examined in more detail.

3.1 Requirement Profile

The toolkit architecture was developed during a research project conducted at CDTM and UC Berkeley. The first step in developing the architecture was to find out about requirements for such a toolkit. A comprehensive requirement profile was compiled based on general characteristics of toolkits for user innovation.

A toolkit for user innovation should encompass five important elements (Hippel 1999): First, a toolkit should allow customers to run complete cycles of trial-and-error learning. Second, the resulting user design shall be producible by the provider. Third, a toolkit should provide libraries of commonly used design elements to let customers design custom solution rapidly. Fourth, it should offer users a concrete delimited solution space that encompasses the designs customers want to create. Finally, a toolkit should be intuitively usable by users.

Putting these five key characteristics into the context of digital service development and analyzing resulting implications led to a comprehensive requirement profile that consists of 42 requirements classified into several categories corresponding to the toolkit characteristics described[4]. These requirement categories include:

- The generation of a functionally complete and executable prototype that allows users to carry out trial-and-error learning efficiently,
- the automatic mapping of users' service designs to a production/ execution system and to a software engineering model to allow for both, an ad-hoc usage of newly created services and a refinement and onward development by in-house developers if needed,
- the provision of composable service units out of which new services can be built by users and the support for a composition mechanism that allows for the composition of service units with an appropriate degree of design freedom,

---

[4] The complete catalogue of requirements can be found in (Kirchmair 2005).

- an appropriate variety of service units that span a proper solution space to increase the likelihood for innovation,
- the adaptability to different target user groups such as novice users, advanced users, expert users, etc.,
- security, privacy, and data protection mechanisms.

Subsequently, the 42 requirements were analyzed through logical reasoning, and implications for an implementation explored. It turned out that a toolkit for digital service creation has to include at least three main elements in order to satisfy the requirement profile:

- An internal formally unique representation of users' service designs,
- the provision of service units, and
- the provision of a composition mechanism.

Service units and the overall service design have to be described in a formally unique way, syntactically and semantically. This is a prerequisite for many of the toolkit's crucial features such as the automatic mapping of a user design to a production/execution system or a software engineering model, and the check of the design for consistency.

Moreover, the definition and verification of functional and non-functional properties has to be supported. Such properties may include safety and liveness properties such as deadlock freedom or livelock freedom to prevent unsafe service states, application-specific properties to ensure the satisfaction of certain service constraints, and properties to ensure data consistency.

Furthermore, the level of abstraction of both, service units and composition mechanism, has to be adaptable to allow for vertical and horizontal adaptation of the toolkit. Vertical adaptation relates to the adaptation to a specific target user group by adjusting the complexity of the composition mechanism visible to toolkit users and the functional abstraction level of service units provided. Horizontal adaptation relates to the adaptation of a toolkit's solution space, e.g. by adding or removing service units.

The architecture proposed in the following is based on the compiled requirement profile and an extensive analysis thereof.

3.2 Overview of the Architecture

The architecture is based upon the interactions between several roles (Fig. 2). These roles include the *user interaction*, the *model generation*, the *model verification*, the *execution* role, and two *model translation* roles.

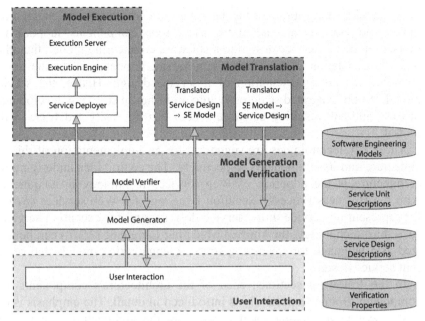

Fig. 2: A conceptual toolkit architecture for mobile service creation

The roles act upon a toolkit's software and data artefacts, namely service unit specifications, service design models, software engineering models, and a set of verification properties.

Any implementation of this architecture consists of components, and component groups respectively, that realize these roles. The interactions between the architecture's components and related actions upon respective artefacts are as follows:

A user creates his service by interacting with the *user interaction component*. The component is responsible for, first, presenting a set of service units, an external composition mechanism, and the service design in progress to the user, and, second, passing service creation related user actions on to the model generator. The *model generator component* then, captures a user's service design in a formal service description, i.e. a service model, utilizing the toolkit's internal composition logic. For this purpose, it interacts closely with the *verifier component* which verifies the service model against defined verification properties. If this check of the service design detects a violation, feedback is given to the model generator which, in turn, notifies the user interaction component. If the check completes successfully, the generated model is passed on to the *service deployer component* which arranges for the *execution engine* to execute the model. The execution engine, finally, executes the service model. Besides bringing the service model to execution, it can be translated to a software engineering model and vice versa. One of the *translation components* supports the translation of the service design to a software engineering model, the other one the translation of a software engineering model back to the corresponding toolkit representation of a service design. Hence, the service model can be integrated seamlessly into an in-house software development process and the resulting software model can be easily fed back to the toolkit.

Three key technologies are suggested for an implementation of this architecture and its components respectively: The central idea underlying the architecture is the adoption of Web services technology in conjunction with the Business Process Execution Language for Web services (*BPEL*) for representing service units, service designs, and for executing services. As a third technology, the Unified Modeling Language (*UML*) can be utilized as a language for specifying software engineering models that represent service designs.

In the following sections, each of the architecture's components and component groups respectively is introduced in detail. The emphasis is on, first, a component's functional role within the architecture, second, the adoption of respective key technologies for this component, and third, the reasoning behind the technologies' utilization with regards to the identified requirements.

3.3 Model Generation

The model generator component performs the following tasks within the architecture:

- First, it manages the actual service design model, i.e. the formal description of a service design. The information necessary to construct this service design model originates from either the user interaction component or the model translator. Whereas in the former case a service description is successively constructed according to the user actions passed on by the user interaction component, in the latter case a yet complete service design description is handed over from the translator component.
- Second, as it is the user interaction component that realizes a toolkit's composition mechanism as it is visible to users, the model generator component has to provide means that allow for the mapping of a user's composition actions made via this external composition mechanism to the toolkit's internal composition logic. Hence, the model generator component offers a programming interface to the user interaction com-

ponent that provides functionality for the construction of a respective service design model. Any service creation related user action is immediately mapped to a toolkit's internal composition logic for building a service design description.

- Third, the model generator interacts with the model verifier component for checking these compositions for validity and for verifying the actual service design model against defined properties. Issues related to this verification processes are described later in this article.
- Finally, the model generator passes the service model that has been model checked and found consistent, complete, and safe, on to the service execution component or service translation component for further processing.

3.3.1 Realizing the Concept of Service Units by Utilizing Web Services

Web services technology seems to be perfectly suitable for realizing the concept of service units, i.e. for implementing and providing their respective functionality. There is substantial similarity between the concept of service units and the concept of Web services:

- Web services are self-contained entities which encapsulate discrete functionality. The same holds true for the concept of service units.
- Web services are reusable entities. Service units shall be reusable as well.
- Web services provide a clearly specified interface (described in a WSDL document) that defines the service's access protocol (SOAP), the access point (an URI), and the public operations including typed arguments and return values. It can be shown that the interface of a service unit needs to provide similar information.

Since Web services are composable, service units realized as Web services are composable as well. By means of proper composition logic, new services with novel functionality can be created. Such composite services, and composite service units respectively, can be described by any language capable of capturing the composition of Web services. Particularly those languages qualify as potential candidates that are workflow-oriented and have high expressiveness. Former, because Web service interaction involves the coordination of control and data flow between services, latter, because of findings in the requirement analysis which suggest that high expressiveness is preferred over low expressiveness. The utilization of BPEL as a description language is proposed in the following section.

Another benefit from utilizing Web services technology is that a toolkit's solution space can be easily enlarged by making external third party Web services available as service units to toolkit users (horizontal adaptation).

3.3.2 Realizing Service Unit Composition by Utilizing BPEL

For a functionally complete description of a service design, a proper service description language has to capture a service's data and control flow completely. BPEL fulfils these requirements.

Data flow is captured due to BPEL's capabilities of declaration of variables and manipulation of XML data structures using XPath expressions.

Control flow is captured by structured activities BPEL provides. In addition, BPEL features several structures and concepts that are highly suitable for the description of complex services. Examples of such concepts are the built-in parallelism or the support for both synchronous as well as asynchronous interaction with Web services.

BPEL defines a full XML-based programming language, a type system, an exception handling model, a message handling model, a threading model, a compensation model, and a process life-cycle model. In fact, BPEL is *turing-complete* and, thus, allows for the description of services of arbitrary complexity. As BPEL is platform-independent, a service design described with BPEL is not coupled to a certain programming, nor execution platform.

Besides the requirement for a functionally complete description of a service design, each service unit has to be described by a proper description method as well. Such a description method has to be capable of covering both a service unit's interface and its behavior, i.e. syntactical and semantical aspects. Moreover, the composition of service units has to occur in a valid way.

Since service units shall be realized as Web services, two properties are relevant in this context: *Syntactical compatibility* as the basic requirement for any Web service composition and, in addition, *semantical compatibility*. In conjunction, both properties serve as a sufficient criterion for checking the validity of a composition.

Syntactical compatibility refers to the correspondence of certain types within the Web services to be composed, namely message and data types that constitute a service interface. The definition of these types is specified in a Web service's WSDL document. Hence, a check on syntactical compatibility of two service units to be composed can completely rely on the respective WSDL specifications (Curbera et al. 2002).

In the context of checking for semantical compatibility, the behavior of the services to be composed is of interest. It has to be ensured that the resulting composition lies within the pre-defined solution space. The behavior of a service is defined by its assigned BPEL process model.

Hence, the combination of WSDL and BPEL constitutes a comprehensive description method for service units that covers relevant syntactical and semantical aspects, namely their interface and behavior, sufficiently.

In order to be able to verify the compatibility (and, thus, the functional behavior) of two service units to be composed, a semantical uniqueness of the service description is required. The problem with BPEL is that the specification of BPEL does not formally specify the language's operational semantics. Whereas the BPEL syntax is formally founded through *XML Schema* which can be easily translated to the *Model Schema Language* (MSL) allowing for various automatic analysis techniques (Brown et al. 2001), its semantics are described textually through several examples only. Nevertheless, there exists consensus on the semantics of the language's most important structures and concepts.

However, there are several attempts to underpin BPEL with a sound mathematical model. The approaches follow one of two strategies: describing BPEL semantics by building on distributed Abstract State Machines (ASM) (Farahbod et al. 2004) or mapping BPEL to Petri-nets (Vidal et al. 2004; Stahl 2004). Unfortunately, none of these approaches is fully matured or completely validated yet. But even though a complete formal semantics is desirable, it is not necessarily required for verifying certain properties on BPEL process specifications. In fact, recently, several approaches emerged aiming at formalizing a subset of BPEL: Only those semantical aspects are considered and incorporated into a mathematical formalism that are relevant for certain verification purposes. The models can then serve as an input for different verification techniques.

3.4 Model Verification

All tasks related to model verification are done by the model verifier component. The support for verification is important at several points throughout the service creation process. First, semantical and syntactical compatibility of two service units to be composed has to be ensured. Second, before passing a service design on for further processing, the design has to be checked against defined service properties. For one, such defined service properties could be properties defined by the toolkit designer, and service provider respectively, to enforce certain aspects on a design (e.g, safety properties). In addition, properties could also be defined by an (advanced) toolkit user or a software engineer for the purpose of verifying a service design's functionality formally grounded.

As highlighted in the last section, the prerequisite for any verification is a mapping of the service description language, in this case BPEL, to a sound mathematical model providing a formal foundation of the language's semantics, or at least relevant parts of it. In literature, several approaches for the modeling and verification of workflow systems, and business processes respectively, have been proposed[5].

Three approaches can be identified that seem reasonable for an implementation of this architecture. Those approaches are particularly tailored to the modeling and verification of processes defined in BPEL:

Foster et al. (2003) describe an approach which relies on finite state processes (Magee and Kramer 1999) and supports the verification of BPEL implementations against abstract functional specification models described in UML, specifically in the form of message sequence charts.

Koshinka and Breugel (2003, 2004) describe an approach for specifying BPEL processes by a process algebra named BPE-calculus[6]. The calculus' syntax and semantics are formally defined. The BPE-calculus is modeled by means of a structural operational semantics (Plotkin 1981), more precisely, a labelled transition system.

Fu and Bultan (2004) describe an approach which allows for the analysis of asynchronous interactions of a set of composite Web services through linear temporal logic model checking (Pnueli 1977). This focus on interaction verification makes the approach highly interesting for an adoption in a toolkit implementation. As the execution of a service design involves the interaction of several composite service units with each other, the support for checking properties on these interactions is beneficial. In a nutshell, the verification process works as follows: Out of a set of interacting Web services specified as BPEL processes with WSDL interface descriptions, an intermediate representation (guarded finite state automata) is generated which then is translated to a verification language (Promela; Holzmann 1993). This language serves as input for a model checker (SPIN; Holzmann 2003).

Whereas the first two approaches focus on checking certain properties on a single BPEL process, the last approach focuses on analyzing control and data flow among several BPEL processes.

The mapping of BPEL to finite state processes allows for the verification of properties such as safety and liveness properties. The mapping to

---

[5] A comprehensive overview can be found in (Hull and Su 2004).

[6] Process algebras are an algebraic approach to formally describe concurrent processes.

BPE-calculus allows for the check for deadlock freedom and the check of temporal properties in general. In the context of mobile services, an exemplary property might be: "At some point, after a service is called, an SMS or MMS is sent". The mapping to guarded finite state automata allows for the verification of properties on both Web service interactions and data manipulations. An example for a property related to data verification might be: "If a send-request to the SMS service contains a picture, the request will eventually be rejected by the SMS service". A property related to service interaction might be: "Every send-request to the SMS service will eventually be followed by either a fault message or a confirmation message to the service manager service".

Even though, in sum, these approaches with their respective distinctive capabilities provide a good starting point for the verification of BPEL service designs, none of the approaches can be considered as fully mature yet, but is work in progress. Besides the fact that each approach suffers from individual drawbacks, some more fundamental challenges in the verification of Web service interaction that have to be addressed in future research can be found in (Kirchmair 2005; Narayanan and Mellraith 2002).

3.5 Model Execution

One of the decisive characteristics of BPEL is that the language is executable. This is utilized in the architecture. The process of service execution is as follows: once a service design described in BPEL has been verified, it is handed over to a service deployer which passes the BPEL specification on to an execution engine that finally executes the service. In the architecture, these components are part of an execution server component.

An execution engine for BPEL, called *Business Process Execution Language for Web Services Java Run Time* (BPWS4J), has been implemented by IBM and is freely available from IBM alphaWorks. A BPEL service design can be directly interpreted and executed by the BPWS4J engine.

3.6 Model Translation

Model translation is performed by two translator components: one supports the translation of a service design description to a software engineering model, the other one supports the translation of a software engineering model back to a service design description. Thus, in-house developers get access to a user created service on a software engineering level enabling them to modify or improve the design by using development tools they are used to.

As a modeling language capable of capturing a service design in a proper software engineering model the architecture utilizes UML, and *activity diagrams* (UML-AD) in particular. Activity diagrams can be used to capture workflow. BPEL, on the other hand, is a workflow description language.

Mantell (2003) describes an approach for mapping UML-AD to BPEL. The approach has been already implemented. The respective tool, namely *UML2BPEL*, is freely available from IBM alphaWorks. As the tool's name suggests, the transformation process currently implemented is only unidirectional. The approach, however, also allows for a bidirectional mapping.

The mapping process between BPEL and UML-AD is illustrated in Fig. 3. The process represented by BPEL and WSDL descriptions is converted by the translator component to a representation in XMI format[7] according to corresponding mapping rules. Subsequently, the XMI representation can be converted to a visual representation, i.e. to UML-AD.

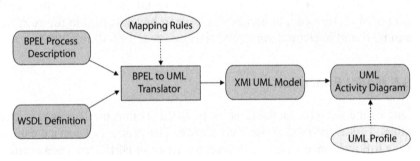

Fig. 3: The mapping process between BPEL and UML-AD

3.7 User Interaction

The part of the architecture that remains to be examined is the user interaction component. Basically this component is responsible for presenting the toolkit to users and making its functionality accessible. The user interaction component encompasses the following functionality: providing a proper user interface, presenting to users the set of service units that can be composed and the service design in progress, providing and presenting the external composition mechanism, and passing relevant (composition-related) user actions on to the model generator component. For a toolkit to

---

[7] XMI, which means XML Metadata Interchange, is an interchanged format for exchanging metadata information via XML. Most commonly, XMI is used as an interchange format for UML although it can be used for other purposes as well.

be adaptable to different user groups the service units' level of abstraction as well as the composition mechanism presented to users has to be adaptable. In the following, it is shown how this adaptation can be realized.

The service units' level of abstraction can be adapted by making use of the toolkit's internal composition logic. BPEL facilitates this adaptation. Starting from a (potentially large) set of provided atomic service units[8], a toolkit designer is able to compose service units recursively to new units until the preferred level of abstraction is reached. These composite service units, whose composition is described with BPEL, can then be made accessible to toolkit users hiding any other service units of lower abstraction from them. The user interaction component presents these service units to the users in whatever form chosen, e.g. graphically or textually.

In contrast to the adaptation of the service units' level of abstraction, the adaptation of the composition mechanism's level of abstraction is meant to be directly implemented in the user interaction component. The external composition mechanism provided by a toolkit abstracts from the internal composition logic's power (and complexity), but has to be mappable to it. Or put differently: every user action related to service unit composition via the external composition mechanism has to be capturable by the internal composition logic. The degree of this abstraction depends on the target users' skills and preferences. Obviously, adaptation in this case cannot be accomplished by means of composition as it is done in the context of varying the abstraction level of service units. Rather, the user interaction component has to implement a dedicated external composition mechanism and then pass composition related user actions on to the model generator component which captures the respective composition with the toolkit's internal composition logic. The model generator, and model verifier respectively, then checks for the validity of this composition and gives feedback to the user interaction component.

The external composition mechanism may be of various kinds, ranging from a powerful visual programming language to a much simpler drag'n' drop mechanism (with graphically represented service units as drag'n'drop elements), or anything in-between. Even allowing a user to access BPEL-specifications directly may be an option, at least when targeting advanced users.

---

[8] Any service can be broken down to single indivisible units providing the most basic functionality available in the respective service domain. These units shall be referred to as atomic service units.

4 A Concept Demonstration of a Toolkit in the Domain of Mobile Services

In this section, the potential of a toolkit for mobile service creation that builds on the architecture proposed and utilizes the outlined technologies and concepts is demonstrated. The demonstration aims to show the following aspects[9]:

- The realization and description of atomic service units, composite service units, and service designs,
- the adaptation of the toolkit to different target user groups,
- the refinement of a service design on different abstraction levels.

The demonstration is based on a fictitious scenario in which a user has an idea for a new service and creates this very service by using the toolkit in "novice mode". Experiencing the limits of this mode's restricted solution space, the user switches to the toolkit's "advanced mode" to refine his service. The domain of mobile services as defined earlier in this article is completely covered by this toolkit. Fig. 4 illustrates this service creation process, the involved components, and their respective tasks.

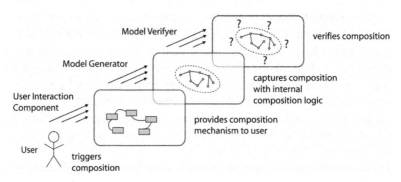

Fig. 4: The process of mobile service creation

In the following, technical details regarding the Web services/BPEL infrastructure used to demonstrate the toolkit concept are outlined. Then, the functionality of the user interaction component in novice mode is explained, followed by a description of how a user creates his first service design and improves it after testing the service in a real use environment. Subsequently, the user interaction component in advanced mode is outlined. It is shown how a user creates an improved service design by utilizing the interaction component's advanced mode features.

---

[9] See (Kirchmair 2005) for a demonstration of additional aspects.

4.1 Technical Infrastructure

This concept demonstration includes an implementation of atomic service units as Web services. However, as the realization of actual mobile services related functionality such as sending text messages to cell phones is quite complex, those Web services are implemented as *test stubs*[10] that deliver fake results. Composite services, i.e. service designs, have been implemented with BPEL.

The technical setup of the demonstration is as follows: Web services are implemented with Java 1.4.1. The respective Java class files have been deployed to an installation of an Apache Tomcat 4.1 application server. The Tomcat installation has been enhanced with Apache Axis, an open source SOAP server.

All service units described below and their composition to complete service designs have been modelled as BPEL[11]. The BPEL specifications of the services have all been successfully tested with IBM's BPWS4J which runs as a Web application within Apache Tomcat.

4.2 The Toolkit in Novice Mode

4.2.1 The Toolkit's User Interaction Component

The component realizes a graphical user interface that represents the provided service units as *building blocks* with n typed input ports and one typed output port. Input ports represent the parameters a building block requires in order to be able to fulfil its functionality. An output port represents the computation result of a building's block program logic. To keep the example simple yet demonstrative, it is assumed that the toolkit for novice users provides only three building blocks. The emerging solution space is obviously very small, but serves the purpose of this demonstration perfectly. The building blocks are:

- A *Radar* building block that is configurable with two cell phone numbers and delivers a result once the distance between these two cell phones is less than 2000 meters. The result contains the coordinates of the second parameter.

---

[10] A test stub simulates parts of a system (in this case, atomic service units) that are called by the tested parts of the system (in this case, BPEL specifications).
[11] See (Kirchmair 2005) for source code, BPEL descriptions, and UML diagrams.

- A *Citymap* building block that requires coordinates as input and delivers, as an image, a city map where the position specified by the coordinates is marked.
- An *MMS* building block that is configurable with three parameters: First, a cell phone number that specifies the recipient of the message. Second, some data, for instance an image, that gets attached to the message. Third, some text that specifies the message's textual content. Only the phone number parameter is required for the service's execution. The text and data parameters are optional. However, without either of those parameters the sent message will be empty.

The external composition mechanism provided by the user interaction component is very simple and straightforward, both in power and usability. A user is able to plug building blocks together via a drag'n'drop mechanism. This external composition mechanism does not provide any advanced control flow structures. Rather, control flow is covered implicitly by the assumption of a sequential flow. On the user interface's section that represents the actual service design, the design's building blocks can be arranged from left to right indicating the direction of the service's control flow. A service's execution process starts with the execution of the leftmost building block. As soon the block's execution has completed, the respective result is passed on to the connected input port of the next building block which is then executed, and so forth. The service stops with the execution of the last, i.e. the rightmost, building block. For a building block to get executed each of its input ports has to be connected - either to an output port of another building block or to a *parameter block* specifying a building block's required parameters. Available parameter blocks include a *text parameter* block and a *phone number parameter* block. These blocks are configurable with a phone number, and a custom text respectively.

Table 1 shows a possible graphical representation of these building blocks and parameter blocks. Dark-colored input ports indicate required parameters, light-colored input and output ports indicate optional connections to another parameter or building block.

Table 1. Building blocks and parameter blocks available in the toolkit's novice mode

Radar Service	*Radar* building block
MMS Service	*MMS* building block
CityMap Service	*Citymap* building block
Phone Number *xxxx*	*Phone Number* parameter block
Text *"xxxx"*	*Text* parameter block

4.2.2 A User's First Service Design

The service idea the user wants to realize is as follows: "Once I activate the service, my friend's position shall be tracked. If my friend comes close to me, I want to get notified by a MMS message."

Given the capabilities of the toolkit's user interaction component and its graphical interface, the user is able to express these requirements for a service as visualized in Fig. 5.

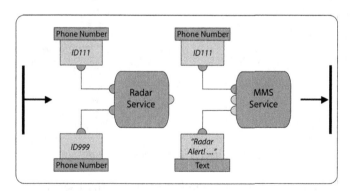

Fig. 5: A user's first service design

In this service design, the result of the Radar Service is discarded, i.e. is not used as an input for the MMS service. Again, according to the control flow semantics described above, the control flow goes from the left to the right: First, the Radar Service is executed. Once the service delivers a result, the MMS Service is executed. Then the service's execution stops. The service design is captured by the toolkit's internal composition logic, that is BPEL.

Obviously, the service fulfils the user's requirements for the service. As outlined before, BPEL processes are directly executable and, thus, the fictious user is able to test his service design repeatedly in the real use environment which facilitates learning by doing.

It is assumed now, that the user is satisfied with his overall design, but recognizes one flaw of the service: The notification he gets, only states that his friend is within a radius of 2000m. Even though the user regards this information as useful, he would also like to know where *exactly* his friend is at the moment. Preferably, by receiving a city map that indicates his friend's position. Consequently, he decides to refine his service design by incorporating another building block that the toolkit provides.

4.2.3 A User's Improved Service Design

The user states his new requirements as follows: "Once I activate the service, my friend's position shall be tracked. If my friend comes close to me, I want to get notified by an MMS message. But also a city map showing my friend's exact current position shall be attached to this message."

The respective service design as it might be created with the toolkit's user interaction component is illustrated in Fig. 6.

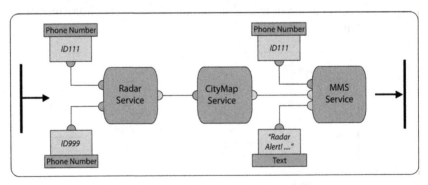

Fig. 6: A user's improved service design

After using his service for a number of times, the user discovers another shortcoming: The sensitivity of the Radar is far too low from being really useful. The user would like to change the Radar's sensitivity from 2000m to 200m. However, he does not have the possibility to do so with the toolkit's version for novice users. The Radar building block can only be used as-is and does not allow for further refinement. Hence, he switches to the toolkit's advanced mode.

4.3 The Toolkit in Advanced Mode

4.3.1 The Toolkit's Advanced User Interaction Component

Switching the toolkit from novice to advanced mode gives rise to a considerably larger solution space. The advanced mode differs in the fact that both the service units' level of abstraction and the external composition mechanism are adapted. This adaptation is done by lowering the service units' level of abstraction and putting a more powerful composition mechanism into place.

In this mode, the user interaction component's composition mechanism offers the user advanced control flow structures such as *while loops* and *if-then-else* branching. Moreover, it allows for the definition of custom variables and basic expressions which can be used, e.g. to formulate a termination condition for a while loop. Hence, this external composition mechanism comes much closer to the toolkit's internal composition capabilities as determined by the power of BPEL.

The user's switch to advanced mode was motivated by the insufficiency of the Radar Service. In fact, the Radar Service as provided in novice mode is already a composite service internally. The service's functionality relies on two other service units which are not accessible in the novice version, but are directly accessible as building blocks in the advanced mode of the toolkit. Those units are:

- A *Locator* building block that takes a cell phone number as input and delivers the coordinates of the current cell phone's position as output.
- A *Distance Calculator* building block that requires two coordinates as input and computes the direct distance between these two coordinates in meters.

Table 2 shows the additional building blocks and structures which can be used by a user to build a service design.

Table 2: Additional building blocks and structures as available in the toolkit's advanced mode

Locator	*Locator* building block	WHILE xxxx	*While loop.* Repeated until condition *xxx* is false.
Distance Calculator	*Distance Calculator* building block	CONTINUE	*No-op* instruction. The service execution continues.
Variable1	User-defined variable named *Variable1*	WAIT xxx [sec]	Stops the service execution for *xxx* seconds.
FALSE / TRUE	Two pre-defined (Boolean) values, one undefined. Can be assigned to a variable.	no xxx yes	*Branches* the control flow depended on the *xxx* condition.

4.3.2 A User's Refined Service Design

The user wants his refined service to provide the following functionality: "Once I activate the service, my friend's position shall be tracked. If my friend is within a 200m range, I want to get notified by an MMS message. But also a city map showing my friend's exact current position shall be attached to this message."

The service design the user created by making use of the capabilities of the advanced interaction component's user interface and as represented by this interface, is shown in Fig. 7.

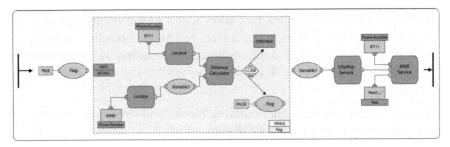

Fig. 7: A user's refined service design

This example demonstrated, how a vertical adaptation of a toolkit can be realized by changing the level of abstraction of the involved service units and by changing the external composition mechanism while leaving the internal composition logic (represented by BPEL) unaffected. This also indicates that BPEL is able to capture a service design on different levels of abstraction.

5 Summary

This article introduced an architecture for user innovation toolkits in the domain of mobile services. However, the architecture is generic and flexible enough to cover various classes of digital services (e.g. web services, E-Mail services, car driver assistance services, etc). The architecture consists of several components, namely a user interaction component that handles the interaction with toolkit users, a model generator component that manages an internal representation of a user's service design, a model verifier component that verifies this representation, two model translator components that serve as a toolkit's interface to external software development processes, and a model execution server that is capable of executing a service. For an implementation of this architecture three key technologies were suggested: Web services technology for the realization of service units, BPEL for the realization of service unit compositions, and UML as a means to represent service designs as software engineering models.

Subsequently, the architecture's main concepts such as the adaptation to different target user groups and the refinement of service designs on different levels of abstraction were demonstrated. For this purpose, a fictitious situation was described in which a user experiences needs for certain mobile services and then uses a toolkit, which is built upon the proposed architecture and technologies, to create and refine these services.

Even though the solution spaces in the concept demonstration are quite restricted, such a toolkit's potential for innovation should have become apparent. This potential increases exponentially with the number of service units provided and with the power of the implemented composition mechanism for those units.

It remains for future research to explore in more detail the possibilities for implementing and utilizing this architecture, particularly in other domains than the mobile service domain.

References

Brown A, Fuchs M, Robie J, Wadler P (2001) MSL - A Model for W3C XML Schema. In: Proceedings of 10th World Wide Web Conference (WWW2001), pp 191-200

Churchman CW, Ackoff RL, Arnoff LE (1957) Introduction to Operations Research. Wiley, New York

Curbera F, Goland Y, Klein J, Leymann F (2002) Business Process Execution Language for Web Services, Version 1.0. Technical report. BEA Systems, International Business Machines Corporation, Microsoft Corporation

Fu X, Bultan T, Su J (2003) Conversation Protocols: A Formalism for Specification and Verification of Reactive Electronic Services. In: Proceedings of 8th International Conference on Implementation and Application of Automata (CIAA), pp 188-200

Fu X, Bultan T, Su J (2004) WSAT: A Tool for Formal Analysis of Web Services. In: Proceedings of 16th International Conference on Computer Aided Verification (CAV)

Farahbod R, Glässer U, Vajihollahi M (2004) Specification and Validation of the Business Process Execution Language for Web Services. Technical Report. Simon Fraser University

Finkel A, McKenzie P (1997) Verifying Identical Communicating Processes is Undecidable. In: Theoretical Computer Science 174:217-230

Foster H, Uchitel S, Magee J, Kramer J (2003) Model-based Verification of Web Service Compositions. In: Proceedings of 18th International Conference on Automated Software Engineering, pp.152-161

von Hippel E (1999) Toolkits for User Innovation. Working Paper No. 4058. MIT Sloan School of Management

von Hippel E, Katz R (2002) Shifting Innovation to Users Via Toolkits. In: Management Science 48(7):821-833

Holzmann GJ (1993) Design and Validation of Protocols: A Tutorial. In: Computer Networks and ISDN Systems 25:981-1017

Holzmann GJ (2003) The SPIN Model Checker: Primer and Reference Manual. Addison-Wesley, Boston

Hull R, Su J (2004) Tools for Design of Composite Web Services. Tutorial abstract. ACM SIGMOD, International Conference on Management of Data

Kirchmair B (2005) Outsourcing Innovation: An Integrated Approach for Service-based Environments. Master Thesis, Department of Informatics, Technische Universität München

Koshkina M, van Breugel F (2003) Verification of Business Processes for Web Services. Working Paper. Department of Computer Science, York University

Koshkina M, van Breugel F (2004) Modeling and Verifying Web Service Orchestration by Means of the Concurrency Workbench. In: Proceedings of 1st Workshop on Testing, Analysis, and Verification of Web Services, ACM SIGSOFT 29:5

Lupp C, Gerstheimer O (2001) Needs versus Technology: The Challenge to Design 3G Applications. In: Dholakia RR, Kolbe L, Venkatesh A, Zoche P (2001) COTIM 2001: From E-Commerce to M-Commerce, RITIM, University of Rhode Island

Lüthje C (2000) Kundenorientierung im Innovationsprozess. Eine Untersuchung der Kunden-Hersteller-Interaktion in Konsumgütermärkten. Gabler, Wiesbaden

Lüthje C (2003) Customers as co-inventors: an empirical analysis of the antecedents of customer-driven innovations in the field of medical equipment. In: Proceedings of the 32th EMAC Conference, Glasgow

Lüthje C, Herstatt C, von Hippel E (2003) Patterns in the Development of Minor Innovations by Users: Bricolage in Mountain Biking,. Working Paper. MIT Sloan School of Management

Mantell K (2003) From UML to BPEL. IBM developerWorks, at www-900.ibm.com/developerWorks/cn/webservices/ws-uml2bpel/index_eng.shtml on December 15th, 2004

Magee J, Kramer J (1999) Concurrency - State Models and Java Programs. Wiley, New York

Magnusson P, Matthing J, Kristensson P (2003) Managing User Involvement in Service Innovation - Experiments with Innovating End Users. In: Journal of Service Research, 6:114-124

Narayanan S, Mellraith SA (2002) Simulation, Verification, and Automated Composition of Web Services. In: Proceedings of the 11th International World Wide Web Conference (WWW2002)

Plotkin GD (1981) A Structural Approach to Operational Semantics. Report DAIMI FN-19, Aarhus University

Pnueli A (1977) The Temporal Logic of Programs. In: Proceedings of the 18th IEEE Symposium on Foundations of Computer Science

Porter, ME (1998) On Competition. Harvard Business School Press, Cambridge

Stahl C (2004) Transformation von BPEL4WS in Petrinetze. Diploma Thesis, Humboldt-Universität zu Berlin

Thomke S, von Hippel E (2002) Customers as Innovators: A New Way to Create Value. In: Harvard Business Review 80(4)

Vidal JM, Buhler P, Stahl C (2004) Multiagent Systems with Workflows. IEEE Internet Computing, 8:76-82

Integrating Users in Discontinuous Innovation Processes: Findings from a Study of Mobile Download Games

Matthias Möller

1 Introduction

User innovation is an intensively discussed topic in theory and practice for raising a company's innovative power. However, the integration of users seems to have certain limitations when dealing with discontinuous innovation projects that exhibit high disruptions in technological capabilities and market applications.

The study introduced in this paper evolved from a three year research project on the development of mobile services for next generation mobile networks.[1] One main goal of that project was to develop an innovation process that can deal with the high discontinuities in technology and market. During the course of the project one particular theme became utterly clear: the difficulty of integrating users in such a discontinuous innovation process.

Innovation in the context of this study is defined as the bridging of knowledge about technological capabilities and market applications.[2] The level of discontinuity of an innovation can thus be defined by the level of missing knowledge in the technology and market dimension.[3]

This article starts with a literature review on discontinuous innovation and user innovation. The next section describes effects of discontinuous innovations on the possibilities of integrating users in the innovation process. Since users have limited knowledge about the new technological capabilities and resulting market applications, their contributions are not assured to be valid and usable. In order to still capitalize on the innovative power of users, the following chapter outlines possible solutions for integrating users in discontinuous innovation processes. Subsequently an explorative study analyzes how to bridge the knowledge gap of and which methods are well suited to achieve this knowledge increase.

---

[1] The project Mobiserve (www.mobiserve.de) was part of the UMTS initiative of the Bavarian State (2001 to 2004) to foster the development of applications that utilize UMTS technology and by doing so helping to amortize the huge investments of the mobile operators in that technology. The goal of the project was to develop location based services in a consortium of a mobile operator, a content provider, a mobile handset manufacturer and a car manufacturer.

[2] (Pfeiffer and Staudt 1975; Picot et al. 1990; Picot and Scheuble 1997; Picot et al. 2003)

[3] (Mensch 1971; Mensch 1972; Mensch 1975; Cooper 1979; Pfeiffer 1980; Abernathy and Clark 1985; Henderson and Clark 1990; Albach 1994; Green et al. 1995; Pfeiffer et al. 1997; Becker 1998; Veryzer 1998a; Veryzer 1998b; Garcia and Clalantone 2002). The level of knowledge can differ from individual to individual. Thus subjective and objective avaible information can be differentiated (Picot and Maier 1993).

2 Literature Review

2.1 User Integration and Discontinuity of Innovations

A central challenge in innovation projects is to recognize needs and demands, since innovations that follow concrete user needs have a high rate of success.[4] Many studies show the increasing importance and success of integrating users in the process of generating new product and service ideas.[5]

Discontinuous innovations through radical disruptions in technological capabilities create potentials for new applications, markets and user needs that differ significantly from habitual consumption patterns.[6] Through this disruption in the logical evolution of technology and market, the knowledge of user needs and possible market applications is not readily available for the company.[7]

2.2 Lack of Knowledge in Situations of Discontinuous Innovation

Also the integration of users to acquire this missing market knowledge poses a challenge on the company.[8] Users express their needs in accordance to their current knowledge base. The level of discontinuity for users

---

[4] (Utterback 1971; Urban et al. 1987; von Hippel 1988; Narver and Slater 1990, Kohli and Jaworski 1990; Geschka and Herstatt 1991; Urban and Hauser 1993; Desphandé et al. 1993; Meyer and Blümelhuber 1997; Lüthje 2000; Lüthje 2003)

[5] (Cooper 1979; von Hippel 1986; Cooper and Kleinschmidt 1987; von Hippel 1988; Zirger and Maidique 1990)

[6] (Veryzer 1998b; Geschka 1986; Lüthje 2000)

[7] (Christensen 2003, p. 165: „Markets that do not exist cannot be analyzed: Suppliers and customers must discover them together. Not only are the market applications for disruptive technologies *unknown* at the time of their development, they are *unknowable*.")

[8] (Veryzer 1998b; Hamel and Prahalad 1994; Christensen 2003; Callahan and Lasry 2004; Lynn et al. 1996 p. 15: „The familiar admonition to be customer-driven is of little value when it is not at all clear who the customer is – when the market has never experienced the features created by the new technology.";
O'connor 1998, p. 158: „In the earliest stages of development, there is no foray into the market, no customer contact, no concept test with lead users. Rather, there is a period of technological forecasting coupled with imagination, or, visioning.")

is represented by the levels of disruption in technological capability and product benefit and the level of associated changes in consumption patterns.[9] Since they have never experienced the possibilities of the new technologies, it is difficult for them to anticipate how their consumption patterns and needs will change when the technology will be available and translated to usable applications.[10]

3 Integrating Users in Discontinuous Innovation Projects

Users must adopt their knowledge to the future situation of a discontinuous innovation project in order to contribute valid and reliable information.[11] „They require to think beyond their current situations and anticipate heretofore unknown potentialities."[12] To reach this knowledge state, users must be conveyed a true sense of the discontinuous innovations. They have to learn how the new technology will change their consumptions patterns and needs and which applications might be useful to satisfy those needs.

This section proposes possible methods for integrating users in their discontinuous innovation projects. The solutions have been developed from experience made in the Mobiserve project and a literature review in this emerging research field. The proposed methods are not mutually exclusive but can be employed simultaneously in user innovation processes.

---

[9] (Veryzer 1998b), p. 137: „The product benefit dimension refers to the new capabilities of the product in terms of the needs that it satisfies as perceived and experienced by the customer or user. The technological capability dimension refers to the degree to which the product involves expanding technological capabilities (…) beyond existing boundaries. The consumption pattern dimension refers to the degree of change required in the thinking and behavior of the consumer in using the product."

[10] (Kaldor 1971; Tauber 1974; Bennett and Cooper 1981; Kohli and Jaworski 1990; Lender 1991; Veryzer 1998a). A good example was the introduction of the SMS service in the market, which was originally thought to have its most successful application area in machine control. Nobody – neither users, nor the companies – could imagine this application to be used for person to person communication and to be the most successful mobile data service so far.

[11] (West et al. 1996; von Oetinger 2005)

[12] (Veryzer 1998b, p.147)

3.1 Increasing the State of Knowledge by Making Experiences

One method is to let users actively learn about their future needs and usage behavior by experiencing the potential of the new technology. This can be achieved by letting users play with instances of the new products or services (e. g. prototypes).[13] By going through these learning-by-doing cycles, users can iteratively specify and concretize their needs and requirements and thus play their way to usable product-need combinations (Fig.1).[14]

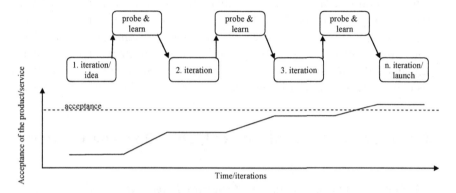

Fig. 1. Increase of acceptance by learning-by-doing

Through probing and learning with concrete instances of the technology, users adapt their state of knowledge to the discontinuous innovation, which increases their ability to test product ideas or generate marketable information in a usable way.[15]

---

[13] (Thomke 2003), p. 25. „Customers are rarely able to fully specify all their needs because they either face uncertainty themselves or cannot articulate their needs on products that do not yet exist. If they have neither seen nor used such a product before, they themselves will have to experiment before arriving at a recommendation."

[14] (Albrecht 1971; Arrow 1974; Geschka 1986; Lynn et al. 1996; Leonard and Rayport 1997; Tyre and von Hippel 1997; Thomke 1997; Thomke 1998; von Hippel 2001; Thomke and Bell 2001; Möller et al. 2003).

[15] (Iansiti 1994, p.521), „Technology integration consists of the set of knowledge-building activities through which novel concepts are explored, evaluated, and refined to provide the foundation for product development."

3.2 Adjustments in the Level of Discontinuity

Another possibility to adjust the level of knowledge of the user to the level of discontinuity in the innovation process is to adjust the level of perceived discontinuity for the user in the integration situation.[16] The perceived discontinuity for the user – as described above – is represented by the dimensions technology, utility and consumption patterns.

This method is especially suitable if the desired progress of knowledge is focused on just one of the above mentioned areas. The perceived level of discontinuity for the user can be lowered by keeping the other two dimensions as compatible as possible with the user's current sate of knowledge. The subsequent study uses this method by keeping the changes in technology and utility moderate, and only exposes the user to a high disruption in his consumption pattern of how games on mobile phones are provisioned.

4 Survey: User Knowledge of Mobile Download Games

4.1 Research Questions and Object of Research

This empirical survey focuses on the methods presented above for integrating users in discontinuous innovation projects. This involves two initial restrictions. Specifically, this explorative study focuses on the following research questions. Does learning occur in contexts in which users do not have a well established frame of reference for usage patterns? How effective are different approaches of facilitating learning for users? Does learning-by-doing yield superior results?

The survey was conducted in a joint effort with O2, a mobile network operator. In 2003, the time of the survey, O2 was facing the challenge of marketing mobile services to customers who had little knowledge of both, the underlying telecommunication technology and the potential changes to their behavior patterns. Consequently, the company was highly interested in examining different methods of facilitating their customers' learning. As noted above, mobile download games were chosen in order to control the degree of discontinuity of a service.

---

[16] This method can be explained by the "Erstmaligkeits-Bestätigungs-Modell" that says that a bit of information should have neither too much new nor too much affirmative elements in order to cause action. (von Weizsäcker 1974; Picot and Maier 1993; Picot and Scheuble 1997)

The latter point will be studied and depicted in more detail in the next section. It follows a section on the methodology of the survey as well as a presentation of the results and their discussion.

4.2 Definition of Degree of Discontinuity of Mobile Download Games

It has been pointed out that the degree of discontinuity of an innovation is an essential factor to consider when integrating customers in the innovation process. After the earlier conceptual treatment, the next sections present the findings of a study on mobile games which was conducted in cooperation with O2. It primarily focuses on different experimental stimuli for new services and how those suffice in changing the users' frame of reference, i.e. the knowledge of a new service.[17]

The study was conducted in 2003. Thus, the context of the study, i.e. the degree of innovativeness and the a priori knowledge of participants in the domain of download games needs to be considered accordingly. Even at that time, mobile download games cannot be considered discontinuous in general terms. However, if one distinguishes between the process of providing and the actual use of the games as well as particular dimensions, a more distinguished picture unfolds and is summarized in Table 1.

Table 1. Degree of innovativeness of mobile download games

	utility	technology	consumer behavior
provision of download games	moderate	moderate	high
use of download games	moderate	moderate	low

Games on mobile phones do not necessarily constitute a revolutionary new or altered perceived *utility* for users: analogies to mobile game consoles and also first rudimentary and pre-installed games on phones do exist. Nevertheless, most users are not familiar with the increasing technological capability of mobile phones, particularly in terms of display resolution, processing power, installed memory and ease of access to game repositories on the internet. Consequently, utility seems to be moderately affected in both the provision and use of download games. In terms of *technology*, there is a combination of different, new technologies such as mobile inter-

---

[17] Note that the study was conducted in 2003. Thus, the context of the study, i.e. a priori knowledge of participants in the domain of download games needs to be considered accordingly. See (Möller 2006) and (Möller and Martens 2004) for more details.

net via WAP, packet-switched data transfer and automated billing by the mobile network operator. This constitutes a novel process of providing games to mobile phones. Finally, the actual *consumer behavior* of using and playing games on mobile phones, e.g. coping with different keypad layouts is not discontinuous by itself. The previous process of choosing, transmitting and paying the game, however, is discontinuous for users since it changes their behavior significantly. The entire process is carried out electronically and differs obviously from familiar behavior of going to a brick-and-mortar store to choose and purchase a game or device. Consequently, the major factor for considering mobile download games to be discontinuously innovative lies within the novel way of providing those games.

The importance of experience and knowledge of individuals for the quality of user generated information has been conceptually shown. Different methods to influence the level of prior knowledge of the users who shall be integrated in the innovation process were also shown. These methods are essential to alter and prepare the users' frame of reference for discontinuous innovations, i.e., in this case, the significantly changed process of providing mobile download games. This study examines the effectiveness of these methods in an explorative way.

4.3 Methodology of Study

4.3.1 Selection of Participants

A total of 250 individuals participated in the experimental study. The sample of the participants was chosen by quota method (Koschnick 1995). This allows for consciously selecting participants by pre-defined criteria. In this study, 40% of the test persons were taken from the age segment of 14 to 24 years and 30% of the segments from 25 to 34 years and 35 to 44 years respectively. Equal numbers of female and male participants compose the sample.

Additional criteria were ownership of a mobile phone and lack of experience with mobile download games. Prior to the experiment participants have neither downloaded nor played a game on their mobile phone. These selection criteria ensure equal preconditions for the impact of different stimuli. Individuals initially considered for the study have furthermore participated in a survey of the cooperating mobile network operator to a similar topic within the previous six months.

4.3.2 Design of Experiment

The experiment was designed to consider ex-ante and ex-post knowledge in respect to different stimuli (Neumann 2001). The 250 test persons participated in a pre-study which examined their knowledge and experience of download games. The entire sample was then separated into four groups. One consisted of 100 individuals who had the opportunity to test and experience the download games with help of specially prepared mobile phones (stimulus "use"). The other three groups of 50 individuals each were given paper-based concepts of mobile games which differed among groups (stimulus "concept"). After being exposed to the different stimuli, an ex-post study was conducted in identical way to the pre-study. The ex-post study again asked for the participants' knowledge towards download games. The results are presented in the following section.

4.4 Results and Discussion

In a first step, the general effect of stimuli on the participants' knowledge of mobile download games is examined. A second step depicts differences in the effects across different stimuli.

4.4.1 General Effect of Stimuli on Knowledge

Due to the design of the survey, almost 80% of the participants in the pre-study had none or very little knowledge on mobile download games. Only 6% claimed to be strongly or very strongly knowledgeable in this area. After being exposed to the stimuli, this assessment changed to 28%. Consequently, the share of participants with none or little knowledge decreased to approximately 36%.

It becomes apparent that the stimuli effectively increase the participants' knowledge of mobile download games. An additional finding is that individuals with minor ex-ante knowledge experienced a more significant increase in knowledge than individuals with prior strong knowledge.[18] There are two interpretations of this finding. First, the stimuli were not informative enough to significantly add knowledge for all participants, particularly not for participants with prior knowledge. Second, the lack of ex-ante knowledge does not seem to have an influence on learning in this context. This may certainly be attributed to the fact that mobile download games

---

[18] A Pearson correlation analysis shows a moderately strong, negative relationship (r=-0.441) between the variables "a priori knowledge" and "increase in knowledge". The relationship is highly significant (p<0.001).

are not strongly discontinuous innovations. Thus, sufficient links to existing knowledge to build upon was available.

4.4.2 Use vs. Concepts: Differences in Learning

After this first overview it is now examined how the different stimuli succeed in building knowledge. Participants exposed to the stimulus "use" are expected to learn more about mobile download games in the course of the experiment. Thus, the change in knowledge due to this stimulus is compared with the average change of all participants. Fig. 2 shows the results. Comprehensibility of download games increased stronger for participants who used download games during the experiment compared to the entire sample. This effect is true in similar magnitude for the assessment of the ease of use of those games.

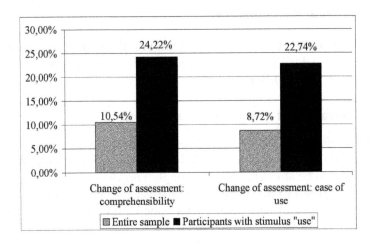

Fig 2. Change of assessment of download games

This finding is underlined by the results of the ex-post survey of the participants (Fig. 3). They show that participants with the stimulus "use" exhibit a higher degree of knowledge than those with the stimulus "concept". Apparently, individuals who use the games and experience them directly are, by the factor of almost three, less likely to have no knowledge at all and at the same time, by the factor of more than three, more likely to be very knowledgeable than individuals who have only received information in form of written concepts. This shows that learning is more profound if users are given the opportunity to experience a novel product rather than only being confronted with written explanations. This way, the frame of reference of understanding the new capabilities can be more easily adapted to novel technologies.

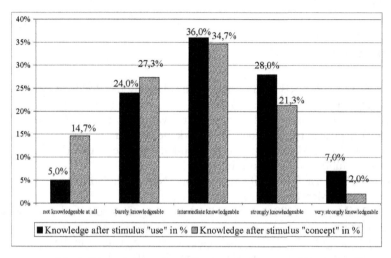

Fig 3. Knowledge of mobile download games after stimuli

5 Conclusion and Outlook

Discontinuous innovations imply a challenge to integrate users in the innovation process. Users must have the right state of knowledge in order to be able to contribute to the innovation process in a reliable and valid way. Two methods of dealing with that problem where proposed. Companies can reduce the perceived level of innovativeness for the user in an integration process or adapt the state knowledge at the side of the user to the discontinuous innovation through learning by doing.

The study showed that users can be brought into higher states of knowledge and that learning by doing is more effective to raise the knowledge state then just plain information.

The results of this explorative study can be helpful for companies when designing user integration processes in discontinuous innovation projects. They have to ask whether users already have the right state of knowledge in order to contribute in a reliable and valid way, or if they have to compensate for the lack of knowledge at the side of the user.

The field of user integration in discontinuous innovation projects is a quite new research area. Future studies could explore which strategies of adapting the knowledge state of users are appropriate at which level of discontinuity. Also the characteristics of users, their actual knowledge state and information processing capacity could prove interesting starting points for future research.

References

Abernathy WJ, Clark KB (1985) Innovation: Mapping the Winds of Creative Destruction. Research Policy, 4, 3-22

Albach H (1994) Culture and Technical Innovation. A Cross-Cultural Analysis and Policy Recommendations, New York, de Gruyter

Albrecht B (1971) Marketing: Die Konzeption für jede marktorientierte Unternehmensführung, Düsseldorf, Econ

Arrow KJ (1974) The Limits of Organizations, New York, Norton

Becker J (1998) Marketingkonzeption, München, Vahlen

Bennett R, Cooper R (1981) Beyond the Marketing Concept. Business Horizons, 22, 76-83

Callahan J, Lasry E (2004) The importance of customer input in the development of very new products. R&D Management, 34, 107-120

Christensen CM (2003) The Innovator's Dilemma, New York, HarperBusiness Essentials

Cooper RG (1979) The Dimensions of Industrial New Product Success and Failure. Journal of Marketing, 43, 93-103

Cooper RG, Kleinschmidt EJ (1987) Success Factors in Product Innovation. Industrial Marketing Management, 16, 215-223

Desphandé R, Farley JU, Webster FE (1993) Corporate culture, customer orientation, and innovativeness in Japanese firms: A quadrad analysis. Journal of Marketing, 57, 23-37

Garcia R, Clalantone R (2002) A Critical Look at Technological Innovation Typology and Innovativeness Terminology: A Literature Review. Journal of Product Innovation Management, 19, 110-132

Geschka H (1986) Markt-Informationen für neue Produkte. VDI-Berichte, 616, 119-138

Geschka H, Herstatt C (1991) Kundennahe Produktinnovation: Ergebnisse einer Befragung. Die Unternehmung, 45, 207-220

Green SG, Gavin MB, Aiman-Smith L (1995) Assessing a multidimensional measure of radical technological innovation. IEEE Transactions on Engineering Management, 42, 203-214

Hamel G, Prahalad CK (1994) Competing for the Future, Boston, MA, Harvard Business School Press

Henderson RM, Clark K (1990) Architectural Innovation: The Reconfiguration of Existing Product Technologies and the Failure of Established Firms. Administrative Science Quarterly, 35, 9-30

Iansiti M (1994) Technology integration: Managing technological evolution in a complex environment. Research Policy, 24, 521-542

Kaldor AG (1971) Imbricative Marketing. Journal of Marketing, 35, 19-25

Kohli AK, Jaworski BJ (1990) Market orientation: The construct, research propositions and managerial implications. Journal of Marketing, 54, 1-18

Koschnick WJ (1995) Standard-Lexikon für Markt- und Konsumforschung: Band 2: L-Z, München, K.G. Saur

Lender F (1991) Innovatives Technologie-Marketing: Grenzen der konventionellen Marktforschungskonzepte und Ansätze zur methodischen Neugestaltung, Göttingen, Vandenhoeck & Ruprecht

Leonard D, Rayport JF (1997) Spark Innovation Through Empathic Design. Harvard Business Review, 75, 102-113

Lüthje C (2000) Kundenorientierung im Innovationsprozess: Eine Untersuchung der Kunden-Hersteller-Interaktion in Konsumgütermärkten, Wiesbaden, Dt. Univ.-Verlag

Lüthje C (2003) Methoden zur Sicherstellung von Kundenorientierung in den frühen Phasen des Innovationsprozesses. IN Herstatt C, Verworn B (Eds.) Management der frühen Innovationsphasen: Grundlagen - Methoden - Neue Ansätze. 1. Auflage ed. Wiesbaden, Gabler

Lynn GS, Morone JG, Albert PS (1996) Marketing and Discontinuous Innovation: The Probe and Learn Process. California Management Review, 38, 8-37

Mensch G (1971) Zur Dynamik des technischen Fortschritts. Zeitschrift für Betriebswirtschaft, 41. Jg., 293-314

Mensch G (1972) Basisinnovationen und Verbesserungsinnovationen. Eine Erwiderung. Zeitschrift für Betriebswirtschaft, 42. Jg., S. 291-297

Mensch G (1975) Das technologische Patt. Innovationen überwinden die Depression, Frankfurt/Main, Umschau

Meyer A, Blümelhuber C (1997) Marketing orientiert sich zuwenig am Kunden. IN Belz C (Ed.) Marketingtransfer: Kompetenz für Marketing-Innovationen; Schrift 5. St. Gallen, Thexis

Möller M (2006) Innovationsexperiment - Kundenintegrierendes Vorgehensmodell zur Entwicklung mobiler Dienste bei diskontinuierlichen Innovationen. Munich School of Management. München, Ludwig-Maximilians-Universität

Möller M, Martens R (2004) Änderung der Einstellung zu mobilen Spielen durch Wissensvermittlung: Eine empirische Untersuchung. Unveröffentlichte Studie in Zusammenarbeit mit O2,

Möller M, Vukovic S, Landgrebe J (2003) Identifiying Customer Requirements for location-based Services. IN Käfer J, Zündt M (Eds.) MoMuC2003. München, Center for Digital Technology and Management

Narver JC, Slater SF (1990) The effect of a market orientation on business profitability. Journal of Marketing, 54, 20-35

Neumann P (2001) Markt- und Werbepsychologie: Band 2 Praxis, Gräfelfing, Fachverlag Wirtschaftspsychologie

O'Connor GC (1998) Market Learning and Radical Innovation: A Cross Case Comparison of Eight Radical Innovation Projects. Journal of Product Innovation Management, 15, 151-166

Pfeiffer W (1980) Innovationsmanagement als Know-How-Management. IN Hahn D (Ed.) Führungsprobleme industrieller Unternehmungen, Festschrift für Friedrich Thomée zum 60. Geburtstag. Berlin, Walter de Gruyter

Pfeiffer W, Staudt E (1975) Innovation. Handwörterbuch der Betriebswirtschaft. 4. Auflage ed. Stuttgart, Poeschel

Pfeiffer W, Weiß E, Volz T, Wettengl S (1997) Funktionalmarkt-Konzept zum strategischen Management prinzipieller technologischer Innovationen, Göttingen, Vandenhoeck & Ruprecht

Picot A, Laub U-D, Schneider D (1990) Comparing Successful and Less Successful New Innovative Businesses. European Journal of Operational Research, 47, 190-202

Picot A, Maier M (1993) Information als Wettbewerbsfaktor. IN Preßmar DB (Ed.) Schriften zur Unternehmensführung, Bd. 49: Informationsmanagement. Wiesbaden, Gabler

Picot A, Reichwald R, Wigand RT (2003) Die grenzenlose Unternehmung: Information, Organisation und Management, Wiesbaden, Gabler

Picot A, Scheuble S (1997) Die Bedeutung von Information für Innovation und Wettbewerbsfähigkeit. IN Mantwill GJ (Ed.) Informationswirtschaft und Standort Deutschland - Der Beitrag der Informationswirtschaft zur Wttbewerbsfähigkeit der Unternehmen. Baden-Baden, Nomos

Tauber EM (1974) How Marketing Discourages Major Innovation. Business Horizons, 17, 22-26

Thomke S (1997) The role of flexibility in the development of new products: An empirical study. Research Policy, 26, 105-119

Thomke S (1998) Managing Experimentation in the Design of New Products. Management Science, 44, 743-762

Thomke S (2003) Experimentation Matters: Unlocking the Potential of New Technologies for Innovation, Boston, Harvard Business School Publishing

Thomke S, Bell DE (2001) Sequential Testing in Product Development. Management Science, 47, 308-323

Tyre MJ, von Hippel E (1997) The Situated Nature of Adaptive Learning in Organizations. Organization Science, 8, 71-83

Urban GL, Hauser JR (1993) Design and marketing of new products, New Jersey, Prentice-Hall

Urban GL, Hauser JR, Dholakia N (1987) Essentials of new product management, New Jersey, Prentice-Hall

Utterback JM (1971) The Process of Technological Innovation within the Firm. Academy of Management Journal, 14, 75-88

Veryzer RW (1998a) Discontinuous Innovation and the New Product Development Process. Journal of Product Innovation Management, 15, 304-321

Veryzer RW (1998b) Key Factors Affecting Customer Evaluation of Discontinuous New Products. Journal of Product Innovation Management, 15, 136-150

von Hippel E (1986) Lead Users: a Source of Novel Product Concepts. Management Science, 32, 791-805

von Hippel E (1988) The Sources of Innovation, New York, Oxford University Press von Hippel E (2001) PERSPECTIVE: User Toolkits for innovation. The Journal of Product Innovation Management, 18, 247-257

von Oetinger B (2005) Nurturing the new: patterns for innovation. The Journal of Business Strategy, 26, 29-36

von Weizsäcker EU (1974) Erstmaligkeit und Bestätigung als Komponenten der Pragmatischen Information. IN von Weizsäcker EU (Ed.) Offene Systeme I - Beiträge zur Zeitstruktur, Entropie und Evolution. Stuttgart, Klett-Cotta

West P, Brown CL, Hoch SJ (1996) Consumption Vocabulary and Preference Formation. Journal of Consumer Research, 23, 120-135

Zirger BJ, Maidique MA (1990) A Model of New Product Development: An Empirical Test. Management Science, 36, 867-883

Distributed Collaboration:
Services and Information Sources in a
Knowledge-based Architecture

Patrick Renner, Bernd Brügge, Martin Ott

1 Introduction

With the evolution of interconnected mobile devices and business-to-business communication through the Internet, distributed organizations such as virtual companies or global teams have become reality. Knowledge management is a key requirement for these organizations to be successful (Fensel et al. 2000).

There are several problems with knowledge management in distributed mobile organizations. The knowledge is not centralized but must be brought together from remote and even mobile information sources, knowledge is not always accessible, and it is represented in different formats, which are rapidly evolving.

We have been exploring communication infrastructures for mobile distributed knowledge management in application domains such as oral surgery, archeology, logistics, personal information management and media asset management.

A communication infrastructure that supports distributed knowledge management must be decentralized, extensible to incorporate new knowledge as well as new knowledge sources. It must also be adaptable to the evolution of access protocols, networking technologies and data formats. In this paper we present a framework for such a communication infrastructure and demonstrate its use in two applications. The Medusa application targets mobile surgeons from different hospitals to exchange knowledge about patients to make or confirm a diagnosis even if they are not at the same location. The OntoMedia application supports teams working at different locations on the distributed production of a feature-length film.

In section 2 we describe several scenarios illustrating the use of our framework. In section 3 and 4 we present the requirements and design goals for a communication infrastructure supporting mobile distributed knowledge management. Section 5 details the architectural style, in particular services, mediation components and mechanisms for knowledge transfer. In section 6 we describe two implementations using the framework, a distributed collaboration application for mobile surgeons and an application supporting large feature film productions.

2 Application Domains

In this section we present two application scenarios for distributed mobile knowledge management. The first scenario illustrates the collaboration of mobile physicians discussing the case of a patient in a distributed setting.

The second scenario describes the distributed production of a film where project relevant information is exchanged in different formats.

To formulate the medical scenarios we conducted an ethnographical study by accompanying surgeons in their daily work over a period of two weeks[1]. The scenarios in the media production domain were produced in a similar way - one of the authors worked in a post production facility for digital movies for over a year and participated in the daily production workflows.

2.1 Surgeon Collaboration

Many different people work together to collect information about patients. This requires access to their medical history and specific medical findings. The information is usually not available in a central location but spread out; not even the patients themselves have access to all the information of their medical background. In an emergency case, for example, a hospital often admits patients with no access to their medical history. In such a case the emergency physician on duty relies only on the information provided by the hospital admission procedure, and this may not be sufficient for an effective diagnosis. Physicians on call could provide additional information, but they in turn do not have direct access to the information from the admission procedure.

This usually forces the physician on call to travel to the hospital for a personal examination of the patient. The results are long waiting periods for patients and unproductive idle times for the treating physician waiting for examination results - which could have been done before he arrives at the hospital. To remedy this problem a medical knowledge management sys-tem is needed that allows the distributed sharing of patient information where physicians can participate remotely.

We collaborated with oral surgeons from two Swiss hospitals, as hospitals in Switzerland share responsibilities in a unique form: University hospitals support regional hospitals and perform on-call service for emergency cases. Physicians on call are assigned to a set of hospitals for which they are responsible. They – and not the patient - must travel to a remote hospital if the local physician needs help in a diagnosis or cannot be instructed remotely when a special skill is needed.

As part of their daily work the surgeons also participate in so-called tumor conferences. A tumor conference is an event where experts from various medical disciplines meet each other in person to discuss complicated

---

[1] For more details we refer to (Dunst and Adamski 2004)

cases of cancer in order to contribute their special knowledge to the case and formulate a plan on how to proceed. Paper documents, flip charts and voice-based communication are the current form of knowledge exchange in this scenario. Sometimes, however, this does not allow the physicians to assess a situation thoroughly. Additional capabilities such as access to a remote expert or remotely available biometric data, high-resolution images and videos of the patient are needed to support the diagnosis.

2.2 Media Asset Management

The central activity of digital film postproduction is the so-called "digital intermediate process". Analog film is digitized and processed in steps such as editing, retouching, compositing of different image sources or final color grading. The management of the digital film data and specially the management of the various meta-data created throughout the production steps is a major challenge for postproduction facilities. The storage needs for a typical movie project easily reach several terabytes of image data, because the scanned original camera negative film, rendered sequences, retouched material, and so on, must be stored. A movie typically consists of thousands of single "shots", each having up to 20 different setups from different tools, often in a variety of versions stored at different locations, because several postproduction facilities work together as a virtual company to finish the movie. Moving an entire movie from one workstation to another takes at least a day even at a local site using fiber channel connections. Much longer transfer times are required if the storage spaces are in different locations accessible only through the Internet.

The proposed solution is a knowledge management system that enables the facilities to work together in one virtual site. Intelligent data management techniques are employed for moving image- and meta-data from high performance storage to lower performance (but cheaper) tertiary storage systems such as data tape libraries or to the high performance storage systems at remote sites.

3 Requirements for Mobile Distributed Knowledge Management

Our scenarios deal with users who need to access distributed information in order to acquire knowledge for making decisions: The physician needs as much knowledge as possible about a patient to make a thorough diagnosis; the production manager needs information about the status of a movie project to decide if timely delivery is still possible. In order to provide access to the distributed knowledge, it must be represented in an appropriate way and knowledge publishers have to be networked to make it available to knowledge consumers. Controlling and restricting the access to the knowledge is an important aspect: For example, the exchange of patient-related information has to follow law-enforced regulations in most countries. Media production companies strictly limit the access to their as-sets during production in order to prevent piracy.

In knowledge-based systems, information "is normally not an eternal truth, but a socially constructed artifact [...] which evolves over time" (Abecker and van Elst 2003). Considering this, the form in which the knowledge is being stored and transferred between users has to be flexible and expressive enough to adopt these constant changes.

In distributed, collaborative scenarios, different knowledge publishers will have different information in different representations for individual concepts. To grant uniform and consistent access to the concepts and to let users gather new knowledge by reasoning over these concepts, it must be possible to merge relevant information. For example, to get an overview of the status of the individual movie clips in a project, information from different servers in different locations of the distributed production has to be collected. To get the entire clinical history of a patient, knowledge from different physicians has to be collected and merged.

In media production, a multitude of tool-specific information formats have to be integrated; Information about patients is represented differently by individual clinical admission systems. This complexity should be hidden from the user, who should be able to focus on the concepts of the collected knowledge. Appropriate means for filtering have to be provided to avoid an information overload that would prevent the user from making fast decisions. The user must also be able to actively search for concepts by defining filter criteria. In addition, the filter criteria should be dynamically adjustable by utilizing the user's current focus of attention. An operator of a special effects workstation does not have to see all the clips of a movie, but only the ones that are important for the special effects he is currently working on. An oral surgeon planning a dental operation does not need x-ray images of the knee of a patient, but all records concerning the jaw and any history of paranasal sinusitis.

Most of today's centralized hospital information systems do not meet the mobile and collaboration-oriented capabilities for knowledge management described in the above scenarios. In fact, many of the interviewed physicians mistrust central knowledge repositories and prefer to have full command of sharing the knowledge about their patients with other physicians.

Existing media asset management systems realize information access similarly - either through distributed access to a central database or through additional export and import functionality. Moreover, they cover only limited portions of the production workflows such as media management or project management (Alienbrain; TMAM). Integration of additional functions is hard because proprietary data formats and predefined user interfaces often prevent the functionality to be added as plug-ins.

4 Analysis and Design Goals

In the following we will address these requirements with an ontology-based framework. Approaches such as the FieldWise (Fagrell et al. 2000) system or the AWARE (Bardram and Hansen 2004) architecture are aiming at similar mobile collaboration scenarios, but they do not focus on merging knowledge from different sources and thus are not utilizing the concept of ontologies. Glossaries or hierarchical taxonomies don't provide the flexibility and extensibility required in the scenarios as they require strict classification (e.g. a directed acyclic graph such as an inheritance taxonomy) and a predefined schema for information entry.

An ontology is defined as the "explicit specification of a conceptualization"(Gruber 1993). The most important feature of an ontology is that it is self-describing: An ontology not only contains information, but it also includes concepts that describe this information on a meta-level. Consumers of a specific ontology can therefore interpret the information and work with it immediately, e.g. infer new knowledge, even if the underlying information origins from different sources. Knowledge publishers can also extend an existing ontology with additional types of information.

In the following publishers and consumers of knowledge are collectively called knowledge clients. An information unit denotes the fundamental entity of communication between knowledge clients. An information unit may be either a concept, which we define as a digital representative of a subject from the real world, or an association between two information units. As information units contain different kinds of data properties such as names and types, they can be represented as a vertex- and edge-colored graph (Kubale et al. 2004). For example an information unit can represent a patient, a medical treatment or the fact that an x-ray image shows the jaw of a certain patient.

Merging of information units is an important feature of ontologies. The merging capabilities are utilized by aggregating information from separate ontologies into an aggregated ontology. The merging activity includes the identification of information units that represent the same subject in the real world. For example, the two information units in Fig. 1 called "fklammer" represent the same subject "Karl Klammer" in separate ontologies.

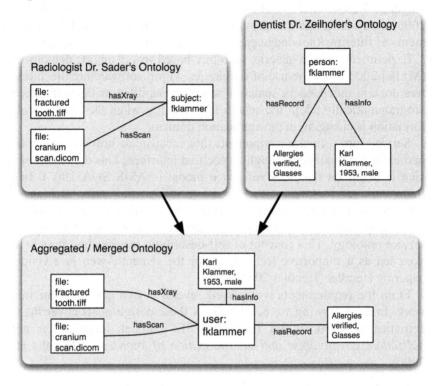

Fig. 1. Merging ontologies: Information for subjects represented in two ontologies is merged to an aggregated ontology. The formerly disconnected information from the two physicians is now available in a merged information unit

Initially we used Topic Maps (Biezunski et al. 2002) as implementation of ontologies. The advent of the Semantic Web framework (Berners-Lee et al. 2001), in particular the OWL (Dean and Schreiber 2003) model, added comprehensive reasoning support to ontologies. We therefore now use OWL as exchange standard for our communication infrastructure framework. OWL is based on the Resource Description Framework (RDF), which provides fine-grained publishing control down to the level of individual resources - corresponding directly to information units such as patient data or movie clips. With OWL, in particular with its variant OWL-DL (Dean and Schreiber 2003), new knowledge can be derived from existing knowledge by reasoning about the subjects in a specific do-main and their relations. For example, if a genetically hereditary disease has been documented for the parent of a patient, the predisposition for the patient can be automatically induced. This is similar to the capability provided by description-logic systems (Baader et al. 2003). Together with the query language RDQL (RDQL 2004) and the upcoming SPARQL (SPARQL 2006) query language this provides the functionality to fulfill the requirements of filtering knowledge appropriate to the user's current situation.

Experiments with a generic, ontology-based search engine demonstrated (Maalej 2005), that the use of ontologies within software architectures offers domain independent semantic search capabilities without the need to programmatically adopt the search functionality when the structure of information is changing in the application domain.

Services are software components that encapsulate how a user can use a particular functionality through a specified interface. This definition of service is based on the SOA reference model (OASIS SOA 2005). In our framework services offer either access to information units, such as a file directory, or to the functionality provided by an existing system such as an archival system. The capabilities of a service are described in the so-called service ontology. This concept of self-describing services has already been sketched as a supportive technology for the semantic web in a visionary paper by Hendler (Hendler 2001).

From the requirements we derived several design goals for our framework. In the following we describe how these design goals cover the four activities in Nonaka's and Takeuchi's SECI model: *socialization, externalization, combination and internalization of knowledge* (Nonaka et al. 2000).

- *Socialization of knowledge*: When a graph of information units created and managed by a knowledge client needs to be shared with another knowledge client, the sharing attribute can not be limited to "make public" or "keep private". Instead, it requires a detailed access control mechanism depending on the organizational relationship to the other client. When sharing information, social aspects such as trust have a strong impact on the way of sharing[2]: The level of trust between clients usually impacts the selection of information to be shared. Physicians, for example, will only share patient data with another physician who treats the same patient. In media asset management projects, postproduction facilities from different companies share media- and metadata only for a

---

[2] As Bonifacio (Bonifacio et al. 2000) stated, the sharing and integration of knowledge is an act of negotiation of meaning and thus "a mechanism of social agreement" – in his terms knowledge con-joins information and dialectics.

specific project. Our framework must meet the requirements of these socially accepted patterns of communication and the organizational associations between the communication partners.

- *Externalization of knowledge:* A system can't externalize directly the tacit knowledge of humans but it can externalize implicit technical knowledge from information sources like file systems or log files. Users leave traces of information during their daily work such as the change of a file or the disk space usage of a workstation. These traces can be meaningful for other knowledge clients. If this information is formalized as information units it can be made accessible by services, for example a service providing knowledge about the utilization of a workstation or the status of a project.

- *Combination of knowledge:* Each service provides it's own ontology - a room booking service provides information about rooms, occupations of rooms and occupation times, a backup service provides information about files, data tapes and the association between them. Often the services will overlap in their ontologies - some subjects represented by information units will appear in several services: A person requiring mobile health care is represented by information units in a health insurance system and in a database storing the x-ray images. Using the merging activity (see Fig. 1) graphs of information units provided by different services can be merged into a combined graph as shown in Fig. 2.

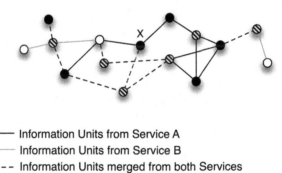

● —— Information Units from Service A
○ —— Information Units from Service B
◉ --- Information Units merged from both Services

Fig. 2. An ontology graph with information units from two separate ontologies that were provided by two services A and B. The visualization of the context of the information unit "x" is presented Fig. 3

- *Internalization of knowledge*: Ontologies frequently grow in size as well as in complexity e.g. by adding new information or new types of information. As the capability of humans for the comprehension of new information is limited, information filtering should be provided that can adapt to the size and complexity of an ontology. We define the situational relevance as a metric for information units with respect to the current focus (the context) of the user. The situational relevance of an information unit is the edge distance to the information unit of current interest; it decreases with the distance between the information units (see Fig. 3). The situational relevance can be used for the selection of information units. For example, if a project manager wants to see the relevant information of the specific scene of a film, the information units that are selected for display are limited to those with the highest situational relevance to the scene. These could be the movie clips or special effect setups used in the scene, or operators and workstations involved in the production of the scene.

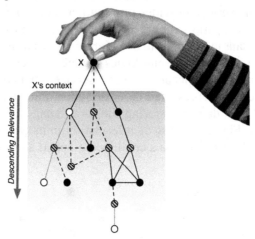

Fig. 3. Visualization of the context of an information unit of current interest "x" defined by the situational relevance. The context consists of information units that may have their origin in different ontologies provided by different services

The design goals for the framework can be summed up as follows:

- Knowledge clients can decide explicitly who can access the information units owned by them (fine grained, resource based access control).
- It must be easy to integrate new components or existing proprietary services into the framework, in particular services must offer an ontology based service description (modularity and extensibility).
- All information units have to be stored in an ontology (self-describable data model), which can be shared between knowledge clients (flexible data model).

- It must be possible to define new ontologies and add them to an existing instantiation of the framework (extensible data model).
- An ontology has to provide appropriate means for filtering the distributed information with respect to the current interest of a user (filtering by situational relevance).

5 Architecture of the Framework

Based on the requirements and design goals described in the previous section we developed an ontology-based service-oriented framework. Fig. 4 illustrates the subsystem decomposition of the framework organized in five layers.

The legacy layer consists of existing components such as databases or directories that provide application-specific data for the higher layers ("enterprise components layers" in SOA (Arsanjani 2004)). The service layer contains basic services providing functionality and information units accessible through the protocol layer. The protocol layer encapsulates communication between knowledge clients and services. The knowledge layer provides a merged ontology. As the sharing of information between services is controlled individually, this merged ontology may be different for each knowledge client. The ontology layer also enables applications in the client layer to apply filters or request the current context of an ontology. Applications access services indirectly through the knowledge layer. This architecture is similar to SOA (Arsanjani 2004), but it focuses on the sharing and processing of knowledge which is not addressed in SOA's architectural template.

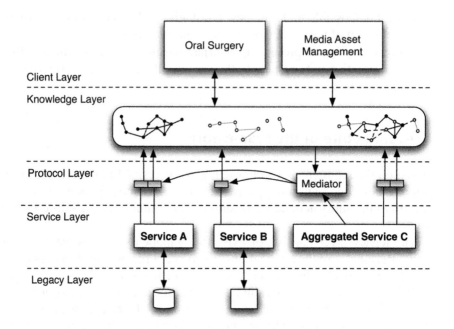

Fig. 4. A five-layer architecture for knowledge-based applications

The basic abstraction of the service layer is the basic service shown in Fig. 5. A basic service offers one type of functionality, for example the allocation of a room or the access to a user-directory. This functionality is implemented in the service layer or it can be provided by an existing component from the legacy layer.

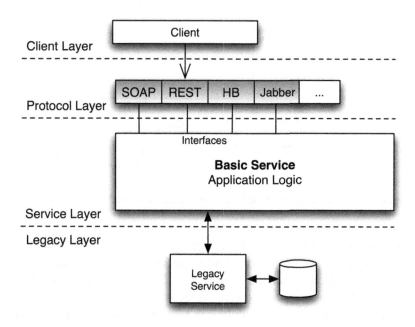

Fig. 5. Service-centric view of the architecture: Access to a service's functionality is decoupled from the access protocol

Access to a basic service is message-based but is not bound to a single protocol. The actual service interface is decoupled from the protocol used by the clients to access the service. The protocol layer is divided into independent partitions encapsulating different access protocols to the service. Examples of access protocols supported by the framework are REST (Fielding 2000), SOAP (SOAP 2003), or XMPP/Jabber (XMPP 2004); other protocols can be added by extending the implementation of the mediator's capabilities of translating protocols (see below).

While applications access services via the protocol layer, the coupling between services is loose. We use the mediator pattern (Gamma et al. 1996) to allow for basic services and applications to communicate with each other. The mediator and the basic service are derived from a generic service interface (see Fig. 6). The mediator acts as a proxy to the basic service and supports transparent access protocol translation to improve interoperability between clients and basic services.

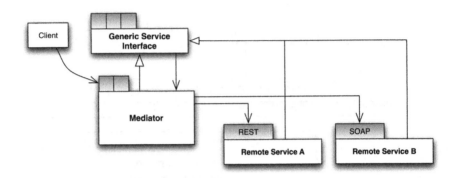

Fig. 6. Mediator centric view of the architecture: The mediator decouples the access to a service from the client

Basic services can be combined to form aggregated services. For example, combining a map service with a real estate service results in service, which offers information about the neighborhood of specific houses. The basic service and the aggregated service are both derived from a generic service interface, but the services usually don't know about each other. Coupling of services is done by a mediator (see Fig. 7).

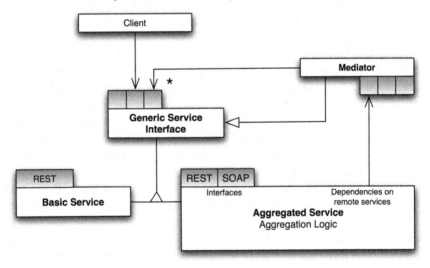

Fig. 7. Aggregator-centric view of the architecture: A service is either a basic service or an aggregation of loosely coupled services, where the aggregation is hidden from the client by a mediator

6 Prototype Applications

In this section we demonstrate the use of the framework in two applications. The Medusa application targets mobile surgeons from different hospitals exchanging knowledge about patients to make or confirm a diagnosis even if they are not at the same location. The OntoMedia application supports teams working at different locations on the distributed production of a large film.

6.1 The Medusa Application

The main user interface of the Medusa application is shown in Fig. 8. The user interface was implemented in Objective-C using the Cocoa framework for Mac OS X, a Java application for maintaining and sharing semantically enriched resources was also implemented. To support devices such as PDAs and mobile phones, a web-service based implementation leveraging the Tomcat web server and Java Server Pages was developed.

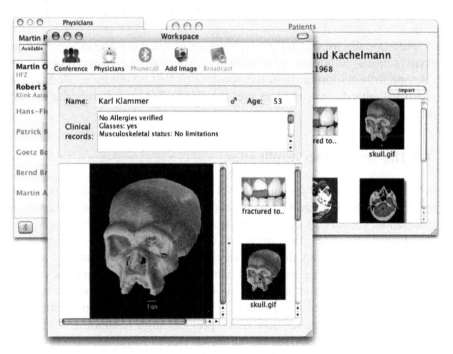

Fig. 8. Screenshot of the Medusa Application. The window in the front shows the representation of Dr. Zeilhofer's ontology after merging it with Dr. Sader's ontology. (Refer to Fig. 1 for the underlying ontologies)

Each physician manages his own ontology (see the example in Fig. 1). The ontologies consist of various types of information units such as image files or medical records. Knowledge is shared in Medusa by publishing a set of information units of a physician's own ontology for other physicians. The published information units are stored in two types of containers named data and key containers. The containers are encrypted symmetrically with AES. The symmetric key itself is encrypted within a key container using asymmetric RSA. The key container is encrypted with the public key of the recipient of the information units. By using two different types of containers data transfer can be reduced: data containers are intended to be accessible by more than one physicians, only one physician accesses the key container.

The communication within the Medusa application is realized in a knowledge network based on a peer-to-peer communication protocol. Each physician runs his own Medusa application, which can act as a knowledge publisher as well as a knowledge consumer. The knowledge publisher peer notifies other knowledge clients when new information units are available. These can then be fetched, decrypted and merged into the ontology of the receiving physician. An example of such a merged ontology is shown in Fig. 1.

Additionally Medusa allows physicians to discuss information units in a synchronous collaboration conference. The participating physicians exchange information units in the con-text of that conference. Medusa uses XMPP/Jabber for notification messages and SOAP to deliver the containers.

6.2 The OntoMedia Application

The OntoMedia application supports the distributed production of feature films. The focus of the implementation is on the integration of various information sources in one virtual working site. The service layer in the framework provides five services: A thumbnail-service, an image sequence-service, a user directory-service, a cutfile-service and an archive-service. Two network protocols - namely the REST web services protocol and a company proprietary active protocol for services that reside behind a firewall – were added to the protocol layer to support the application.

The thumbnail-service lets users preview high-resolution images and movie clips. Together with the cutfile-service (an aggregated service), the application provides functionality to visually manage sets of movie clips without having direct access to a workstation. Another service delivers additional organizational project information for movie clips: it extracts in-

formation such as project membership, sequence names and time codes
from the clip file's path information (Hallama 2006). The user directory-
service provides access to the information of an LDAP directory. A rudimentary version of an archive-service is also available, providing information about archived file tapes in a tape robot.

The services were not implemented at once, but were added to the
framework incrementally in different projects. Each of the services was realized in the same manner: Implementing the service using the service interface of the framework; choosing a communication protocol from the
protocol layer; and generating an OWL-ontology describing the ser-vice's
functionality and the structure of the provided information units.

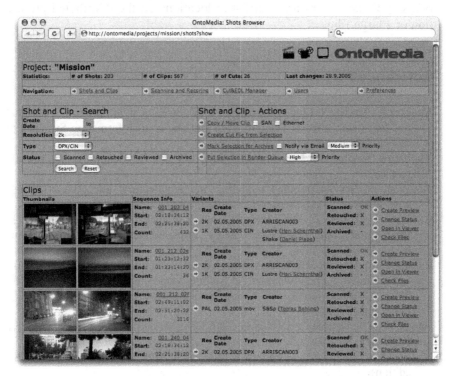

Fig. 9. The screenshot shows a the user interface of a browser for image sequences
in a film project. The different information displayed for an image sequence
(thumbnails, creator's ID, time codes, status etc.) originates from different services. The overlapping ontologies provided by these services are merged in one
ontology used by the framework. In the upper part of the screen shot filtering criteria can be chosen to further narrow down the set of displayed information units.
Hyper links invoke functionality in different services such as "Create Preview" or
"Create CutFile"

7 Conclusion

In this paper we introduced an ontology-based, service-oriented framework for knowledge management in distributed virtual organizations. The key of the framework is a layered architecture combining the concepts of ontologies and services. To decouple knowledge publishers and knowledge consumers, the framework uses mediators and aggregators for the composition of services independent from the network architecture and the availability of individual services.

We demonstrated the use of the framework in two applications supporting the collaboration of mobile surgeons exchanging knowledge about patients and teams working at different locations on the distributed production of a large film.

References

Abecker A, van Elst L (2003) Ontologies for knowledge management. In St. Staab and R. Studer, editors, Handbook on Ontologies in Information Systems, pp 453–474, Springer Verlag, Berlin

Alienbrain Studio, Avid Technology, Inc., http://www.alienbrain.com/products/features

Arsanjani A, Service-oriented modeling and architecture, http://www-128.ibm.com/developerworks/webservices/library/ws-soa-design1/, Nov 2004.

Baader F, Calvanese D, McGuiness DL, Nardi D, Patel-Schneider PF (2003: The Description Logic Handbook: Theory, Implementation, Applications. Cambridge University Press, Cambridge, UK

Bardram JE, Hansen TR (2004) The AWARE Architecture: Supporting Contextmediated Social Awareness in Mobile cooperation. In Proceedings of the 2004 ACM conference on Computer supported cooperative work. ACM Press, pp. 192–201

Berners-Lee T, Hendler J, Lassila O (2001) The semantic web. Scientific American 284(5):34–43

Biezunski M, Bryan M, Newcomb S (2002) ISO/IEC 13250, Topic Maps (2nd edition)

Bonifacio M, Bouquet P, Manzardo A (2000). A distributed intelligence paradigm for knowledge management

Dean M, Schreiber G. (2003) OWL Web Ontology Language Reference. W3C Working Draft. http://www.w3.org/TR/owl-ref/

Dunst M, Adamski M. (2004) Ubiquitäres, mobiles, kooperatives Computersystem zur Unterstützung von Arbeitsprozessen in der Kieferchirurgie. Diploma Thesis, Technische Universität München, Feb. 2004

Fagrell H, Forsberg K, Sanneblad J. (2000) FieldWise: A mobile knowledge man-age-ment architecture. In Proceedings of CSCW 2000. (Philadelphia, Dec. 2–6, 2000), 211–220

Fensel D, v. Harmelen F, Klein M, Akkermans H (2000) On-to-knowledge: On-tology-based tools for knowledge management. In Proceedings of the eBusi-ness and eWork 2000 (EMMSEC 2000) Conference, Madrid, Spain, Oct. 18–20

Fielding R (2000), Architectural Styles and the Design of Network-based Soft-ware Architectures, Dissertation, University of California, Irvine

Gamma E, Helm R, Johnson R, Vlissides J (1996) Design Patterns. Addison-Wesley Publishing Company, New York, 1st edition

Gruber T (1993) A Translation Approach to Portable Ontology Specifications. Knowledge Acquisition, 5(2):199--220

Gruber TR (1993) Towards Principles for the Design of Ontologies Used for Knowledge Sharing, Kluwer Academic Publishers

Hallama P (2006) DIAMOND, Distributed Media and Information Management with Semantic Web Technologies, Diploma Thesis, Technische Universität München, January 2006

Hendler J (2001) Agents and the semantic web. IEEE Intelligent Systems Journal, 16(2):30–37, 2001

Kubale M et al. (2004) Graph Colorings. American Mathematical Society

Maalej W (2005) Domain Independent Generation And Management Of User Queries In Semantic Web Applications, Diploma Thesis, Technische Univer-sität München, October 2005

Nonaka I, Krogh G, Ichijo K (2000) Enabling Knowledge Creation, Oxford University Press, June 2000

OASIS SOA (2005) Reference Model, http://www.oasis-open.org/committees/tc_home.php?wg_abbrev=soa-rm

RDQL - A Query Language for RDF, W3C Member, http://www.w3.org/ Submis-sion /RDQL/, Submission 9 January 2004

SOAP (2003) SOAP Specifications, http://www.w3.org/TR/soap/

SPARQL Query Language for RDF, W3C Working Draft http://www.w3.org/TR/rdf-sparql-query/, 20 February 2006

Technicolor MAM (Media Asset Management), Thomson, http://www.technicolor.com/Cultures/En-Us/Services/PostProduction/MAM.htm

XMPP (2004) Specs, http://www.xmpp.org/specs/

VI Location-based and Ubiquitous Services

Business Potentials of Ubiquitous Computing

Uwe Sandner, Jan Marco Leimeister, Helmut Krcmar

1 Introduction

The term *ubiquitous computing* was coined by Weiser (1991) and focuses on the increasing number of computing devices that are surrounding humans in everyday life. Physical objects, information and processes merge providing economical, social and individual benefits, such as new products, services, and business models, increased security and safety, and higher convenience for consumers. In UbiComp people will no longer be aware of their usage of IT systems since these have "disappeared" and become part of everyday products, so called Smart Devices (e.g. an intelligent fridge ordering automatically goods and services on demand, etc.) Today, UbiComp receives attention under the label Radio Frequency Identification (RFID).

RFID is, first of all, a technology that allows wireless communication and identification building on radio waves between objects. Secondly RFID means a system that includes not only the communication interface but hardware and software components that reach from physical infrastructure to applications, and thirdly, it enables some of the concepts that are necessary for building UbiComp systems. RFID systems allow the automatic data collection caused by real-world events and therefore the automation of many manual data collection activities in and between companies (e.g. real-time monitoring of goods, etc.) The full exploitation of the potentials is by far not yet reached today, the full impact is still to come (Sheffi 2004). Today, automotive, manufacturing, pharmaceuticals, healthcare, and logistics are among the most important industries for RFID usage (Furness 2005; Strassner and Fleisch 2005; Strassner and Fleisch 2002; Fleisch and Dierkes 2003). This chapter gives an overview about potentials and challenges of ubiquitous computing (UbiComp) for business management. The objective is to introduce applications and usage scenarios that might be supported by UbiComp. The analysis starts with a definition of an UbiComp system and its components. Potentials of UbiComp are identified categorized into three major areas: as an identification and information technology, as an enabler for improving processes and decisions in a real-time enterprise, and as a driver for the long-term vision of the "internet of things". For each area challenges and issues are identified. In concluding we highlight aspects managers should consider when thinking about their future IT landscapes and business opportunities.

2 RFID Technology

The basic technology in a RFID system consists of an information and communication technology (hardware) layer including objects, tags, readers, sensors, and actuators, and an information system layer including middleware, applications, and interfaces as software components (Fig. 1).

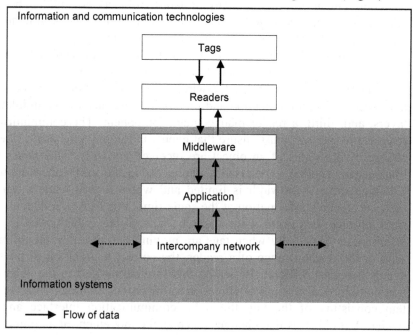

Fig. 1. UbiComp system

An *object* is a physical item, for example a good, a machine, an asset, a resource, a container, a vehicle, a pallet, or a living being, such as an animal or a person, that is equipped with a tag. To identify persons, tags may be attached to an object the person possesses like a garment, a passport, or a key. All objects in the RFID-system covering a specific sector of the "physical world" have a tag.

A *tag* is a piece of hardware attached to an object and able to communicate with a reader. Tags store data and the most important data is a unique ID for the object. They may possess additional storage capacity and interfaces to sensors. Tags are attached to the objects for enabling their automated identification and they come in several flavors which differ in size, price and technical capabilities. Among the most important tag characteristics are the need for power supply (i.e. passive tags need to internal power supply), communication range, capacity of data storage, ability to perform calculations and logic, and interfaces to sensors. To protect the tag from its environment different bodies are used, like glass or plastic coils or the tag is applied on paper or foil or directly printed on the object. The tags communicate with readers on a wireless radio interface. Since the physical characteristics as the materials (metal, fluid) of the object might influence the communication, and in many situations objects are hidden beneath other objects, packed together on pallets or in containers or shielded by other objects, the place of the tag must be selected properly.

A *reader* is a device that communicates on one side with tags, on the other side with a backend system. Readers can be split into several components again. The reader has first, a wireless communication interface to the tags, second, a communication and processing interface to the middleware layers, and, third, a reader management component. The communication interface to the tags must ensure that events in the physical world like the change of the status of an object are received correctly. This raises data transmission challenges, especially in areas where several readers are used. Communication bandwidth is limited and when several readers want to send and receive information at the same time, this causes collisions. The same problem can occur when there are several tags which want to send information. Especially when tags are moving and are only for a limited time in the reading range of a reader, the correct recognition of physical events becomes difficult. Basically, this limitations lead to the phenomenon that physical changes of objects are not recognized properly in the system consisting of the tag, the radio communication interface and the reader. A problem is that changes (such as the movement of an object) are completely missed and not grabbed by the reader. Strategies to alleviate this problem include the coordination between several readers to reduce collision and the prioritization which changes and which objects are most relevant.

The second component of the reader is the interface to the middleware, where raw data events are transformed and transmitted to middleware servers. Some of the functions like prioritization, cleansing, filtering and aggregation can be done in the reader, reducing the amount of data to be communicated to the middleware. This is especially relevant if reader and middleware communicate over channels with limited bandwidth or discontinuous connectivity, for example with mobile readers and mobile communication networks. The reader management component becomes relevant in usage scenarios where there are many devices, for example at a production site. To reduce the effort to administrate and check the reader hardware which might be placed in difficult to reach locations and to ease collaboration between several reader devices. With ongoing technology development, the capabilities of readers will grow and shift more functions from the middleware to the readers.

The *middleware* is a component that performs data processing tasks like aggregation and filtering and makes the raw data from the reader usable by applications. A lot of raw physical events, which are not relevant for any application, are gathered by the reader, so strategies for distributing and forwarding only relevant data are necessary. Data cleansing, filtering and aggregation are also necessary. The middleware also takes part of the management of the infrastructure and should hide problems on the communication layer (Krishna and Husak 2005; Floerkemeier and Lampe 2005).

The *application system* connects the UbiComp applications with other IT systems in an organization, for example for supply chain management and resource planning. It includes functions to support management decisions and to control and monitor processes.

While the application system focuses on the single enterprise, the *inter-company system* connects several organizations across the value chain. The application system also includes infrastructure and services that deal with information exchange, interoperability and directories.

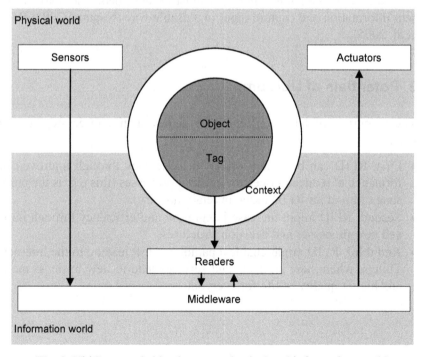

Fig. 2. UbiComp as bridge between physical and information world

Context is information about an object including the unique ID, sensor data, and information gathered or created during the lifetime of the object. Context information may be stored on the tag or by the backend system (Finkenzeller 2002).

A *sensor* is a piece of hardware that is able to gather information about its environment such as position, temperature, pressure, brightness, or moist. Sensors might be placed at the object and communicate directly with tag or might be external source that are connected to the UbiComp system (Dongwon et al. 2005).

An *actuator* is a device that influences its environment physically, for example a machine, a robot, or a display. It might be controlled by an UbiComp system to adapt the environment and process actions for objects.

UbiComp systems bridge the gap between the physical world and the information world, in this case by merging physical world objects with tags (Fig.2). Thus it becomes possible to process automatically an object's context. The middleware does not only provide access to via readers to this artifact, but also to sensors and actuators.

To make information accessible to humans and make the potentials of UbiComp usable for improved convenience, productivity and efficiency, adequate *human-machine interfaces* must be designed. They have to present information and capture input in a usable way (Nagumo 2002; Raskar et al. 2005).

3 Potentials of UbiComp

The potentials of UbiComp could be achieved in a three step roadmap (Fig. 3).

- First, RFID can become a driver for efficiency through improved performance at reduced prices for existing processes (this e.g. is the current state of mind for RFID usage in retail industry).
- Second, RFID might increase integration and efficiency through improved new processes and decision structures.
- And third, RFID might enable a paradigm shift leading to the Internet of Things, where new products and services lead to new business models and higher quality of life for everyone.

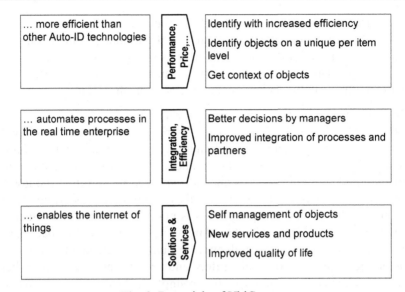

Fig. 3. Potentials of UbiComp

3.1 RFID as Enabler for More Efficient Identification Technology

In this stage RFID serves primarily as identification and information technology. The potentials and benefits of UbiComp lie in more efficient processes (e.g. in automated goods receipts in retail or manufacturing, etc.), with higher performance at cheaper prices. RFID systems combined with optimized processes allow better management of information in companies and organizations and to solve problems and shortcomings of existing processes.

3.1.1 Potentials

Identify with increased efficiency
Since costs for identification are reduced, identification can be used more often and in finer granularity throughout the process chain, where first applications are seen in logistics and supply chain management (Kinsella 2003; Twist 2005). This leads to decreased cost of identification of flows of goods, since UbiComp makes the identification of objects faster, easier and more error prone compared to traditional identification methods as barcodes or labels. Readers do not need a line of sight to the objects, which allows the scanning of objects packed together or stored in containers.

Tags are more resistant against dirt, damage or other environmental influences. Identification can be automated without human interaction and thus human mistakes. Furthermore it is faster since many objects can be recognized at the same time. This can for example be used in logistics, where a large number of objects have to be processed in short time.

Identify unique objects on an item level
Objects are identified not only on a generic class level, but each item has a unique electronic identity. Customers and consumers can be protected against fraud (e.g. by storing the unique identification number and the way of the good through the sales channel) and can be sure that the good they own does not only look like the one they wanted but was originally manufactured by a certain company. This is not only relevant at product piracy in industries with high value brand name items, but also for spare parts and products where a possible reduction in quality or changed technical characteristics can cause damage. Safety and security are increased, when objects are easier to distinguish, for example in health applications, where correct drugs and treatments should be applied to the correct patient, or for homeland security and access control.

Get context of objects
The identification of objects always comes with at least one type of context data: the information that the object was in the proximity of a reader (which has a position) at a certain point of time. This context can be used to make it easier to prevent theft (e.g. by detecting when a good leaves a certain area or by verifying the original owner), to locate items in a warehouse, in production facilities or container management or on promises for logistics. When the identification information is merged with sensor data and these data are stored historically, objects can be traced. Single items of a production series are in many cases difficult to distinguish when they arrive at the customer. When problems are discovered that occurred earlier in the process chain (e.g. hidden defects) it is a complex and expensive task to trace all products and repair the defect. For some items it is also important that an item was not processed in certain locations, by certain persons or organizations because negative influence or the alteration of the item could lead to security of safety problems. When an object can be identified uniquely, this can be used to access information related to this single object and does process items not only based upon a general object class and its general characteristics. In manufacturing and logistics a higher flexibility and granularity can be reached.

3.1.2 Challenges

Reliable hardware level

According to experience reports on current implementations of RFID, the reliability of processes on a hardware layer is a challenge. Defective tags may lead to objects invisible to a system, as limited bandwidth, errors occurring on the air interface between readers and tags, interference by external sources or unfavorable environmental conditions. The 100% prevention of such failures might be impossible or cause significant costs.

Availability & accessibility of information

When information and context is stored in a system which is interconnected by a communication network, an entity which requests data is confronted with problems of availability, consistency and security. Information might be stored at several physical or logical locations and might be replicated to increase efficiency. Directories are necessary to find this storage location and transmission of data must be protected against tampering.

Privacy and access control

In many situations it must be assured that only a limited number of organizations are able to use information stored on the tag (identification) or information connected to the context of an object. This leads to concerns in regard of privacy but also to complex decision who can access information (Data X was collected by organization Y at time T and is stored at Z – who is allowed to access or change this data?) (Ohkubo et al. 2005; Peslak 2005).

Precision and quality of information

Context information coming from sensors and external sources is available in several degrees of precision. Especially for position information the quality of data might be more a probabilistic assumption and not sufficient to support certain applications. Applications must be able to cope with these diffuse data and be able to use other technologies where necessary.

Standards

Since hardware such as readers and tags come from different manufacturers, there should be standards to hide specialties of single implementations. This abstraction (e.g. of hardware types, communication protocols, data exchange formats) must not only cover technical details but also include standards to exchange information about context, its representation, and logic to control and manage hardware.

3.2 RFID as Enabler for the Real-time Enterprise

UbiComp might enable managers and organizations to make faster and better decision and to better plan and control processes. This is the core of the vision of the the Real-Time Enterprise (RTE), a vision coined by Gartner Research and others. The fundamentally idea is that an enterprise can gather real-time information, allowing it to change its operational characteristics dynamically in response to changing external parameters and to generate new sources of revenue, avoid unnecessary business expenses and significantly improve business processes (Neil and Clark 2003). In a RTE managers can use the information about identification and context to manage their enterprises in real time and use resources more efficiently. On the other hand, control can be moved down from a central Enterprise Resource Planning system to the location much closer to the processes and questions involved, leading to new problem solving strategies.

3.2.1 Potentials

Better decisions by managers
UbiComp provides managers and consumers with more information and leverages better, more efficient and faster decisions (Smith and Mckeen 2005). The abundance of information does not come for free, since the representation and processing of data must be in a format that does not overstrain human abilities. Decisions must be supported in a proper way and the interface to users must be appropriate. For some items the process of the identification of the item and the provisioning of connected information (handling instructions, details about characteristics) is complex from a process view including human interaction. These processes can be simplified, for example in a shop floor environment where consumers receive details about a product or in a manufacturing process where workers receive handling instructions.

Improved integration of processes and partners
UbiComp can improve the integration of processes and partners in enterprises by providing better and more detailed information about the status of goods in the supply and the production chain (Van Nunen and Zuidwijk 2004; Krikke et al. 2004). Management can react faster to challenges and changing internal and external requirements which allows providing additional value to customers and taking market changes into account. For outbound logistics and after sales services higher service levels can be reached and sold.

3.2.2 Challenges

Information retrieval

More information does not automatically lead to better decisions when the excess of data is not analyzed and aggregated in a way managers can understand and use. This challenge has been addressed for more than two decades in the context of management information systems (MIS) and many challenges (e.g. as to adequate task-technology fit of such MIS or information retrieval needs of managers, etc.) have to be taken into consideration. The design of human-machine interfaces and the representation of relevant information is a challenge that must be solved before UbiComp can leverage all potentials.

Middleware and applications

The middleware in UbiComp systems is a key component to connect to hardware from several manufacturers and information systems in companies. Due to the diversity of existing products and legacy systems already in place the flexibility and ability to integrate those solutions is critical. Application systems must not only be able to analyze and monitor the surplus of information made available by UbiComp, but also support control structure and processes. Furthermore, the amount of generated data increases which presents challenges to the communication and information system infrastructure. Necessary up front investments to make middleware and applications available have to be weighted out against benefits.

3.3 RFID as Enabler for the Internet of Things

UbiComp can not only lead to more distributed processes in companies, but also allows a stronger interconnection of organizations in the value chain: From manufacturers, suppliers, retailers, service providers, up to customers and consumers. Companies can keep an information link to every physical object they processed, shipped, manufactured or used at any time which allows new business models shifting the focus from the single specific step in the value chain to a more holistic view where solutions and services become more prominent (Fleisch 2001).

3.3.1 Potentials

Self management of objects

The vision of the internet of things, where every item as simple as a light bulb (Gershenfeld et al. 2004) is connected to the internet, leads to the question which form of problem solving (centralized vs. distributed) and control (company centric vs. holistic) does provide benefits for certain tasks and physical goods and how business models can realize these benefits. Processes are not planned centrally, but autonomous, decentralized "smart" units solve problems on their own. The shift of problem solving from a central location to multiple single processes is also an area of research in other fields, like organic computing.

Items can report information about themselves (identification), their status and their environment with the help of sensors, be able to communicate with other objects, possess computational power to process data, and influence their surrounding with actuators. Given that many objects are smart they form a swarm which leads to a distributed, decentralized system. In an enterprise context, this idea can be broken down into the vision of the virtual enterprise where all resources (people, goods, products, assets) and their related processes are monitored and controlled in real time.

This changes the location where information is stored and processed and where processes are changed. When a machine in the production line is recognized to cause problems or stops working, an alternative production setup can be discovered by objects and they can "decide" to use an alternative machine for the next step. Objects can use actuators to adapt their environment so it fits their needs, leading to self-healing processes.

New services and business models

Ubicomp enables companies to keep a connection to the products and goods manufactured or processed through the whole product lifecycle, even when the object is located at the premises of the customer. This allows completely new services and business models where solutions become more important. Not only do physical characteristics of a product define the benefit it delivers, but also connected and surrounding services. Furthermore, different pricing and billing models are possible, from price discrimination based on more information on customers to billing on a per-usage base. Processes can be divided in more granular and individual steps, leading to finer measurement of the value contribution of single players and virtual organization forms (Banavar et al. 2005).

Improved quality of life

Although UbiComp is seen as a threat for privacy, it has the potentials to improve the quality of life for everyone. As a consumer, people receive more information about products leading to higher safety and security, for example in areas such as food or drugs. In health and emergency response applications, faster response times and fewer mistakes become feasible. The usage in homeland security plays an important role in countries that face the danger of terrorist attacks. This sector is becoming a major driver for research & development on UbiComp technologies.

3.3.2 Challenges

Standards
If the potentials of UbiComp should be exploited fully, an application must not only focus on single organizations but should be able to span across the whole value chain and integrate multiple players along the value chain such as suppliers and retailers. This needs first common standards and data exchange structures to allow sharing identification, information, and context about objects, but also interfaces to connect processes and decisions. Different solution providers and manufacturers as well on the information and communication technology layer as on the information systems need to make their solutions able to communicate with each other.

Global infrastructure
To allow the interconnection of enterprises and their UbiComp applications there is a need for a technical infrastructure that enables these interconnections. Similar structures are already present in the World Wide Web, for example the domain name service. Also, the organizational aspects of these structures (operation of the infrastructure, management of unique IDs, certification of players) have to be discussed, where for example EPCGlobal could play an important role.

Acceptance and Privacy
UbiComp provides vast opportunities for consumers, but also faces challenges in regard to privacy. Companies, lobbyists and governments have to inform and educate the public (Eckfeldt 2005; Günther and Spiekermann 2005) and inform about risks and privacy issues. At the same time, technical solutions must be found to allow people to control their privacy, to identify UbiComp technology in products they buy or use.

Intelligent objects
When objects should sense their environment, plan ahead, interact with other objects and decide, algorithms are requires which give objects these capabilities and intelligence. Research fields like organic computing, semantic modeling, swarm intelligence and agents can give important input to solve these problems (Brock et al. 2005; Bodendorf and Zimmermann 2005).

4 Outlook

UbiComp provides vast benefits in several areas, from replacing current identification technologies to having large impact on society and economy.

In a first step, it can become an efficiency driver for optimizing existing processes and realize cost benefits. Afterwards it will allow rebuilding and automating processes to a higher degree than today by giving management the tools to decide better and faster. At the same time, control over processes will move from central application systems to the locus where problems arise and enable smart objects to shape their environment. Enterprises can integrate internal and external steps of the value chain to a larger extend, making economy more effective. With the help of a global infrastructure, the internet of things might have huge impact on economy and provide individual benefits to everyone.

But there are also challenges and risks from technical problems on the hardware layer, question on the algorithms of intelligence for objects, up to privacy issues in the social and legal framework. Standards and the question of integrating existing systems to make the vision possible also need further research.

Companies should keep in mind that the importance of RFID as a core technology of UbiComp is already rising, and cannot be ignored for much longer. It will not only be about replacing barcode, but will affect a lot more processes, products or services. They also should be well aware of the fact that RFID usage is not only a thing of their own choice, but can also be declared necessary or even compulsory on the part of business partners, as happened in the cases of Wal-Mart and Metro. It is therefore essential to keep watch of the RFID activities of close neighbours in the supply chain. Companies are well advised to concretize and substantiate their RFID visions in order to know their needs and possibilities and to develop an action plan they can refer to.

References

Banavar G, Black J, Cáceres R, Ebling M, Stern E, Kannry J (2005) Driving Long-term Value from Context-aware Computing. Information Systems Management, 22, 32-42

Bodendorf F, Zimmermann R (2005) Proactive Supply-Chain Event Management with Agent Technology. International Journal of Electronic Commerce, 9, 57-89

Brock DL, Schuster EW, Allen SJ, Kar P (2005) An Introduction to Semantic Modeling for Logistical Systems. Journal of Business Logistics, 26, 97-117

Dongwon J, Young-Gab K, Hoh I (2005) New RFID System Architectures Supporting Situation Awareness under Ubiquitous Environments. Journal of Computer Science, 1, 114-120

Eckfeldt B (2005) What Does RFID Do for the Consumer? Communications of the ACM, 48, 77-79

Finkenzeller K (2002) RFID-Handbuch, München, Wien, Carl Hanser Verlag

Fleisch E (2001) Business perspectives on Ubiquitous Computing

Fleisch E, Dierkes M (2003) Ubiquitous Computing aus betriebswirtschaftlicher Sicht. Wirtschaftsinformatik, 45, 611-620

Floerkemeier C, Lampe M (2005) RFID middleware design: addressing application requirements and RFID constraints. Proceedings of the 2005 joint conference on Smart objects and ambient intelligence. Grenoble, France, ACM Press

Furness V (2005) The RFID Market Outlook - New applications, best practices and future profit opportunities. Business Insights

Gershenfeld N, Krikorian R, Cohen D (2004) The Internet of Things. Scientific American, 291, 76

Günther O, Spiekermann S (2005) RFID and the Perception of Control: The Consumers View. Communications of the ACM, 48, 73-76

Kinsella B (2003) THE Wal-Mart FACTOR. Industrial Engineer: IE. Institute of Industrial Engineers

Krikke H, le Blanc I, van de Velde S (2004) Product Modularity and the Design of Closed-Loop Supply Chains. California Management Review, 46, 23-39

Krishna P, Husak D (2005) Simple Lightweight RFID Reader Protocol.

Nagumo T (2002) Innovative Business Models in the Era of Ubiquitous Networks. NRI Papers. Nomura Research Institute

Neil D, Clark W (2003) The Real-Time Enterprise and the Network. Gartner

Ohkubo M, Suzuki K, Kinoshita S (2005) RFID Privacy Issues and Technical Challenges. Communications of the ACM, 48, 66-71

Peslak AR (2005) An Ethical Exploration of Privacy and Radio Frequency Identification. Journal of Business Ethics, 59, 327-345

Raskar R, Beardsley P, Dietz P, van Baar J (2005) Photosensing Wireless Tags for Geometric Procedures. Communications of the ACM, 48, 46-51

Sheffi Y (2004) RFID and the Innovation Cycle. International Journal of Logistics Management. International Logistics Research Institute

Smith HA, McKeen JD (2005) Developments in Practice XV: Information Delivery: IT´s Evolving Role. Communications of AIS, 2005, 197-210

Strasser M, Fleisch E (2005) Innovationspotenzial von RFID für das Supply-Chain-Management. Wirtschaftsinformatik, 47, 45-54

Strassner M, Fleisch E (2002) Segment Evaluation Automotive - Applications of RFID Technology.

Twist DC (2005) The impact of radio frequency identification on supply chain facilities. Journal of Facilities Management, 3, 226-239

van Nunen JAEE, Zuidwijk RA (2004) E-Enabled Closed-Loop Supply Chains. California Management Review, 46, 40-54

Weiser M (1991) The Computer for the 21st Century. Scientific American, 265, 94

A Novel Approach to Ubiquitous Location-Based Service Architectures Using Mobile Communities

Maximilian Zuendt, Peter Dornbusch

1 Introduction

There are many different Location-Based Services (LBS) solutions available on the market today. Despite of their diverse nature, underlying location platforms (LP) with respective supporting positioning technologies have similar approaches on providing the best possible location information on entities such as people or other target objects such buildings, parcels etc. Although many solutions exist, currently no LBS solution is capable of covering all usage environments. Each positioning source, be it indoors or outdoors needs a location server and geographic information entity in order to make use of the location information in its designated usage environment. GPS and the future Galileo satellite positioning systems will be able to provide a good global coverage providing location information, yet certain weather conditions, urban canyons, inner-cities or indoor building conditions will still set limitations there (Eissfeller et al. 2005). The abundance and almost ubiquitous coverage of heterogeneous wireless networks in our daily living environment (e.g. GSM/UMTS, WLAN or Bluetooth networks especially for indoors) and positioning systems realized using them (Dornbusch and Huber 2003; Connelly et al.; Wong et al. 2005) will hence be a key component for future ubiquitous location information access.

This "multi-facetted" wireless provider and technology landscape, as well as lack of standardisation for inter-working and "easy access" to this heterogeneous technology information necessary for location determination systems, makes it difficult to effectively "capture" the potential diversity and distributed nature of positioning systems for ubiquitous, homogeneous location-information provisioning for LBS. Furthermore, there is a continuous evolution especially in the case of short range wireless networks (e.g. WLAN, Bluetooth) in our daily living environment, hence making it even more difficult to provide a reliable and up-to-date positioning system based on such technologies.

As a result, due to the slow evolvement towards 4G architectures for seamless heterogeneous network inter-working, a paradigm shift has evolved towards autonomous, multimode mobile clients being able to discover potential access networks by themselves. Extending on this principle, such "mobile sensors" can even collect certain wireless data for maintenance and site-mapping purposes, or even distribute local information such as accidents, weather warnings or other events to potential user communities via centralized knowledge databases (Zhang et al. 2005). Based on such principles, community-, operator independent- or often called "open-oasis"-based approaches to next-generation network design and service provisioning platforms provide a potential competitive alternative solution (Dornbusch and Huber; Zuendt et al. 2003).

In this book chapter, we will introduce a novel approach to ubiquitous LBS provisioning architectures based on such community-based principles. We believe that community-platform approaches are very capable of handling and capturing the location information derived from heterogeneous wireless networks and mobile operators, using mobile devices as sensors in the environment for automated, as well as additional manual user collaborative location information generation.

The remainder of this chapter will talk about the following: We will start by giving a generic LP architecture model similar to all common LBS solutions. Example mobile operator (centralized) and client-based (decentralized) LP approaches will be briefly presented followed by a general discussion on the advantages and disadvantages involved in each case. Introducing mobile communities and collaborative value generation aspects, we will then show how these concepts can be used for location information generation and provisioning effectively. Having established the foundations of our approach, we will present a distributed community-based location service architecture using heterogeneous positioning systems as well as multiple inter-working location server and geo-information databases for specific usage environments. We will end up by introducing a seamless location-based service navigation prototype as a proof of concept for our architecture approach.

2 The LBS Environment and Aspects Involved with Location Information Provisioning

In order to understand the LBS environment, we will discuss the issues involved with generating and providing location information for application service providers from potential targets such as users or other objects more closely. We will start by giving a definition on LBS types and frameworks for location provisioning. Following examples of current LBS solutions, we will discuss the advantages and disadvantages involved with centralized and/or decentralized location information provisioning, concluding with a potential "silver bullet" approach.

2.1 LBS Classifications and a Generic Definition of a Location Platform

The key idea behind LBS is to use the user's current physical position information as a "filter" for delivering localized services and/or information relevant to a certain area related to his position. The kinds of services offered can be classified into two main types (3GPP 2004) as illustrated in Fig. 1(a): Services which are triggered by an application service provider when a user arrives or enters a certain geographic location e.g. push advertisements in a shopping mall or localized weather warnings, are classified as type 1 services (also called "push" or "triggered services"). Services which are typically information services requested by a user from an application service provider e.g. finding nearby restaurant/gas-stations or navigation services, are classified as type 2 LBS (so called "user-requested" or "pull services").

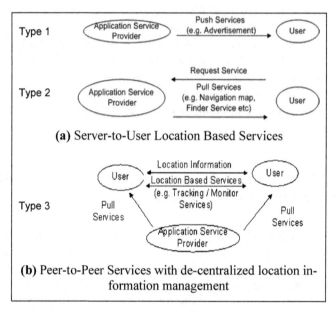

Fig. 1. Location-based service classifications

The two types illustrated in Fig. 1(a) are server-to-user LBS where location information is managed by central location server (OMA 2004) i.e. a centralized LP approach as followed by mobile operators primarily. Access to location information i.e. to 3rd party application providers, is only being made available through mobile operator network entities in this case. A third type of peer-to-peer LBS (Fig. 1b) represents a different approach to type 1 and 2 LBS, in that location information is directly exchanged by communicating peers, but LBS can be still provided by a 3rd party. This de-centralized location information provisioning approach has considerable advantages concerning privacy and user control over location information (Zuendt et al. 2005).

Stand-alone solutions such as in-car- or mobile PDA-based navigation using GPS and static geo-information data stored locally on the device for outdoor navigation can be seen as a decentralized LP approach. Furthermore, dynamic information such as traffic-conditions can be made available via radio broadcast or other communication channels. The issue of (de-)centralized location information provisioning and associated research approaches will be discussed in later sections of this chapter in more detail.

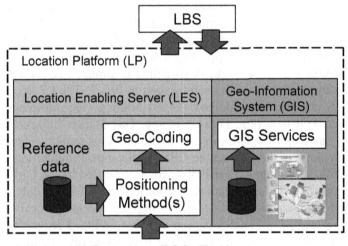

Fig. 2. A generic LP model

LPs enabling any kind of LBS all share a common structure as depicted in Fig. 2. The main difference in LPs is how location information is generated from respective positioning systems (i.e. from device, network or both) as well as how additional location content is provided (e.g. map data, navigation functions, Point Of Interest, POI data etc.). The LP itself can be broken down into two major components: a Geo-Information System (GIS) holding appropriate map and point-of-interest (POI) data, and a Location Enabling Server (LES) providing the location information of a positioned target in some meaningful format for the GIS system. The LES generates appropriate location information in the following way: a network identifier, timing or received signal strength information is received from a senor or communication interface. A positioning method is performed using this information and some pre-recorded reference values, generating some form of difference value (error estimation) which then can be transformed to meaningful location information using a respective geo-coding function. The GIS system can provide additional basic services such as routing, navigation and find_nearest_POI functions.

2.2 Current Location Platform Solutions

Mobile operator LBS are improving as better end-devices with higher usability as well as more cost effective and accurate positioning technologies become available (e.g. Assisted GPS, A-GPS), but regulatory and privacy issues hinder an efficient global deployment, as we will talk about later.

For current mobile operator networks, the Open Mobile Alliance (OMA) standardisation group provides a LP framework providing the functionalities required supporting LBS via standardised interfaces from the operator's core network. A so called centralized LP approach implemented by mobile operators can be seen in Fig. 3. The LP is comprised of the LES and the Geo-Toolbox (GTB) holding Geo-information such as Map and POI data (e.g. Hotel, Cinema, Gas Station Information etc.) as well as basic services as explained in the previous section. These functions are provided via the LES to the LBS Application Provider via a standardized XML API using the MLP protocol as specified by the OMA, formerly known as the LiF consortium (LiF 2002). This API is the only interface to the LBS Application Provider providing the necessary location information. The position estimates as seen in step 4. in Fig. 3 are performed in the access network by the corresponding network entity[1], handset[2] or hybrid positioning method (e.g. A-GPS), then forwarded back to the LP via the GMLC *Le* interface.

One of the additional primary tasks of the LES is to perform privacy and access control including temporary storage of user data, provide configurable user privacy profiles for each subscriber and handle access rights quotas of external application providers. As a user privacy database is maintained, privacy-enabled location-based services can be provided without impact to the mobile operator HLR. Last but not least, it also supports LBS roaming and production of appropriate LBS billing records.

---

[1] e.g. Time (Difference) Of Arrival (TOA, TDOA) positioning methods
[2] e.g. Enhanced Observed Time Difference (EOTD) positioning method

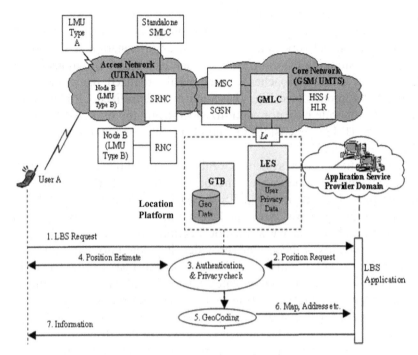

Fig. 3. A LP implemented by mobile operators

The Secure User Plane Location (SUPL) framework has now been specified by the OMA (OMA 2004), ensuring better user location information privacy and security, as well as location information control from various location sources with no impact to the core network infrastructure. Currently released solutions[3] focus on advanced mobile-network (WCDMA and GSM) as well as -positioning support (enhanced cell ID and A-GPS).

The mentioned network and handset-based positioning methods use available radio resource management information supporting service and mobility in access networks. The simplest mean to determine a mobile device position is via the Cell ID[4] of the base station in the access network the user is currently booked into and being served from. This positioning method is common and virtually supported by every mobile device attached to a wireless network (e.g. GSM, WLAN etc.) being the most lucrative approach for community-based positioning approaches.

Thus, another LP approach found quite commonly apart from the well known stand-alone solutions as previously mentioned is a device-centric

---

[3] The Nokia iGMLC 4.0 platform, http://www.nokia.com
[4] Cell Of Origin (COO) positioning method

middleware or decentralized LP approach, also often called an operator-independent positioning solution (Dornbusch and Huber 2003). Here, communication network data or GPS sensor information is directly provided for positioning from the mobile client to the LBS or requesting peer. Peer-to-Peer LBS approaches can be easily realized using the device-centric LP approach (see Fig. 1b). Such a decentralized LP can even co-exist with a mobile operator centralized LP using the future IP Multimedia Subsystem (IMS) extension in future mobile operator core networks (Zuendt et al. 2005).

The Location-Trader system (Dornbusch and Huber 2003) is based on the device-centric middleware concept providing an operator-independent decentralized LP, supporting GPS, GSM Cell ID, and WLAN hotspot-based positioning. It was developed from a mobile community background (e.g., www.nobbi.com, www.hotspot-locations.com), where each member of the community collects and provides location information for other members in the community as well as potential 3rd party providers of location-based services. The accumulated interaction of each user of the community allows for the generation of location information (GSM Cell IDs with GPS coordinates, street names, points of interest e.g., hotels, events etc.) in the Location Trader database. We will further discuss the Location Trader[5] concept and its efficient use of mobile community generated location information later on in this chapter. This will then provide the basis for our novel distributed community-based location service architecture approach.

2.3 Comparison of Centralized and De-Centralized Location Information Provisioning

Current mobile operators prefer centralized LP approach for 3rd Party application service providers. The most common and readily available positioning method in mobile operator networks uses the base station Cell ID where a user is currently booked into. This method however is not very accurate since its accuracy depends on the base station service area (cell size) which can range from a few hundred meters to several kilometers. The more accurate positioning methods such as EOTD/OTDOA, TOA or AOA are not implemented in current mobile networks due to the high upgrade costs (hardware and software) in the access network and mobile devices. Instead, mobile operators plan to roll-out the new hybrid A-GPS standard which can provide high positioning accuracy within a few meters, having

---

[5] See also http://www.getlocal.de

little impact on the existing access network infrastructure as well as low mobile device integration costs. As it is the case with standard GPS (without the initialization problems), location information is generated at the mobile device, but only capable of being accessed from the mobile network (Hulls 2004). Hence control over the user's location information, thus user privacy control remains on the operator's side.

The mobile operator's intend is to keep control over location information access, thus being able to generate revenue from LBS. Privacy control is implemented by querying the mobile user whether he wants to let himself be positioned before he can carry out the LBS. This legally upholds the user's privacy rights, but does not give any indication to which 3rd party this location information is handed to.

Mobile operators with their LPs and proprietary location information are, by nature, limited to their own networks and can only serve their own mobile customers – who have agreed to be tracked – with LBS, unless roaming mobile users from other operators are willing to pay higher rates to receive those services. Furthermore, the LP is bound to the positioning capabilities available within its network, therefore resulting in restricted availability and accuracy (poor performance of GSM Cell ID, A-GPS mainly outdoors).

A decentralized LP can always offer the best possible positioning information, since it works independently in heterogeneous network environments – clearly its strongest feature. The mobile user always "knows best" about his current physical position, hence satellite- (e.g. GPS, A-GPS) (Eissfeller et al. 2005), indoor- (e.g. WLAN) (Wong et al. 2005) and short-range- (e.g. RFID, IrDA, Bluetooth) based positioning systems can currently deliver the best possible and most up-to-date positioning accuracy as the positioning information here is actually generated at the mobile device. The downside of this approach is that each time a location update is needed, the mobile device has to be queried and the location information returned to the requesting peer through the currently available communication network. Using GPRS or UMTS for data communication can be quite costly, although flat-rate data fees are dropping steadily. In the mobile operator centralized LP case, the signaling stays within the mobile operator's core network resulting in less signaling overhead and minimal user-incurred costs.

The positioning currently provided by the mobile operator LP solutions do not require special modifications on the client, hence being future-proof and capable of supporting legacy mobile devices. The decentralized LP middleware would require a software client to be adapted to each new mobile client system. This again could also have an effect on increase mobile device power consumption.

Last but not least, privacy is a two-fold issue: The mobile user should be able to control his privacy and whether or not he wants to be localized. Location information is provided only to a (trusted) known requesting peer or application service provider of the user's choice, thus offering him full control over his location information and hence over his privacy. A decentralized system where location information is directly exchanged and completely controlled by participating peers increases user awareness and trust for LBS (Zuendt et al. 2005). On the other hand, a mobile operator should be more trustworthy compared to a mobile community-controlled environment. Especially in the case of the previously mentioned Location Trader system (Dornbusch and Huber 2003), there also needs to be a critical mass of users, generating "reliable" location and GIS information in the community databases, whereas the mobile operator with his LES system does not need to worry about that. For a community-based LP system to be a competitive alternative solution in the market, the issue on location privacy, security and reliability needs to be taken very seriously.

Due to the distributed nature of location information, the ideal solution is clearly a combination of both centralized and decentralized LP approaches. The multitude of different technologies – GSM, UMTS, WLAN, GPS, and A-GPS – on the user side and on the network side requires a standardized, open platform to generate, store, and provide location information.

For such a system to be successful and widely accepted, a standardized generic interface is required, enabling location-based service providers to access location and GIS information without knowing the specific positioning technology-related features.

Scalability is another important issue. There needs to be an interworking between globally available and localized positioning systems, as well as corresponding GIS databases (Zuendt et al. 2004). The interworking between outdoor- and indoor-based positioning systems is essential, since the potential technologies readily available in indoor environments (e.g., WLAN, IrDA, Bluetooth, RFID or even Ultra Wide Band) clearly have the edge over their outdoor-focused counterparts, such as GPS or GSM/UMTS-based systems. This is due to their smaller service/radio coverage allowing for more accurate positioning (in some cases, less than one meter). The most dominant and widely spread technology here is the Wireless LAN IEEE802.11x standard. Positioning systems based on RSS calculations can provide accuracies of up to 1-5 meters, however they require an extensive training (and potentially re-training) period depending on the size, complexity and dynamics of the indoor environment (Zuendt et al. 2004). Since WLAN is very common in well-equipped buildings such as offices, airports or shopping malls, this is still the most competitive indoor-navigation and positioning solution.

An essential but difficult-to-achieve feature will be the possibility of combining multiple positioning sources to allow for the required positioning accuracy. There are several projects dealing with the "sensor fusion" aspect of such systems using probability calculations, one of them being the "Location Stack" (Hightower 2003) project at the University of Washington.

3 Using Mobile Communities for Location Information Generation

In this section we introduce a community based approach to initialize a location database, which has first been introduced in (Dornbusch and Huber 2003). The presented results have been mainly taken from the Location-Trader project. In a novel approach the Location Trader system aims to collect location data by users and help to establish a generic positioning platform that fosters the development of innovative and diverse location-based services.

In the following we use the Location Trader system as a case study for general location collecting platforms. As mentioned earlier in the chapter, this introduces an interesting way for network based positing system where in the beginning most of the location data is missing (e.g. location systems for WLAN networks). Form an economic point of view these concepts are strongly related to the topic of unintended value co production.

A location data pool (e.g. a new hot spot location system) will not contain a lot of information at the time the service is launched. Therefore it has to be assured that the location data pool is constantly enriched to further attract additional users and to improve the quality of service. The task of filling and updating the data basis can be managed in a cost efficient way by initiating an "open source" like user community that supports the systems (Lerner and Tirole 2000).

At the time of the service kick off, only a very small user community is interested to use the service. These initial users are curious about the service and may support it by adding new user positioning information to the location data pool. As the database is getting larger and more accurate, the Location Trader service will also become more interesting for a broader user community and attract additional service providers. This implies that our concept has a strong tipping behavior as it is driven by network externalities. The "tendency of one system to pull away from its rivals in popularity once it has gained an initial edge" is described in more detail by Katz and Shapiro (Katz and Shapiro, 1992).

A simulation of the evolution of usage patterns is shown in Fig. 4. The x-axis represents the time after a community location system has been launched. The y-axis represents the probability for each of the three possible ways of usage of the patterns. The three usage probabilities do always sum up to 100%. This figure is now explained in detail.

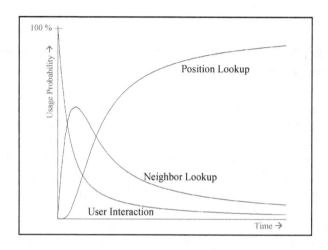

Fig. 4. Service usage evolution

3.1 User Interaction Evolution

When the service is launched the location data pool is assumed to contain only very little data nodes. So users are in most cases forced to add user positioning data by themselves. This user information is stored in the location data pool to increase the quality and accuracy of future service requests. This pattern is called user interaction. Over the time, the probability of this usage pattern decreases to a low value as other ways of usage gain dominance.

3.1.1 Neighbor Lookup Evolution

The neighbor lookup curve depicts a usage pattern where the actual positioning information is unknown, but can be interpolated using historic network node data and adjacent network node information. The adjacent nodes table is empty at the service kick off time, so there is a zero possibility of the neighbor lookup pattern at this time. After a while, when a certain amount of information is stored in the location data pool, the neighbor lookup is getting more and more important. Positioning information for the current network node may not be available, but there is an increasing possibility to have positioning information available for one of the adjacent network nodes. This neighbor information is used to calculate the current user position. The pattern will reach a peak and decrease after some time, as the probability of positioning requests served with the even more accurate position lookup pattern will dominate over the time.

3.1.2 Position Lookup Evolution

The position lookup curve itself shows a clear tipping behavior. The location data pool is empty in the beginning, so this usage pattern is not very effective at that time. As more and more information is stored and critical mass is reached, the probability of this pattern rises increasingly. After some time, most requests will be served by the position lookup pattern.

3.1.3 Success Factors

First of all, it is important to understand the economic principle of such a system: the key concept here is the interaction and cooperation of users within a user content network. Most of the positioning data is originally provided by the users themselves. Therefore the service user is a member of the systems user content network who contributes to the service in the context of her own service request.

We now have a look at the concepts of value co-production and customer integration in the context of the system. Our solution integrates the user into the entire process of value creation and usage. The Location Trader system is an illustrative example of value co-production and customer integration. Although the system is able to perform some heuristics to produce positioning information even without accurate location pool data, at least in the initial phase a large part of the positioning information has to be provided by the user. It is possible to enter user location information into a special user interaction form inside special client application.

To sum all this up in a economical sense: every user has two roles in the Location Trader system, first as a producer of incremental, small content parts, second as a consumer of the public good that was produced by the entire community. Besides to the intended value creation by users, there is even non-intended value creation within the Location Trader system (Huber 2004). The bivalent process of usage and built-in self-improvement is beneficial for both user and Location Trader service. The user benefits by the service as he uses the service intentionally and therefore gains a positive value. Additionally, a co-produced value from user interaction is realized by the Location Trader system. This value is tangible in a steadily improved location data pool, which is enriched by the automatically generated list of adjacent network nodes. It is an example for non-intended value creation by variation within the Location Trader system.

Co-creation in the case of Location Trader is enabled by cellular communications technology and the Internet in connection with the fact that the created value is immaterial information which can be transmitted and processed very cost-efficiently using these technologies.

Analyzing this value creation constellation from an implementation point of view suggests considering the following *risks*: Privacy concerns of service users may prevent them from contributing to the system. When they feed the data pool with location information they effectively disclose their current location. As they are requesting a location-based service this is actually required and will be plausible to them. However, as the system stores this information in the data pool, service users may be concerned that this information is used to track or trace back their movements. It needs to be credibly assured that the information they contribute is stored anonymously and therefore cannot be associated with their identity at any point of time.

Legal risks play a minor role in the co-creation process of Location Trader as the contribution process is well defined and the contributed information is always mere location information. However, it has to be ensured that intellectual property issues are considered.

Crucial for motivating users to contribute is to minimize the effort of contribution: Contribution in the case of the Location Trader co-creation process is a very structured and invariable task that can be highly automated. As most users are naturally used to disclosing their current location when requesting a location-based service they do not even perceive an additional effort. In fact, each user's average effort is reduced as contributions do not have to be made every time, but will automatically be reused in the future. There is a greater effort on the side of the positioning service to enable the co-creation of value through service users, but this effort has to be accepted as it constitutes the core of the whole concept.

Interrelated with these two challenges is the issue of equity of returns. The return to each service user for the disclosure of their current location is the provision with a location-based service. It has to be ensured that the value of these services is perceived equitable to effort by each service user.

Applying *best practices* of value co-creation to the Location Trader concept yields the following insights:

The objective of co-creation in the case of Location Trader is clearly defined: Service users disclose their current location so that the positioning platform can associate this location with the user's current positioning in a cellular network and can reuse this information in the future for positioning services. So co-creation takes place at the production stage. It also takes place at the maintenance stage once there is sufficient data available and further contribution are just used to refined the data pool and keep it up to date.

The channel that the positioning service can use to monitor and control user contributions is the list of incoming locations. They should be checked for plausibility before they are added to the core data pool.

Service users need to be enabled to contribute by providing them with the required Location Trader Client Applications and by making the contribution process as easy and self-explanatory as possible.

The users' incentives to contribute need to be explicitly communicated and managed. There is the immediate incentive of being provided with a location-based service that otherwise would not be available. However, there are also more indirect incentives such as the idea of the Location Trader platform as an independent, open source-like data pool where contributors can identify themselves with this vision. A competitive and signaling incentive can be created by allowing the association of a particular network cell with the nickname of the user who first "discovered" and contributed the cell to the data pool. Other incentives can be thought of.

An important aspect of value co-creation in the case of Location Trader is that it takes place automatically and not necessarily intentionally: The basic co-creation process is automated and users need to be involved only if their current location is not known to the system yet. Only then they become aware that they need to submit information in order to be provided with a location-based service. However, they are not necessarily aware that this information will also be reused at a later stage and therefore they are not aware that they are actually co-creating value. This kind of integration is denoted as *variation* as it is non-intended, non-creative and non-innovative.

3.2 Quantitative Computer Simulation of Value Co-Production with the Location Trader

In addition to the theoretical and qualitative analysis of the Location Trader system in the previous section, this section presents a more quantitative analysis based on a computer simulation as a second approach to understanding the system's mechanics.

The simulation models the service usage behavior of a certain number of Location Trader users within a certain area and over a certain period of time. It takes into account several factors such as contribution of locations, individual satisfaction and completeness of the data pool. By varying initial settings and comparing the effects on the resulting simulations, the importance of particular factors is determined.

It is important to bear in mind that all conclusions are based on an idealized model of the real world and cannot be taken for granted. Nevertheless they can help to identify general interdependencies and trends. Furthermore the simulation should serve as an interactive model for playing around and experimenting.

3.2.1 The Model

The model of the Location Trader system assumes a certain number of users in a certain quadratic area. This area is partitioned in equal-sized squares where each square represents an idealized network cell in a cellular network. Every user is unambiguously located within one of these network cells, however, as in real life one cell can accommodate several users.

Each user in the model has the properties requests, contributions, satisfaction and frustrations. *Requests* counts for each user how frequently the user requested a services. *Contributions* represents the number of locations that the user contributed to the data pool. *Satisfaction* measures the satisfaction of each user by incrementing the current value each time the user requested a service and was automatically provided with the service without the need of contribution. *Frustrations*, on the contrary, counts the situations when a user requested a service and had to provide the current location manually.

Each cell has the property *locations* which counts how many locations have been mapped to the cell's cell ID. If a cell is mapped to at least one location the model assumes that a service request in this cell can be satisfied.

In addition, it can be set how many more frustrations than satisfactions a user can stand before abandoning the system (*discouragement threshold*). The *recruitment threshold* determines how many more satisfactions than frustrations a user has to experience in order to start recruiting new users. The probability of a successful recruitment can be set, too.

Finally, it can be varied how frequently the systems asks the user to contribute the current location although the data pool already contains a location for the current cell (*redundant location request*). This is to maintain the integrity of the data pool and also to increase positioning quality.

The previously described model was implemented using the software StarLogo 2.0[6] by the Media Lab at the Massachusetts Institute of Technology (see Fig. 5 for a screenshot).

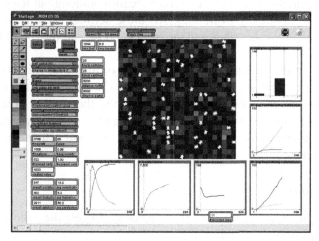

Fig. 5. Computer simulation of the Location Trader concept in StarLogo

3.2.2 The Simulations

As a structured approach to simulation, two scenarios and a set of basic initial settings have been chosen. They serve as a basis for comparison with simulations where selected parameters have been varied.

For example the urban scenario tries to model an urban environment where there are smaller and more network cells in a certain area. Based on reported average cell sizes the cell radius has been set to 100 meters with 25 times 25 cells. The resulting area of 5 times 5 kilometers approximates the area covered by the city of Munich.

Based on different basic initial settings several simulations have been run. A comparison of the results of simulations with the same initial settings has shown that outcomes are converging and are therefore representative for the selected initial settings.

In 20 different simulation setups five basic initial settings have been varied along a single dimension each time in order to single out and identify their effects on the simulation outcome. Different scenarios were considered. The simulation was run for a simulation time period of 8 weeks to allow a comprehensive overview of the launch period.

---

[6] StarLogo website: http://education.mit.edu/starlogo/

The five settings that were varied are: the initial number of users, frequency of usage, mobility of the users, the users' discouragement threshold and the redundancy of contribution (the percentage of cases in which a user is required to provide the current location although at least on location information is already available). All these settings were both halved and doubled one after the other and the effects on the simulation outcome were examined.

The examination was based on the value of nine indicative figures at the end of the simulation: the completeness of the data pool, the total created value based on the valuation as described in 0, the number of users, the total numbers of requests and contributions and the users' average number of requests, average number of contributions, average satisfaction and average frustration.

3.2.3 Results

An example outcome for the urban scenario suggest the following interdependencies (see also Table 1):

Both the initial number of users and the frequency of usage seem to have the greatest effect on the completeness of the data pool. While an almost complete coverage is achieved in almost all cases after at least 8 weeks, these two factors speed up the process. They also increase the total created value and the overall number of requests and contributions. The initial number of users has an even higher impact on the latter two, whereas the frequency of usage increases the average number of requests per user. This is understandable as both factors have a direct effect on the number of locations contributed to the system and therefore have a direct impact on the quality of service and the satisfaction of users. Frequent usage further pushes average satisfaction which can be explained with the more frequent satisfaction that users experience. On the other hand, a greater initial number of users helps to extremely decrease average frustration as the disappointment of having to provide the current location manually is spread across more people.

In fact, the initial number of users is mission critical as in all simulations for the urban scenario a great loss of users occurs in the beginning. If the initial number of users is too low (less than 75 in the simulation) the initial great loss may even be unrecoverable and the system may fail completely. (The user loss is due to the frequent frustrations that user experience with a not-yet-complete data pool in the beginning.) On the other hand, the higher the initial number of users is, the more users the system will have in the future. In fact, this seems to be a super-proportional relation.

Table 1. Simulation outcomes for the urban scenario

Effect of higher ... on ...	Number of users	Frequency of usage	Mobility of users	Discour. Thresh.	Redund. of contrib.
Completeness of data pool	+	++.	0	0	0
Created value	-	-	0	0	0
Number of Users	++	-	0	-	0
Total number Requests	++	+	0	-	0
Total contributions	++	+	0	-	0
Average requests	0	+	0	0	0
Average contributions	0	-	0	0	+
Average satisfaction	0	++	0	0	0
Average frustration	--	0	0	0	0

-- invers proportional, - sub proportional, 0 insignificant,
+ proportional, ++ super proportional

Surprisingly, user mobility as an indicator for the spatial distribution of service usage has very little effect on any of the indicative figures. It seems that a high number of users already provides sufficient spatial distribution.

The discouragement threshold proves to be another mission critical factor. Simulations show that users must accept at least two frustrations more than satisfactions before abandoning the system to keep the system running. Otherwise the number of users drops dramatically and the system fails. In the simulation a discouragement threshold of three is sufficient. A higher threshold has only a moderate positive effect on the number of users and requests.

Requiring the user to redundantly provide the current location has an interesting effect on several factors. Of course, it increases the average number of contributions per user and maintains the quality of the data pool. On the other hand it decreases average satisfaction and therefore the number of users. But this is only true for redundancy rates of more than 20% in the simulation. Below this value these negative effects are negligible, but improvements in completeness and quality of the data pool are still gained. A moderate rate of redundancy does therefore make sense.

In conclusion in the urban scenario the initial number of users and frequency of usage are the most effective levers on the number of service requests and the future number of users. The initial number of users is mission critical, but at the same time most effective for increasing the number of users. There needs to be a certain level of resistance of users against frustrations in the beginning. Redundant manual contributions seem to be acceptable to users within certain boundaries. All results including additional scenarios you can find in (Dornbusch et al. 2004).

3.2.4 Simulation Conclusion

Value co-creation takes place between service users and the positioning platform. The major risk involved with this is that privacy concerns of service users may prevent them from contributing to the system. It has therefore to be credibly assured that the location information cannot be associated with their identity at any point of time. The Location Trader approach naturally ensures that the goals of both parties are satisfied in the co-creation process: the positioning platform improves its data pool and service users are provided with a location-based service. Requiring a contribution only if necessary further reduces the effort of co-creation. In order to ensure equity of returns, the quality of the offered services has to be guaranteed. For encouraging service users to contribute their expectations have to be managed and they have to understand why they sometimes have to disclose their location. A major incentive will be to fascinate them for and make them identify themselves with this independent and open source-like approach. Still, contributions have to be checked for intentionally corrupt information. Finally, as the co-creation process is nearly completely automated, some users may not even perceive it as such.

The basic observations are the same for all scenarios: Initial number of users and frequency of usage have the greatest effect on build-up speed and the future number of users. Users have to tolerate a certain number of frustrations in the beginning when required to manually provide their location. However, a certain level of redundancy in requiring contribution is acceptable.

4 Development of a Novel Community-Based LP Architecture

Having established the foundations and approaches of LPs, as well as having shown the potential and importance of user-communities for collaborative location information generation, we now show how we can combine them effectively to a future competitive LP approach. We will begin by discussing the requirements for a globally distributed location service LP. Describing our novel community-based architecture we will demonstrate how to fulfill these requirements, ending with a brief introduction of a first proof of concept prototype of a seamless LBS running on our current LP implementation.

4.1 Architecture Requirements for a Distributed Location Service Using Heterogeneous Positioning Technologies

There is a clear need and trend towards developing a globally available system for providing ubiquitous location information of mobile and stationary users. The matching of the quality of location information needed should be done using all the available distributed positioning sources as best as possible considering the user privacy wishes and security in each case. Solutions should be operator independent and provide a low barrier for LBS developers to provide innovative new LBS solutions (Dornbusch and Huber 2003) as depicted in the previous sections.

In order to be able to offer a ubiquitous location service for LBS, multiple, inter-working LES/GIS entities for various usage environments are needed. Fig. 6 shows a possible hierarchical model of multiple LES/GIS with commonly available positioning technologies in each case. Furthermore, the Open Mobile Alliance (OMA) specifications on Location - Platform (LP) i.e. LES/GIS models have been adopted in each usage environment case to an extend providing a basic framework for LBS provisioning (Zuendt et al. 2006b).

On a country-wide and city level scale, existing LES/GIS solutions used by mobile operator LBS, or GPS-based solutions such as in-car and PDA-based navigation solutions provide good LBS support for outdoor situations. City-wide solutions might additionally use more comprehensive GIS databases for additional valuable location-based content e.g. city tour-guides, local classified advertisements etc. In these usage environments, GPS and the mobile operator pushed A-GPS standards provide the state-of-the-art and most accurate positioning technology.

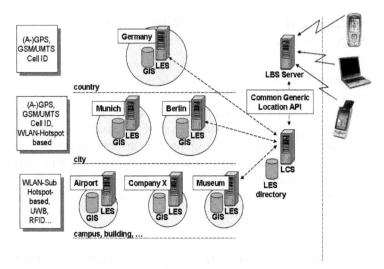

Fig. 6. A hierarchical model using multiple LES/GIS Entities for "ubiquitous" location provisioning

In dense inner-city scenarios, WLAN hotspot-based positioning can be used as additional positioning support for non-GPS-based devices due to the small radio-coverage area / cell size of WLAN Access Points (Dornbusch and Zuendt 2003; Zuendt et al. 2003; LaMarca et al. 2005).

Especially in these inner city environments with abundance and almost complete coverage of heterogeneous networks, the device-centric location sensor approach of collaboratively collecting this network data into centralized LES knowledge databases for location information generation and provisioning is most valuable (Dornbusch and Huber 2003; Zhang et al 2005).

On a campus and indoor building environment, localized LES and GIS pairs are essential for building maps, local-services and -information e.g. museum tours, shopping malls, service technicians/asset tracking etc. So far, only WLAN-, UWB-based and RFID supported positioning technologies are able to provide the necessary positioning accuracies below 10m to roughly <1m necessary for indoor navigation and tracking. WLAN sub-hotspot-based positioning methods such as RSS-triangulation and finger-printing methods (Dornbusch et al. 2003; Zuendt et al. 2004; Wong et al. 2005), or hybrid approaches using additional RFID position triggers are capable of providing satisfactory positioning performances.

It is obvious that no LES/GIS pair will be able to cover all usage areas alone due to the sheer data volume and heterogeneity of location data, as well as performance aspects (scalability issues). Not all LES/GIS solutions use standardized location formats such as WGS84 but use proprietary, relative coordinates systems, especially when dealing with indoor solutions. Hence inter-working will most definitely require some form of translation into standardized location formats. To satisfy these and further requirements for seamless LBS, a central coordination entity, the Location Core Server (LCS) is responsible to manage and harmonize the location information from multiple LES/GIS entities, considering privacy and common AAA procedures in each case (Zuendt et al. 2005). In order to achieve a required LBS Location QoS (Funk and Miller 2001) (e.g. accuracy, location update interval) location information fusion from multiple LES should be possible as well (Hightower 2003). A central LES directory is needed to identify the usage area and "scopes of responsibility" of each, as well as possible relationships between LES/GIS pairs (e.g. hierarchies). For a global system, eventually multiple LCS entities will also be needed concerning scalability for managing high numbers of LBS users and providers.

What is not shown in Fig. 6 is the relationship between mobile clients and LES systems. The location information (e.g. GPS) or radio signal data discovered from the wireless networks in the environment is captured by the mobile client and transmitted to the appropriate LES system for further location data processing. We also assume that each mobile client is attached to at least one LES/GIS pair at all times e.g. country level LES/GIS as fallback.

Coming from these requirements, we have developed the Location-Aware Community-Based Architecture (LACBA) (Zuendt et al. 2006a) – an open, scalable, self-learning, low-cost community-based location service architecture for enabling seamless adaptive location based services using heterogeneous network technologies as well as distributed positioning systems. LACBA focuses on the collaborative generation and filtering/refinement of the location information derived from heterogeneous wireless networks and positioning systems in our every-day living environment. To help in this, self-learning capabilities are built in to discover wireless network environment changes as quickly as possible.

The concept of using and fusing location information derived from heterogeneous network radio signals and other positioning systems is not new (Pfeifer and Popescu-Zeletin 1999). Frameworks and localization platforms with different approaches to location information delivery have been developed since then.

Intel's PlaceLab (LaMarca et al. 2005) is quite similar to LACBA in that it uses radio beacons from GSM and 802.11 networks and beacon reference databases to determine the position of the mobile client. However, the primary goal of Placelab is to maximize the coverage and availability of the LP, but considering positioning accuracy only secondly. Furthermore, location server discovery, scalability and handover issues are not covered.

The Nimbus framework (Roth 2005) is very similar to LACBA in that it proposes a decentralized location service using distributed location servers. Nimbus focuses on providing semantic and physical location estimates from heterogeneous location sources as well as providing means for organizing multiple location server hierarchies, modeling the distribution of service domains among- and relations between location servers. The positioning calculation in Nimbus is performed via "positioning drivers" and the fusion as well as provisioning logic of location data for LBS is based on a three stage "Virtual Positioning System" framework on the mobile client. LACBA in contrast uses "dumb" clients as sensors in the environment having the location server entities perform these tasks and provide the location information.

Other generic architecture concepts (Hightower 2003; Pfeifer 2005) focus on fusing different context information sources together in order to achieve better confidence about identifying a user/object and his/its current location through redundancy of potential location sources. Models on how to capture different context information from various sensors (e.g. visual, biometric, pressure pad, network, user device type etc.) are being developed and simulated. LACBA focuses on generating location information from ubiquitous heterogeneous network environments and readily available positioning technologies using similar approaches explained in the next section.

Both (LaMarca et al. 2005) and (Roth 2005) see the availability of appropriate, cultivated reference databases and broadcast mechanisms for LES discovery as a perquisite. The novel concept of LACBA is that it provides a generic location server framework for specific indoor/outdoor usage environment deployment, additionally supporting community-based collaborative collection, value generation and common knowledge database data sharing principles (Dornbusch and Huber 2003).

4.2 The Location-Aware Community-Based Architecture

The LACBA System can be broken down into three main parts: The LACBA enabled clients (LC) roaming about in the daily environment; the Location Core Server (LCS) acting as the central location management hub, and last but not least the Location Enabling Server entities (LES) with the responsibility of providing location information to specific geographic regions and/or buildings (Fig. 7).

The LACBA enabled clients (LC) gather heterogeneous network signalling information from the environment e.g. WLAN, GSM and UMTS base stations. Additional location inference information derived from GPS devices and RFID tags are supported and can be processed by the client as well. The client software is kept lightweight and modular, aimed to be deployable for a broad range of mobile device platforms. Whilst primarily providing server side positioning calculation, the LC can be configured to cache location data and perform positioning calculation locally. This is mostly performance related regarding device capabilities and LBS usability, or due to privacy issues (Zuendt et al. 2005). Concerning control on location data generation, the LC currently operate in two modes: 1) Initialization and training of the community-LES location databases performed by "trusted" LCs. 2) Positioning mode performed by all LCs in the community. Both modes can run simultaneously as well.

The LACBA Core Server (LCS) is the heart of the LACBA system. LBS Providers are seen as external entities capable of retrieving location information from the LCS via the Common Generic Location API. The generic interface is modelled after the OMA-LES specification implemented by many commercial location platform solution providers[7]. The LCS core functionality is to coordinate the inter-working of the various LES entities, provisioning of user positioning data, and matching of LBS requirements concerning location accuracy, update intervals etc – all within specified privacy and security policies.

The LES Agent manages the inter-working between the different global and localized LES entities validating user and service provider access rights in each case. All LES servers are registered in the root LES database along with their geographic service area. In future, it may be needed to define hierarchical LES models with appropriate LES service broadcast mechanisms (Roth 2005). However, we are currently investigating a more efficient structured peer-to-peer DHT-based approaches using ring hierarchies for a more efficient LES discovery and allocation mechanism for our community approach (Zoels et al. 2006).

The user's current position estimate from available location sources (GPS, GSM, WLAN etc.), history location data, and corresponding user privacy settings are stored in the LCS User profile. The User Agent task is to provide user access to the LCS and enforce privacy rules set for other users and service providers.

The Service Agent manages the LBS registered with LACBA along with their location QoS requirements (Funk and Miller 2001) and LES access rights in the service profile database.

---

[7] Siemens LES V2.0 Developer's Guide, http://via.vodafone.com

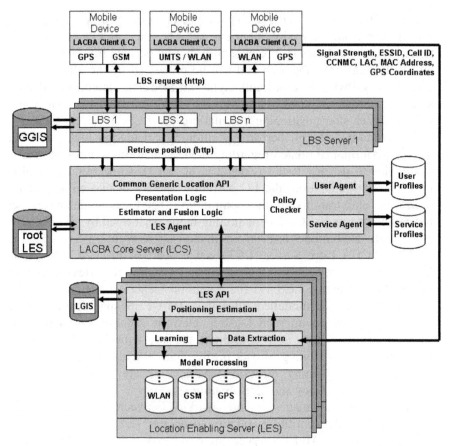

Fig. 7. The Location-Aware Community-Based Architecture

The task of the Service Agent is to monitor that the required parameters are met and signal this to the LBS accordingly via the Presentation Logic. The Presentation Logic is responsible for the LBS session initialization, location QoS negotiation, adaptation and termination. The Estimator and Fusion Logic performs sensor fusion as in (Hightower 2003). We currently support simple center of gravity probability-based fusion methods for GPS, WLAN and GSM positioning types (Ng et al. 2003).

The Location Enabling Server entity processes the environment data (e.g. wireless network data, RFID tags, GPS location information etc.) collected by the roaming LC within its designated geographic service area and generates usable location information from it. As a world-wide known location information format we have chosen WGS84 which is also used by GPS. Initialization mode driven clients are equipped with commercially available GPS receivers and standard communication hardware e.g.

WLAN, GSM, UMTS interfaces. As explained earlier, heterogeneous network data is collaboratively collected by roaming LCs and consolidated in the appropriate LES model database. The LES entity uses appropriate initialization models in each case (Connelly et al. 2005), capable of geocoding and generating "cell-maps" of the wireless network base-stations in its geographic service area (e.g. outdoors: WLAN-hotspots, GSM cells), or possibly signal strength fingerprint maps (e.g. indoors: WLAN RSS-based positioning). In "positioning mode", LCs roaming within the same geographic service area also transmit detected network environment data to the corresponding LES entity. With the implemented positioning methods in place (Ng et al. 2003, Wong et al. 2005), a LC can then be positioned using the reference data generated by initializing LCs from the corresponding LES database. Being a community-based system, LACBA needs a critical mass of roaming LCs (Dornbusch and Huber 2003), using and training the existing LES databases within their geographic service area, as well as potential re-training depending on the environment evolution rate on wireless networks, especially related to WLAN Hotspots in inner cities which might be replaced, moved, or updated on a regular basis. This issue is common to both outdoor- and indoor-based LES systems.

A more detailed description on the initialization, heterogeneous positioning and fusion, as well as feedback and optimization processes can be found in (Dornbusch et al. 2004; Zuendt et al. 2006a). The whole issue on LES discovery, handover-methods and -triggers (e.g. manual or automated using RFID tags, edge networks etc.) has been discussed thoroughly in (Zuendt et al. 2006b). Last but not least, the strategies possible in constructing seamless LBS sessions i.e. having ad-hoc LES discovery or performing LES pre-signalling if a navigation route involving changing indoor and outdoor environments is known with high probability, are also discussed here (Zuendt et al. 2006b) in more detail. We will pick-up on some of these issues in our next section, when we introduce our first seamless LBS prototype using our currently implemented LACBA system.

4.3 Realization of a Seamless Navigation Prototype

In order to prove the concept of LACBA, a first seamless indoor-outdoor navigation service has been developed within the Ariadne[8] project at the University of Technology in Munich (TUM). The main goal here was to demonstrate a distributed location service by inter-working of heterogeneous positioning technologies and using multiple LES/GIS entities.

---

[8] Further Information on the Ariadne project can be obtained from http://www.lkn.ei.tum.de/~max

A picture of the working LC prototype with attached network/positioning devices can be seen in Fig. 8. The various communication interfaces (GSM, UMTS, WLAN) as well as other sensor devices such as GPS and RFID are used for positioning purposes. The gathered information is transmitted via UMTS to the LACBA server components. It can be expected that future multimode mobile devices will have these most common technologies integrated.

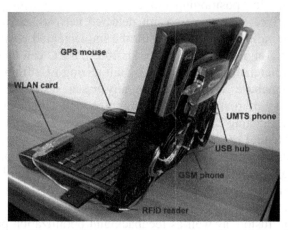

Fig. 8. Current LACBA Client (LC) prototype based on with peripherals

The current LACBA server setup involves two LES/GIS pairs: The global LES (GLES) provides the outdoor navigation part, which is performed using GPS and geo-coded WLAN hotspot or GSM Cell ID information from the inner-city district around the TU Munich. A readily available commercial map server[9] solution is used as a global GIS (GGIS). The indoor navigation system part is provided by a local LES and GIS entity (LLES, LGIS). The LGIS provides appropriate floor maps of the TUM building where our institute is situated. The LLES provides indoor location information using WLAN-RSS-based positioning (Stamoulakatos et al. 2003), as well as RFID Tags as waypoints, object identification and indoor route-calculation/navigation to rooms, electronic devices etc.

The Ariadne client navigation application running on the LC (Fig. 9) shows the currently available positioning sources for the user from his LCS user profile, along with map data and additional navigation information obtained from the respective LGIS and GGIS entities.

---

[9] Microsoft MapPoint Server web service

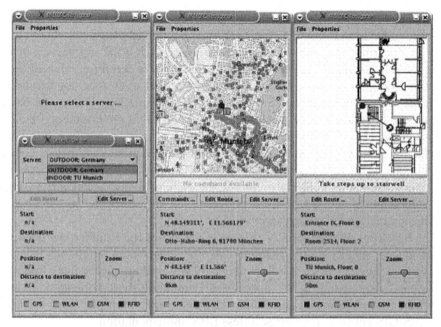

Fig. 9. Ariadne application screenshots. From left to right 1) manual selection of available LES entities, 2) outdoor-navigation using GPS, 3) indoor-navigation using WLAN and RFID

The information on the current LC position and currently available LES entities can be obtained by invoking respective methods of the generic web service API via the LCS.

A more detailed description of the seamless navigation and LACBA system prototype, as well as performance characteristics on positioning accuracies obtained in respective indoor and outdoor environments can be obtained from here (Zuendt M et al. 2006a).

5 Summary and Conclusion

In this chapter, we have introduced a novel positioning framework approach for providing a distributed, ubiquitous location service. We have shown that community-based approaches can provide a viable enhancement to existing LP solutions and ambitions. We believe that such an approach is currently the only solution capable of capturing the abundance and distributed nature of providing location information from heterogeneous wireless networks and readily available positioning systems for future ubiquitous LBS. Furthermore, a future LP will involve both centralized and decentralized location service provisioning due to the distributed nature of location information and various LBS requirements.

Concerning the user community aspects of such a LP approach, a quantitative analysis of the service usage behavior of a certain number of location community users within a certain area and over a certain period of time was modeled in an idealized computer simulation. The model based on the Location Trader platform takes into account environmental factors such as network cell size and initial number of users as well as individual factors such as frequency of usage, number of requests, number of contributions, each user's satisfaction level, frustration level and tolerance towards frustration before abandoning the system. By systematically varying certain initial settings of these parameters, their effect on the outcome of the simulation have been analysed.

Based on the community principle, an architecture model has been introduced, specifying the requirements for a distributed ubiquitous location service. We have shown how the LACBA system meets these requirements, demonstrating its distributed community-based location service from heterogeneous positioning systems and multiple inter-working LES/GIS entities on a first seamless LBS implementation.

References

3GPP (2004) 3GPP 23.271 Technical Specification Group Services and Systems Aspects; Functional stage 2 description of Location Services (LCS), June 2004

Connelly K et al (2005) A Toolkit for Automatically Constructing Outdoor Radio Maps, International Conference on Information Technology: Coding and Computing (ITCC'05), April 2005

Dornbusch P, Zuendt M (2003) Realisierung von Positionsortungen in WLAN, ITG-Fachtagung "Technologie und Anwendungen für die mobile Informationsgesellschaft" 2002

Dornbusch P, Huber M (2003) Generierung von Ortsinformationen durch User-Communities, Proceedings of 6. Internationale Tagung Wirtschaftsinformatik 2003

Dornbusch P, Fuchs F, Huber H (2004) Simulating Collaborative Mobile Services – An Approach to Evaluate a New Location Enabling Service 4th International Conference on Electronic Business (ICEB2004) December 2004

Eissfeller B, Teuber A, Zucker PR (2005) Special Report on: Untersuchungen zum GPS-Satellitenempfang in Gebäuden. Universität der Bundeswehr München, March 2005

Funk HB, Miller CA (2001) Location Modelling for Ubiquitous Computing: Is This Any Better?, Workshop at Ubicomp 2001, September 30

Hightower J (2003) From Position to Place, in Proceedings of the 2003 Workshop on Location-Aware Computing, Oct. 2003

Huber M (2004) Kolloborative Wertschöpfung, Deutscher Universitätsverlag, ISBN: 3824481901, September 2004

Hulls W (2004) IP-Based Assisted-GPS Solutions – The Technical Benefits, IIR's Sixth Annual LBS Forum; Budapest, June 2004

Katz ML, Shapiro C (1992) Product introduction with network externalities, in: Journal of Industrial Economics, 40, S. 55-83.

LaMarca A et al (2005) Place Lab: Device Positioning Using Radio Beacons in the Wild; In proceedings of Pervasive 2005

Lerner J, Tirole J (2000) "The Simple Economics of Open Source", HBS Finance Working Paper No. 00-059, October 2000

LiF (2002) LIF TS 101 Specification, Location Interoperability Forum, Mobile Location Protocol, Version 3, June 2002

Ng JKY et al (2003) A Study on the Sensitivity of the Center of Gravity Algorithm for Location Estimation, Department of Computer Science Hong Kong Baptist University, May 13, 2003

OMA (2004) OMA-RD-SUPL-V1_0-20040930-C, Secure User Plain Location Requirements Candidate Version 1.0 30-September 2004

Pfeifer T, Popescu-Zeletin R (1999) A Modular Location-Aware Service and Application Platform; 4th IEEE Symp. On Computers and Comms, ISCC, 1999

Pfeifer T (2005) Redundant Positioning Architecture; Computer Communications, Vol. 28 (2005) 13, pp. 1575-1585, August 2005

Roth J (2005) A Decentralized Location Service Providing Semantic Locations, Informatik Bericht 323, Habilitationsschrift, Fernuniversität Hagen, January 2005

Stamoulakatos T, Kyriazakos S, Sykas E (2003) Hidden Markov Modelling and Macroscopic Traffic Filtering supporting Location Based Service. Dept. of Electrical and Computer Engineering, Technical University of Athens, 2003

Vicenty T (1975) Direct and Inverse Solutions of Geodesics on the Ellipsoid with Application of nested Equations, Directorate of the Overseas Surveys, Survey Review XXII, 176, April 1975

Wong WH, Ng JK, Yeung WM (2005) Wireless LAN Positioning with Mobile Devices in a Library Environment, 25th IEEE International Conference on Distributed Computing Systems Workshops (ICDCSW'05), June 2005

Zhang T et al (2005) AC-CDS: Autonomous Collaborative Collection, Discovery, and Sharing of Information for Mobile Users and Devices; 3rd International ITRE'05 IEEE Conference, June 2005

Zoels S, Eichhorn M, Tarlano A, Kellerer W (2006) Content-based Hierarchies in DHT-based Peer-to-Peer-Systems, 2nd Workshop on Next Generation Service Platforms for Future Mobile Systems (SPMS 2006), January 2006

Zuendt M, Dornbusch P, Schaefer T, Jacobi P, Flade D (2004) Integration of Indoor Positioning into a Global Location Platform", 1st Workshop on Positioning, Navigation and Communication 2004, ISBN 3-8322-2553-6

Zuendt M, Deo G, Naumann M, Ludwig M (2005) De-centralized Location Management: Minimizing Privacy Concerns for Location Based Service; 3rd International ITRE'05 IEEE Conference, June 2005

Zuendt M, Ippy P, Laqua B, Eberspaecher J (2006a) LACBA – A Location-Aware Community-Based Architecture for Realizing Seamless Adaptive Location-Based Services, In 12th European Wireless Conference (EW2006), April 2006

Zuendt M, Ippy P, Laqua B (2006b) Seamless Adaptive Location-Based Services using Heterogeneous Positioning Technologies and Multiple Location Servers, In 6th International Workshop on Applications and Services in Wireless Networks (ASWN'06), May 2006

Zuendt M, Tabery P, Bachmeir C (2003) Seamless Handoff in Community-Based and Location-Aware Heterogeneous Wireless Networks, MoMuC Conference 2003, ISBN 3-9808842-9-5

Context-sensitive Content Provision for Classified Directories

Thomas Hess, Barbara Rauscher, Christoph Hirnle

1 Objective and Structure of the Overall Project

The mobile communication innovations of the last decades have, amongst other technological novelties, substantially changed society: it has become more flexible and faster paced. While mobile telephony has arrived at a certain saturation point, the now mobile society also demands other services to be mobile, too. Context-sensitive service provision is one way of providing additional mobile services in a manner which takes advantage of location information.

As a test case for context-sensitive service provision, the overall goal of this research project was to develop and to test a context-sensitive service for GelbeSeiten, a cooperation of regional German classified directories companies. In short, three phases were gone through. First, based on economic considerations, a specification of the context-sensitive service was put up. Parts of this specification were then implemented in a second step. In the final evaluation phase, a field experiment yielded insights both for the economic evaluation of the business model "context-sensitive services for classified directories" and on adaptation processes from a communication science point of view (see Fig. 1).

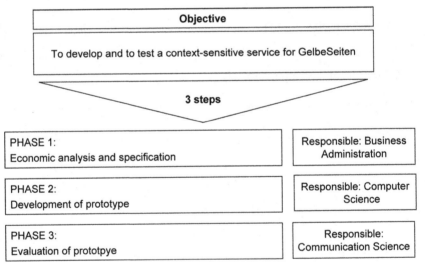

Fig. 1. Objective and project structure

Four institutions were involved in the conceptual design, its realization and the empirical studies: GelbeSeiten Marketing Services, Keller Verlag Munich, its IT-subsidiary IT2Media, and the University of Munich (LMU). From the academic side, within the research project intermedia, three disciplines were involved: business administration, computer science and communication science. Every phase was lead managed by one of the three fields.

2 Phase 1: Economic Analysis and Specification

The first phase of the project was concerned with the economic analysis and the specification of the context-sensitive service.

A context-sensitive service is a service that is able to adapt to the context and thus to the situation of the user. The term context is defined as every piece of information about an entity that is relevant for the interaction of user and application (Dey 2001). The special benefit to users of context-sensitive services lies in the automatic adaptation of services to the current situation and the preferences of the user. This facilitates personalization of content which in turn is extremely helpful when considering the limited display possibilities and time restrictions of mobile communication equipment and mobile applications.

For these reasons, the classified directories editor GelbeSeiten considered the usage of new positioning technologies as highly relevant. In a first step, different business models based on the technology of context-sensitive services were developed for GelbeSeiten. Later on, these business models were evaluated making use of market-based and resource-based views (see Porter 1999; Barney 1991). The context-sensitive service solution for classified directories appeared to be of advantage from both perspectives.

2.1 A Market-based View

The market-based view on the business models was to examine which competitive forces GelbeSeiten is facing and how strong these forces are. At the time of analysis, YelloMap and KlickTel were identified as the dominant competitors. This result indicates that direct competition on the market is quite low. Thus, it is rather simple to evaluate the relative strengths of the competitors. Due to this constellation, measures enhancing rivalry will not stay undetected and are therefore rather unlikely. The sector for mobile classified directories is quite young and still grows slowly. It is obvious that in such a small and slowly increasing market players are struggling to win more market shares for themselves. How-ever, because of the expected growth, competitors can grow organically with the market which again reduces rivalry. High exit barriers can also increase competition as even non profitable firms would rather stay than retreat. Nevertheless, as the supply of mobile classified directories requires no specific assets and no high fixed costs are to be worried about, exit barriers can be considered to be quite low. In addition, these low barriers for resigning stabilize the profits in a sector and competition decreases.

Rivalry could increase by new market entrants because of growing capacities and therefore falling prices. A market sector is protected by certain entry barriers which have to be overcome by new competitors. Nevertheless, GelbeSeiten faces low barriers if it wants to enter the market for mobile classified directories. It can realize high economies of scope as many functions and operations already exist and will not have to be set up; examples include the database, a sales force and a large customer base. Furthermore, GelbeSeiten owns an attractive brand name. That way, it is cheaper for GelbeSeiten to enter the market than it would be for other competitors who would have to set up material and immaterial assets. Experience and size of GelbeSeiten are factors that should not be neglected and can also cause cost advantages. Entering a new market in an early stage minimizes the risk to have to compensate switching costs of competitors' customers.

The threat from substitutes is another competitive force that GelbeSeiten has to face. Substitutes lower potential profits. They level the upper price limit for a service in case they offer functions similar to a mobile classified directory. In the case of classified directories such services have the potential to cannibalize the branch if they replace advertisements or match supply and demand in another way. For instance, search engines, online catalogues or Ebay-like services can all be used via mobile phones using WAP technology.

Customers are also putting strain on the attractiveness of a sector. They demand better service or lower prices and have the power to play some competitors off against the others. This is especially dangerous if customers are concentrated and responsible for the major part of revenues of a provider. In the case of GelbeSeiten this threat is limited as customers as well as advertisers are widely dispersed. Hence, almost no bargaining powers can be bundled. Additionally, costs for advertisers can be kept low and therefore lower price sensitivity can be assumed.

The last competitive force is the bargaining power of suppliers. They can increase prices or decrease quality. Concerning mobile classified directories, the most important suppliers are mobile network operators and DeTeMedien. As DeTeMedien is invested in GelbeSeiten, they will not use their bargaining power as forcefully as they could. On the other hand mobile network operators are a concentrated group of suppliers whose service can not be substituted. It is possible that they threat forward integration and thus limit the bargaining power of GelbeSeiten. Fig. 2 sums up the results of the market-orientated analysis. As a conclusion, GelbeSeiten can in essence use their existing strong brand name in the field of classified directories without facing too fierce a competition.

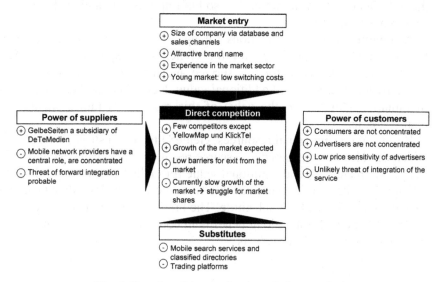

Fig. 2. Results of the market-based view analysis

2.2 A Resource-based View

From this point of view, existing information about the sector can be used to extend sales channels by additional mobile ones. A high quality database and its updating are the basic resources for a mobile online classified directory. For customers, this resource is of critical value and therefore has value-creating effects for GelbeSeiten. Such a database is exclusively kept by GelbeSeiten. This underlines the immense worth of this resource. The complexity of the data stock and the complexity of its further development can easily prevent imitations and protect the value of the resource. The database has a high strategic value for GelbeSeiten because it is asymmetrically distributed in favor of GelbeSeiten.

Another important competency is the processing of data through value added services like e.g. geo-coding or updates of data. While the current database of GelbeSeiten is already geo-coded, the necessary routines for updating entries by the advertisers themselves are not yet implemented. Such a function would be rare on the market and would generate additional value for customers and advertisers. GelbeSeiten could skim it. In case GelbeSeiten can close this resource-gap, they could profit from first-mover advantages. Developing this competency can initially bring relative advantages against competitors; further development can permanently save them. Protection from imitation is also built up this way and profits can be acquired effectively.

Analogous to missing functions for updating data stocks, GelbeSeiten has no explicit competencies for the contextual supply of content. Resources are fundamental for this service and have the potential to create first-mover advantages and additional value. Nevertheless, there is a threat of imitation. Altogether, the value of this resource is rather operational than strategic.

Besides these functional resources, GelbeSeiten has a strong brand name which can also be considered as a scarce resource. The awareness and publicity can create trust and additional value for GelbeSeiten. As building up a brand is quite time-consuming, this resource is a lasting advantage and very difficult to imitate or substitute. The brand and brand name have high strategic value and bring along benefits in competition. Fig. 3 summarizes this resource-based view analysis.

Process oriented value chain

Acquisition of basic data, acquisition of advertisers	Assignment and coverage of the sector, updating of database	Value added services: geo-coding, editing of current contents by advertisers	Transfer / connection: context-depending supply	Navigation / user interface

Database	Data processing	Context-sensitive supply
(+) Value added for consumers	(+) Data already geo-coded	(+) First-mover advantages
(+) Unique resource	(+) Rare data in high quality	(-) High threat of imitation
(+) Difficult to imitate, sustainable value	(+) Securing the resource by moving first	(-) Scarcity not securable

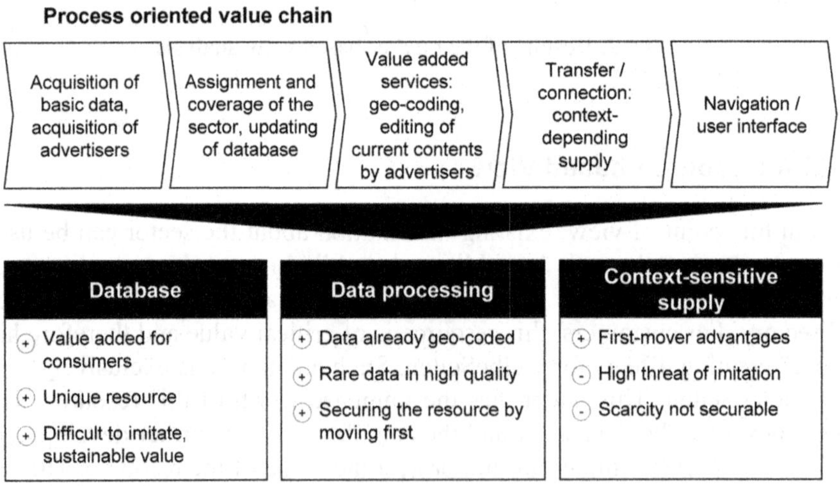

Fig. 3. Results of the resource-based view analysis

On the basis of these economic considerations, a concept for a mobile classified directory was developed. It served as a template for the later realization of a prototype in phase 2 and will not be introduced here in further detail.

3 Phase 2: Development of a Prototype

In the second phase of the project, a prototype for a context-sensitive service was developed. To simplify the implementation in the first step, the restaurant sector was chosen as a test case. In effect, a restaurant locating service was implemented (see use case diagram in Fig. 4).

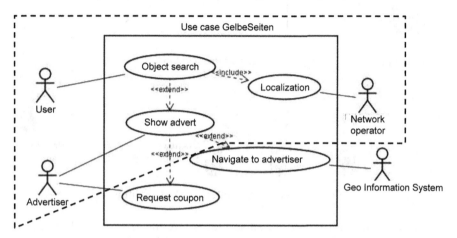

Fig. 4. Use case diagram for the RestaurantFinder

In cooperation with IT2Media, a subsidiary of the cooperation partner Keller Verlag, a specification was put up which integrated the existing infrastructure and the databases. This architecture is displayed in Fig. 5. For using this service, a client for mobile phones was developed based on J2ME. The user can retrieve the service via an easy-to-use interface. The current position of the user of the RestaurantFinder can be determined by a mobile GPS receiver which transfers data to the mobile phone via Bluetooth. This context-information is transferred to the RestaurantFinder when called and then processed. Preferences of users are stored in a profile database which again is linked to the restaurant server. Additional context-information for the second version of the service is provided using CoCo as a middleware (see Buchholz et al. 2004; Hochstatter and Krause 2004). CoCo stands for Context Composition and links functions for context-acquisition, -processing and -distribution. Context-information is provided by context information systems (CIS) as displayed in Fig. 5.

The RestaurantFinder service is run on the mobile phone of the user and links itself to the databases of Keller Verlag via the respective servers. In detail, the service was implemented in two different versions.

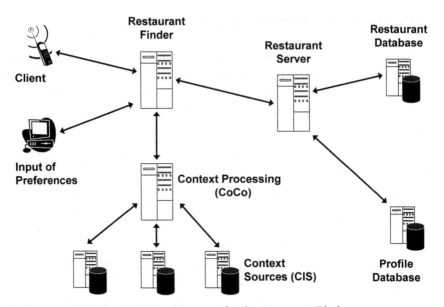

Fig. 5. IT Architecture for the RestaurantFinder

The first one is a location based service where the service is adapted to the position of the user; the second one additionally reacts to context-information retrieved from other sources such as preferences concerning cuisine, payment, seating, type of the restaurant (café, bar, etc.) or information concerning the location like opening hours. Fig. 6 provides an overview of the basic functions.

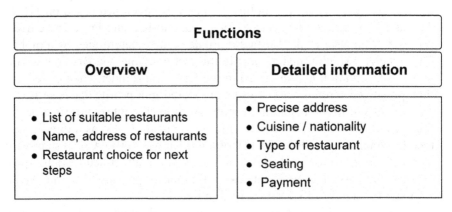

Fig. 6. Implementation of the RestaurantFinder

4   Evaluation of the Prototype

4.1 Specification of the Empirical Study

The empirical analysis represents the third and final phase of the joint project. Several findings were gathered at this stage. In all, the studies were to be integrated into the academic research project intermedia and hence had to yield results of scientific significance. The empirical study was on the one hand basis for further interdisciplinary research of the GelbeSeiten project; on the other hand it was meant to answer relevant discipline-specific questions. For example, the functionality of a context-sensitive service had to be supported from a technical point of view.

From a communication science perspective, the study served as an analysis for adaptation processes in the case of context-sensitive services. As a basic assumption, we presupposed that the success of the additional services would only show after adaptation. Adaptation is regarded as the further integration of the innovation into the daily life of the user after his first decision to buy.

Adaptation is a highly complex process that results from many psychological and social factors (e.g. profiling or network effects, see Wirth et al. 2005 on details). Basically adaptation can be seen as a two-dimensional haggling process. The first dimension is the negotiating of usage and handling, the second dimension is the negotiating of prestige and image (see Fig. 7). The process of adaptation is finished when one ore more patterns of usage and handling or one or more prestige-values have stabilized.

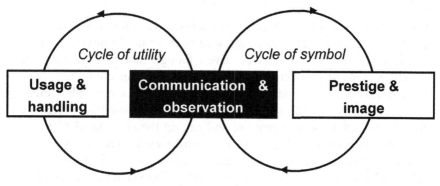

Fig. 7. The adaptation process (Wirth et al. 2005)

From an economic viewpoint, this phase of the project was used to analyze the value of an actual context-sensitive service. Quantitative as well as qualitative aspects were to be examined. In detail, the research questions besides the technical realization problem concerned the service's economic advantages and the adaptation by users:

- How do users integrate the service into their daily life - considering both the dimensions of usage and identity?
- How much context-sensitive information should a context-sensitive service provide and to what extent should it be personalized and individualized?

Additionally, a survey among the test persons established practical recommendations for the partner companies in respect to the design of the prototype itself.

The experiment was conducted with 48 participants in three waves. The participants were grouped into two samples: one was equipped with a RestaurantFinder which only used location based information; the other was supplied with a version that also included additional context-information. Participants were allowed to use the service for free for two weeks. To analyze adaptation and usage depending on the integration of context-information, all relevant usage data was stored on the servers. In addition to that, the participants were interviewed in a structured manner after the test phase. These guidelines mainly dealt with prestige of the service and meta-communication (i.e. communication about the service within the own peer group) and usage (with special focus on context-information).

4.2 Results of the Empirical Study

Concerning the prestige effect of the service we found that overall it was positively received. This can be traced back to the 'innovation' and 'dynamics' features of the service. Even though mobile restaurant finders cannot be seen as innovative from an academic perspective these days, users consider it to be brand-new and innovative. The service also refers to a dynamic and active lifestyle, which is on the one hand supported by the mobile extraction of information, and can on the other hand be presented towards other people. This was also confirmed by the fact that a lot of meta-communication was observed. Nevertheless, some user statements indicated that the prestige effect was not stable yet which means that the initial interest in the innovative service can also decrease in later stages.

Concerning the integration of context information, two major findings are worth mentioning. On the one hand, positioning (which was integrated in both versions) was acknowledged to be essential value added. In fact, the structured interviews highlighted that to users the positioning system was a good alternative to traditional recommendation systems. However, concerning the usage of other context information such as preferences regarding to the cuisine offered, no positive effects were noted. First, the log-files showed no differences in information retrieval between the two RestaurantFinder versions. Second, it was pointed out during the interviews that the integration of additional context-information did not leave a positive impression; this was mainly because of the static implementation of the input of preferences via the web-interface. Some users requested a mobile option for input or changes of preferences. Others complained that some restaurants which do not match the specified preferences are not displayed even if they are near to the current position of the user.

5 Conclusion

During the three phases, major findings could be derived from a business angle, a technological point of view and a communication science perspective.

From the business point of view, GelbeSeiten could benefit from a fast market entry as the market for context-sensitive services currently is in a very early stage of development. As a pioneer, GelbeSeiten could achieve high loyalty of its customers. When entering the market, the high quality brand name GelbeSeiten could support the new service. On the other hand, building up new resources would be necessary to hold on to competitive advantages. For example, GelbeSeiten would have to negotiate conditions with mobile network providers concerning sales channels or for the gaining of positioning data - in case positioning would not be realized with GPS. Furthermore, existing data stocks of GelbeSeiten would have to be enriched by context-sensitive data. Costs for construction and enhancements of the technological infrastructure must also be taken into consideration.

From the information technology perspective, RestaurantFinder is a complex system consisting of several prototypes. In addition, the profile based search requires a different kind of data collection and standardized storage as it is currently implemented at Keller Verlag. Also, the independence of the database which would theoretically be very reasonable is not given in practice. Further, two hardware problems remain to be solved. First, the Bluetooth communication between the Bluetooth mouse and the mobile phones was problematic. Second, GPS positioning often was slow and quite imprecise.

Concerning the communication science point of view, the most important finding is that positioning is seen as a value added. The idea of the service is perceived as a good alternative to existing recommendation systems. Nevertheless, personalization should be adjusted to usage and handling in daily life, i.e. the creation of profiles should be configured more dynamical. The average user evaluates the creation of profiles to be critical if it is not highly flexible and hence allows to quickly adapting to situational contexts. As main suggestions for improvement the integration of GPS mice and mobile phone on one device, the integration of maps of surroundings, an expansion of the data basis and the integration of a rating system were put forward.

References

Barney J (1991) Firm Resources and Sustained Competitive advantage. Journal of Management, 17, 1: 99-120

Buchholz T, Krause M, Linnhoff-Popien C, Schiffers M (2004) CoCo: Dynamic Composition of Context Infor-mation. In: Proceedings of the First Annual International Conference on Mobile and Ubiquitous Computing (MobiQuitous), Boston, no pagination

Dey AK (2001) Understanding and Using Context. Personal and Ubiquitous Computing Journal, 5: 4-7

Hochstatter I, Krause M (2004) Strategies for On–The–Fly Composition of Context Information Services. In: 11th International Workshop of the HP Open-View University Association (HPOVUA 2004), Paris

Höflich JR (1998) Computerrahmen und Kommunikation. In: Prommer E, Vowe G (eds) Computervermittelte Kommunikation - Öffentlichkeit im Wandel? Konstanz: UVK, pp 141-174

Porter, M. E. (1999) Wettbewerbsstrategien: Methoden zur Analyse von Branchen und Konkurrenten. 10th ed, Campus-Verlag, Frankfurt/Main

Reichwald R, Meier R, Fremuth N (2002) Die mobile Ökonomie - Definition und Spezifika. In: R. Reichwald (ed.), Mobile Kommunikation - Wertschöpfung, Technologien, neue Dienste. Gabler, Wiesbaden, pp 3-16

Rogers EM (2003) Diffusion of Innovations, 5th ed, Free Press, New York

Wirth W, von Pape T, Karnowski V (2005) New technologies and how they are rooted in society. In: 55. annual reunion of the International Communication Association (ICA), New York , no pagination

List of Contributors

Angerer, Christoph
Laboratory for Software Technology
ETH Zürich, Computer Systems Institute
Clausiusstr. 58, CH-8092 Zürich, SWITZERLAND
christoph.angerer@inf.ethz.ch

Brenner, Michael
Munich Network Management Team
Ludwig-Maximilians-Universität München
Oettingenstraße 67, 80538 München, GERMANY
brenner@mnm-team.org

Broy, Manfred, Univ.-Prof. Dr. Dr. h.c.
Lehrstuhl für Software & Systems Engineering
Technische Universität München, Department of Informatics
Boltzmannstr. 3, 85748 Garching, GERMANY
broy@in.tum.de

Brügge, Bernd, Univ. Prof. Ph.D.
Chair for Applied Software Engineering
Technische Universität München, Department of Informatics
Boltzmannstr. 3, 85748 Garching, GERMANY
bruegge@in.tum.de

Danciu, Vitalian A.
Munich Network Management Team
Ludwig-Maximilians-Universität München
Oettingenstraße 67, 80538 München, GERMANY
danciu@mnm-team.org

Diepold, Klaus, Univ.-Prof. Dr.-Ing.
Department for Electrical Engineering and Information Technology
Technische Universität München
Arcisstraße 21, 80333 München, GERMANY
kldi@tum.de

Dornbusch, Peter, Dr. rer. nat.
CDTM – Center for Digital Technology and Management
Technische Universität München, Department of Informatics
Arcisstr. 21, 80333 München, GERMANY
dornbusch@cdtm.de

Eberspächer, Jörg, Univ.-Prof. Dr.-Ing.
Institute of Communication Networks
Technische Universität München
Arcisstrasse 21, 80333 München, GERMANY
joerg.eberspaecher@tum.de

Fiedler, Marina, Dr. MBR
Institut für Information, Organisation und Management
Munich School of Management
Ludwig-Maximilians-Universität München
Ludwigstr. 28, 80539 München, GERMANY
fiedler@lmu.de

Garschhammer, Markus, Dr. rer. nat.
Munich Network Management Team
Leibniz Supercomputing Center of Munich
Boltzmannstraße 1, 85748 Garching, GERMANY
garschha@mnm-team.org

gentschen Felde, Nils
Munich Network Management Team
Ludwig-Maximilians-Universität München
Oettingenstraße 67, 80538 München, GERMANY
felde@mnm-team.org

Gross, Thomas, Univ.-Prof. Dr.
Laboratory for Software Technology
ETH Zürich, Computer Systems Institute
Clausiusstr. 58, CH-8092 Zürich, SWITZERLAND
thomas.gross@inf.ethz.ch

Hanemann, Andreas
Munich Network Management Team
Leibniz Supercomputing Center of Munich
Boltzmannstraße 1, 85748 Garching, GERMANY
hanemann@mnm-team.org

Hegering, Heinz-Gerd, Univ.-Prof. Dr.
Munich Network Management Team
Ludwig-Maximilians-Universität München
and Leibniz Supercomputing Center of Munich
Boltzmannstraße 1, 85748 Garching, GERMANY
hegering@mnm-team.org

Hess, Thomas, Univ.-Prof. Dr.
Institute for Information Systems and New Media
Ludwig-Maximilians-Universität München
Ludwigstrasse 28, 80539 München, GERMANY
thess@bwl.uni-muenchen.de

Hirnle, Christoph, Dr.
Institute for Information Systems and New Media
Ludwig-Maximilians-Universität München
Ludwigstrasse 28, 80539 München, GERMANY
hirnle@gmail.com

Kern, Eva-Maria, Dr. mont. Dr.-Ing. habil.
Department for Business Logistics and General Management
Hamburg University of Technology
Schwarzenbergstraße 95, 21073 Hamburg, GERMANY
e.kern@tu-harburg.de

Kirchmair, Bernhard
Center for Digital Technology and Management
Arcisstraße 21, 80290 München, GERMANY
kirchmair@cdtm.de

Kirstädter, Andreas, Dr.-Ing.
Siemens AG
Corporate Technology
Otto-Hahn-Ring 6, 81730 München, GERMANY
andreas.kirstaedter@siemens.com

Krcmar, Helmut, Univ.-Prof. Dr.
Chair for Information Systems
Technische Universität München
Boltzmannstr. 3, 85748 Garching, GERMANY
krcmar@in.tum.de

Leimeister, Jan Marco, Dr.
Chair for Information Systems
Technische Universität München
Boltzmannstr. 3, 85748 Garching, GERMANY
leimeister@in.tum.de

Mayrhofer, Philip
Center for Digital Technology and Management
Arcisstraße 21, 80290 München, GERMANY
mayrhofer@cdtm.de

Möller, Matthias, Dr. oec. publ.
Center for Digital Technology and Management
Arcisstraße 21, 80290 München, GERMANY
moeller@cdtm.de

Nagel, Michael
Chair for Applied Software Engineering
Technische Universität München, Department of Informatics
Boltzmannstr. 3, 85748 Garching, GERMANY
nagel@in.tum.de

Ott, Martin
Chair for Applied Software Engineering
Technische Universität München, Department of Informatics
Boltzmannstr. 3, 85748 Garching, GERMANY
ott@cs.tum.edu

Picot, Arnold, Univ.-Prof. Dr. Dres. h.c.
Institut für Information, Organisation und Management,
Munich School of Management
Ludwig-Maximilians-Universität München
Ludwigstr. 28, 80539 München, GERMANY
picot@lmu.de

Pramateftakis, Michael, Dr.-Ing.
Department for Electrical Engineering and Information Technology
Technische Universität München
Arcisstraße 21, 80333 München, GERMANY
pramateftakis@tum.de

Rauscher, Barbara
Institute for Information Systems and New Media
Ludwig-Maximilians-Universität München
Ludwigstrasse 28, 80539 München, GERMANY
brauscher@bwl.uni-muenchen.de

Renner, Patrick
Chair for Applied Software Engineering
Technische Universität München, Department of Informatics
Boltzmannstr. 3, 85748 Garching, GERMANY
renner@in.tum.de

Sailer, Martin
Munich Network Management Team
Ludwig-Maximilians-Universität München
Oettingenstraße 67, 80538 München, GERMANY
sailer@mnm-team.org

Sandner, Uwe
Center for Digital Technology and Management
Arcisstraße 21, 80290 München, GERMANY
sandner@cdtm.de

Schiffers, Michael
Munich Network Management Team
Ludwig-Maximilians-Universität München
Oettingenstraße 67, 80538 München, GERMANY
schiffers@mnm-team.org

Schmid-Egger, Arno
Siemens AG
Power Transmission and Distribution
Humboldtstr. 59, 90459 Nürnberg, GERMANY
arno.schmid-egger@siemens.com

Zuendt, Maximilian
Center for Digital Technology and Management
Arcisstraße 21, 80290 München, GERMANY
zuendt@cdtm.de